USEFULLY USELESS

EVERYTHING YOU'D NEVER LEARN AT SCHOOL { BUT MAY LIKE TO KNOW }

MARK HANKS

■ SQUARE PEG

Published by Square Peg 2011

2 4 6 8 10 9 7 5 3 1

First published in Great Britain in 2011 by
Square Peg
Random House, 20 Vauxhall Bridge Road,
London SW1V 2SA

www.rbooks.co.uk

Addresses for companies within The Random House Group Limited
can be found at: www.randomhouse.co.uk/offices.htm

The Random House Group Limited Reg. No. 954009

A CIP catalogue record for this book
is available from the British Library

ISBN 9780224086639

The author and the publishers have made every effort to trace the holders
of copyright in quotations. Any inadvertent omissions or errors may be
corrected in future editions.

The Random House Group Limited supports The Forest Stewardship
Council (FSC), the leading international forest certification organisation.
All our titles that are printed on Greenpeace approved FSC certified paper
carry the FSC logo. Our paper procurement policy can be found at
www.rbooks.co.uk/environment

Printed and bound in Great Britain by Clays Ltd, St Ives PLC

To Bernard Kennedy, a minefield of information both useful and useless. And to his family, for listening to it.

ACKNOWLEDGMENTS

I would like to thank Rosemary Davidson at Square Peg for commissioning this tome over a nice cup of tea, and my wonderful agent Barbara Levy.

use·ful *adj* \'yüs-fəl\

capable of being put to use

———————

use·less *adj* \'yüs-ləs\

incapable of being put to use

Very useless things we neglect, till they become
old and useless enough to be put in Museums: and so
very important things we study till, when they become
important enough, we ignore them – and rightly.

Samuel Butler

★ ☆ DEAR READER, ☆ ★

When a person in a group yawns, over half the group will yawn within five minutes.

Yawning is involuntary – we do it before we are born. Research has shown that foetuses yawn at 11 weeks.

A child will begin yawning contagiously by the time it is two years old.

Chimpanzees yawn when they see other chimps yawning.

The average human yawn lasts for six seconds, and men tend to yawn for longer than women.

There is a theory that one's ability to yawn contagiously (you yawn when someone else does) is a measure of one's ability to empathise with others. Autistic people have been shown to give no response when watching videos of people yawning.

I HOPE THIS BOOK DOES NOT MAKE YOU YAWN . . .

☆

MARK HANKS

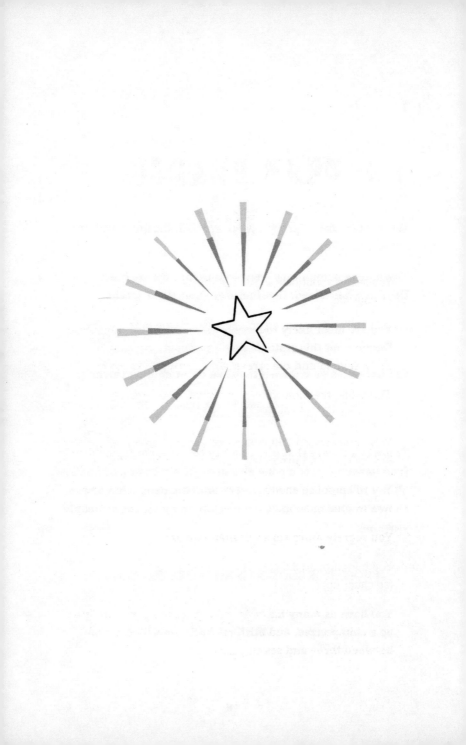

★ ☆ YOU ☆ ★

* You spend about half an hour as a single cell at the beginning of your life.

* **You are most likely to have a heart attack on a Monday. Doctors put this statistic down to people overdoing it at the weekend and the stress of returning to work.**

* The colder the room you are sleeping in becomes, the more likely you are to have a nightmare.

* **You have around 250,000 sweat glands in your feet, which is why they can produce up to a pint of sweat a day.**

* You will produce enough saliva in your lifetime to fill roughly two swimming pools.

* **You secrete more earwax when you are afraid.**

* You burn around 3.5 calories each time you laugh (so cheer up).

* **You have as many hairs per square inch on your body as a chimpanzee, and each of them has a lifespan of between three and seven years.**

✳ You could dissolve razors blades with the acid in your stomach (and fortunately you get a new stomach lining every three to four days).

☆ **You give off enough heat in 30 minutes to bring half a gallon of water to a boil.**

✳ You do not have white bones – they are different shades between beige and brown.

☆ **You will spend around three years of your life on a toilet.**

✳ You are more likely to get attacked by a cow than a shark.

☆ **You have no stronger muscle than your tongue.**

✳ You can calculate your height to within a centimetre or two by measuring your arm span.

☆ **You could cover a tennis court with the surface area of your lungs.**

✳ You will normally hiccup for no longer than five minutes.

☆ **You (if you are an average human) will walk the equivalent of three times around the world in your lifetime.**

✳ The more intelligent you are, the more zinc and copper you will have in your hair.

☆ **You will need nearly half a year to grow a fingernail from cuticle to fingertip.**

✳ You will fall out of a hospital bed twice as often as a woman (if you are a man) and half as much as a man (if you are a woman).

✧ **You have enough iron in your body to make an 8-centimetre nail, enough sulphur to kill all fleas on an average dog, enough carbon to make 900 pencils, enough potassium to fire a toy cannon, enough fat to make seven bars of soap, enough phosphorous to make 2,200 match heads, and enough water to fill a ten-gallon tank.**

☆ FIRST THINGS FIRST ☆
(THE 1ST – AFTER YOU, NATURALLY)

✳ ABBA used the first letter from each of their names – Agnetha, Bjorn, Benny, Ani-frid – to create their name.

✧ **The first episode of *Columbo* was directed by Steven Spielberg.**

✳ Keanu Reeves's first name is Hawaiian for 'cool breeze over the mountains'.

✧ **Charlize Theron landed her first agent in a bank. He signed her after witnessing her throwing a fit at a bank teller who refused to cash her cheque. Her first language is Afrikaans.**

✳ Patrick Swayze's first crush was on original Charlie's Angel Jaclyn Smith.

✳ **Marilyn Monroe was the first ever *Playboy* centrefold.**

✳ Christopher Reeve was not the first choice to play Superman. Paul Newman, Robert Redford and Steve McQueen all turned down the role.

✳ **Vanessa Feltz left Cambridge with a first-class degree in English. Her first snog was with DJ Pete Tong.**

✳ Princess Diana was the first royal bride not to have the word 'obey' in her wedding vows.

✳ **At the age of four, Leonardo DiCaprio was axed from his first job on children's show *Romper Room* for being disruptive.**

✳ Pamela Anderson was born on 1 July 1967, in British Columbia, Canada, and made headlines as the first baby of Canada's centennial year.

✳ **Hugh Jackman's first job was as a petrol station attendant on the midnight to dawn shift.**

✳ Tickets for the first London concert of 'The Return of the Spice Girls' sold out in 38 seconds. (The group was originally called Touch.)

✳ **Matthew Kelly's first job after leaving school was as a bingo caller.**

✳ Robert Redford was the first choice to star in *The Graduate*. Dustin Hoffman only got the part when Redford declined it.

✳ **The first song Bruce Springsteen was able to strum on his guitar was 'It's All Over Now' by The Rolling Stones.**

TREE-CLIMBING GOATS

Morocco is the place to see a goat climbing a tree (or attempting to, at any rate) for, unlike most goats in the world, Moroccan goats have good reason to be scaling branches: they can't get enough of the olive-like fruit of the argan tree. For many years, farmers encouraged goats to clamber up and eat away to their heart's content, as they were part of a valuable production process. Argan oil comes from the argan tree, and is located in the pit of the fruit, which goats cannot digest. The pits would be collected from the goats' droppings and the extraction of the oil would begin. But the day eventually came when the goats were suddenly out of a job. Marketers of the oil believed the international market would buy more of the oil for use in food and cosmetics if they were assured that their product was not collected from goat excrement. So if you see a goat up a tree in Morocco these days, it is probably trespassing

★ ☆ BANANA FACTS ☆ ★

※ Bananas are giant herbs of the same family as lilies, orchids and palms. They grow upwards, rather than down. Unlike other fruits, bunches of bananas do not hang down from the plant, but, rather, grow upwards.

※ **Around 80 million tons of bananas are consumed worldwide every year.**

✳   A cluster of bananas is called a hand, which consists of 10 to 20 bananas, which are known as fingers (the word *banan* means 'finger' in Arabic).

Unlike most fruits, bananas ripen best when off the plant. If left on, the fruit splits open and has a cotton-like texture and flavour.

✳ Banana beer is made in Africa. In Kenya, it is called *urwaga*, in Uganda *lubisi* and in Rwanda *urwagwa*.

One of the first records of bananas dates back to Alexander the Great's conquest of India in 327 BC.

✳ 'Yes! We Have No Bananas' was a 1923 song by Frank Silver and Irving Cohn. Homer sings it at the end of a medley during 'Bart's Girlfriend', an episode of *The Simpsons*.

Reindeer love to eat bananas.

✳ Banana paper is around 3,000 times stronger than regular paper.

Bananarama's hit song 'Robert De Niro's Waiting' was originally called 'Al Pacino's Waiting', but De Niro's name fitted better with the music so the song was changed.

✳ Peter Dowdeswell holds the world record for banana eating – in 1987 he put away 17 peeled bananas in 1 minute 47 seconds.

Because of their potassium content, bananas are radioactive enough to cause false alarms on radiation sensors used to detect smuggled nuclear material at ports.

☆ CELEBRITY DOGS ☆

Sidi Bloom – while in Morocco filming *Kingdom of Heaven*, Orlando Bloom rescued and adopted his black Saluki dog, Sidi.

George Carrey – Jim Carrey's Great Dane. The tallest dogs in the world, Great Danes were bred from the medieval boarhound to hunt boar and deer by the Danir tribe of Denmark.

Bo Obama – after announcing to the world he was looking for a dog for daughters Sasha and Malia, President Barack Obama eventually settled on Portuguese water dog Bo, a gift from Senator Edward Kennedy. Named after singer Bo Diddley, he is known as the First Dog. In 2009, the White House released a baseball card of Bo, with his portrait on one side and statistics about the pet on the other.

Tinkerbell Hilton – most comfortable when travelling inside a designer handbag, Paris Hilton's Chihuahua resides in a $325,000 dog house. Briefly, Tinkerbell played second fiddle to a kinkajou (or honey bear) called Baby Luv, but it was a short-lived romance – the creature bit Paris on the arm in 2006 and hasn't been seen with her since the star got out of hospital.

Buster Cole – *X Factor* judge Cheryl Cole once admitted that her Chihuahua buries her G-strings in the garden. The pooch also made Girls Aloud more than an hour late for a gig because he refused to let Cole leave the house.

Norman and Dolly Aniston – Jennifer Aniston's Welsh corgi-terrier Norman and German Shepherd Dolly are always faithful friends, and Norman can regularly be found on set with the actress.

Arthur John – Elton John's much-adored cocker spaniel was best man at John and David Furnish's civil partnership ceremony.

Indo Smith – Will Smith's Rottweiler has a treadmill on which to go walkies when the actor is too tired to take him out to the park.

Max Clooney – not a dog, but just as good as far as George Clooney was concerned. The actor owned his beloved potbellied pig for 18 years. Max and George's friendship began in 1989 and the 130-kilogram pig was often seen on film sets. After a charmed and happy life, Max passed away peacefully in 2006.

BAFFLE YOUR FRIENDS

1. Ensure you have the attention of your audience.
2. Write down a number (2 x the current year. i.e. 2011 x 2 = 4,022) on a piece of paper, and fold.
3. Put paper in an envelope and seal. Pass to audience for inspection.
4. Ask for a volunteer. Hand volunteer paper and pen.
5. Ask volunteer to write the following: date of birth, year they first began working, age at the end of current year, number of years since began working.
6. Ask volunteer to add up the four numbers.
7. Ask volunteer to open envelope. Their total should tally.
8. Enjoy the puzzlement of your audience.

ON BURPING

The average person belches 15 times a day. The sound of a burp comes from the upper oesophageal sphincter, a muscle above the oesophagus that vibrates when gas passes through it. In Bahrain, it is a compliment when a guest burps after a meal because it's a sign that the food was enjoyable. Every year, cows in the US burp about 50 million tons of gas. If these gases could be harnassed, the annual burps of ten average cows could keep a small house heated for a year. In New Zealand, sheep are burping with such abandon that it is damaging the environment – they produce more than half the country's greenhouse gases.

☆ IDENTICAL TWINS ☆

* Identical twins Jim Lewis and Jim Springer were separated at four weeks old and taken by two adoptive families. Though each boy was informed he had a twin (Lewis when he was five, Springer when he was eight), the brothers were not reunited until the age of 39. On getting to know each other, Jim and Jim were truly amazed by their similarities.

* **Same names aside, both weighed precisely 81 kilograms, had owned a childhood dog named Toy, and had been married twice (both their first and second wives were called Linda and Betty respectively).**

＊ One Jim's son was called James Allan, and the other's answered to James Alan.

☆ **Each twin had owned a light-blue Chevrolet and regularly driven it on family holidays to Pass-a-Grille beach, Florida, and both men enjoyed Salem cigarettes and Miller Lite Beer.**

＊ To top it off, both the Jims had at one time been part-time sherrifs.

☆ **They bit their fingernails, suffered from migraines and enjoyed leaving love notes around the house for their wives.**

SWEAR IN SHAKESPEAREAN

Begin with 'thou' and combine one word from each column.

ARTLESS	BASECOURT	APPLE-JOHN
BAWDY	BAT-FOWLING	BAGGAGE
BESLUBBERING	BEEF-WITTED	BARNACLE
BOOTLESS	BEETLE-HEADED	BLADDER
CHURLISH	BOIL-BRAINED	BOAR-PIG
COCKERED	CLAPPER-CLAWED	BUGBEAR
CLOUTED	CLAY-BRAINED	BUM-BAILEY
CRAVEN	COMMON-KISSING	CANKER-BLOSSOM
CURRISH	CROOK-PATED	CLACK-DISH
DANKISH	DISMAL-DREAMING	CLOTPOLE
DISSEMBLING	DIZZY-EYED	CODPIECE
DRONING	DOGHEARTED	COXCOMB
ERRANT	DREAD-BOLTED	DEATH-TOKEN
FAWNING	EARTH-VEXING	DEWBERRY
FOBBING	ELF-SKINNED	FLAP-DRAGON
FORWARD	FAT-KIDNEYED	FLAX-WENCH

FROTHY	FEN-SUCKED	FLIRT-GILL
GLEEKING	FLAP-MOUTHED	FOOT-LICKER
GOATISH	FLY-BITTEN	FUSTILARIAN
GORBELLIED	FOLLY-FALLEN	GIGLET
IMPERTINENT	FOOL-BORN	GUDGEON
INFECTIOUS	FULL-GORGED	HAGGARD
JARRING	GUTS-GRIPING	HARPY
LOGGERHEADED	HALF-FACED	HEDGE-PIG
LUMPISH	HASTY-WITTED	HORN-BEAST
MAMMERING	HEDGE-BORN	HUGGER-MUGGER
MANGLED	HELL-HATED	JOITHEAD
MEWLING	IDLE-HEADED	LEWDSTER
PAUNCHY	ILL-BREEDING	LOUT
PRIBBLING	ILL-NURTURED	MAGGOT-PIE
PUKING	KNOTTY-PATED	MALT-WORM
PUNY	MILK-LIVERED	MAMMET
QUALLING	MOTLEY-MINDED	MEASLE
RANK	ONION-EYED	MINNOW
REEKY	PLUME-PLUCKED	MISCREANT
ROGUISH	POTTLE-DEEP	MOLDWARP
RUTTISH	POX-MARKED	MUMBLE-NEWS
SAUCY	REELING-RIPE	NUT-HOOK
SPLEENY	ROUGH-HEWN	PIGEON-EGG
SPONGY	RUDE-GROWING	PIGNUT
SURLY	RUMP-FED	PUMPION
TOTTERING	SHARD-BORNE	PUTTOCK
UNMUZZLED	SHEEP-BITING	RATSBANE
VAIN	SPUR-GALLED	SCUT
VENOMED	SWAG-BELLIED	SKAINSMATE
VILLAINOUS	TARDY-GAITED	STRUMPET
WARPED	TICKLE-BRAINED	VARLET
WAYWARD	TOAD-SPOTTED	VASSAL
WEEDY	UNCHIN-SNOUTED	WAGTAIL
YEASTY	WEATHER-BITTEN	WHEY-FACE

☆ ✳ YOUTUBE ✳ ☆

✳ If you press pause during any clip, then press the up and left arrow keys together, a game of Snake will start while the video continues.

✳ **The first ever video uploaded is titled 'Me at the zoo' by Jawed Karim (one of the site's founders). The clip went up on 23 April 2005 and is 18 seconds long.**

✳ YouTube has 490 million unique users worldwide per month.

✳ **Ninety-two billion page views are recorded each month.**

✳ We spend around 2.9 billion hours on YouTube in a month – that's over 325,000 years.

✳ **About 200,000 videos are uploaded every day, and it would take more than 400 years to watch all the videos on YouTube.**

✳ 'Rickrolling' is the practice of deceiving a person into clicking on a link that, against their expectations, takes them straight to a YouTube clip of Rick Astley's hit song 'Never Gonna Give You Up'. Rickrolling began in 2007, and by 2008 was one of the most common online practical jokes. A survey at the time estimated that over 18 million Americans had been rickrolled.

✳ **In September 2005, Brazilian footballer Ronaldinho's 'Touch of Gold' Nike advert became the first video to receive a million views.**

✳ In December 2007, the Queen launched the Royal Channel, which features her annual Christmas Day message and shows recent and historical footage of the royal family.

✳ **For Valentine's Day 2009, YouTube turned their site upside down.**

✳ Not counting music videos, the most viewed video of all time is 'Charlie bit my finger', with nearly 300 million views.

✳ **Each week, footage the length of 60,000 Hollywood films is uploaded.**

✳ The total bandwidth used by YouTube today is roughly the same as that used by whole of the internet in 2000.

TWENTY-FIRST-CENTURY
PALINDROME DATES

10-02-2001	01-02-2010	11-02-2011
02-02-2020	12-02-2021	03-02-2030
04-02-2040	05-02-2050	06-02-2060
07-02-2070	08-02-2080	09-02-2090

(1961 is the most recent year that can be written upside down and appear the same. The next year this will be possible is 6009.)

CLASSIC RIDDLE # 1

You are on a game show. The host shows you three doors. Behind one door is a suitcase with £1 million in it, and behind the other two doors are sacks of sand. You must point at the door of your choice. Once you have done so, the host opens one of the other doors. It swings open to reveal a sack of sand.

'I will give you a choice,' says the host. 'You can stick with the door you originally chose, or you can switch to the other unopened door.'

Should you switch doors, stick with your original choice, or does it not matter?

ANSWER TO CLASSIC RIDDLE # 1

You should switch doors.

There are three possibilities for the first door you picked:

You picked the first wrong door – if you switch, you win.

You picked the other wrong door – once more, if you switch you win.

You picked the correct door – if you switch, you lose.

Each of these cases is equally likely, so switching means there is a two in three chance that you will win (because there is a two in three chance that you are in one of the first two cases listed above), and a one in three chance you'll lose.

MORE THAN A MOUTHFUL - THE BIZARRE WORLD OF COMPETITIVE EATING

American pie-eating contests have been going for donkey's years, but nowadays there's a competition for scoffing almost any food imaginable. The most famous event is Nathan's Hot Dog Eating Contest, held annually on the fourth of July on Coney Island. 'Gurgitators' (the opposite of regurgitators) have been forcing dogs down since 1916, and today the IFOCE (International Federation of Competitive Eating) oversees a confounding variety of events all around the world. Here are some staggeringly true statistics from events at which being more than a little peckish is *de rigueur*.

Food	Quantity	Time (min./sec.)	Hungry person
Baked beans	2.72 kg (27 cans)	1	Don Lerman
Glazed doughnuts	49	8	Eric Booker
Hard-boiled eggs	65	6/40	Sonya Thomas
Quarter-pounders	11	10	Don Lerman
Chicken nuggets	80	5	Sonya Thomas
Deep-fried calamari	3 kg	10	Patrick Bertoletti
Hot dogs (with buns)	68	10	Joey Chestnut
Pickled jalapeño peppers	266	15	Patrick Bertoletti
Mayonnaise	3.6 kg	8	Oleg Zhornnitskiy
Oysters	576	10	Sonya Thomas
Spam	2.7 kg (nearly 8 tins)	12	Richard LeFevre
Waffles	29 x 227 g	10	Patrick Bertoletti

EXPLODING-HEAD SYNDROME

Non-24-Hour Sleep-Wake Syndrome is one of the rarer sleep disorders. Most humans have a circadian rhythm of around 24 hours, but those with Exploding-Head Syndrome have unstable body clocks that make normal sleep patterns an impossibility. Some unfortunates have a 72-hour cycle, which means they remain perfectly awake for 48 hours, and then sleep for 24. The syndrome is common in blind people.

☆ ★ 'ONLY' FACTS ★ ☆

* Abraham Lincoln is the only US president ever to be granted a patent. He invented a hydraulic device for lifting ships over shoals.

* **Up until the 1730s, India was the only source of diamonds in the world.**

* Antarctica is the only continent without reptiles.

* **Elvis Presley made only one television commercial – an advert for Southern Maid Doughnuts that ran in 1954.**

* Hawaii has the only royal palace in the United States – 'Iolani Palace.

* **Libra – the Scales – is the only inanimate symbol in the zodiac.**

* Some only children: Hans Christian Andersen, Lance Armstrong, Raymond Chandler, Eric Clapton, Carey Grant, Charlton Heston, James Earl Jones, Ted Koppel, Ivan Lendl, Barry Manilow, Maria Montessori, Jack Nicholson, Al Pacino, Elvis Presley, Franklin D. Roosevelt, Jean-Paul Sartre, Frank Sinatra, Robin Williams, Tiger Woods.

Liberia is the only country with a capital city named after an American president. Monrovia is named after James Monroe.

* The hummingbird is the only bird that can fly backwards.

The king of hearts is the only king without a moustache on a standard playing card.

* The only Englishman to become Pope was Nicholas Breakspear – Pope Adrian IV, 1154–9.

The only married couple to fly together in space were Jan Davis and Mark Lee, who flew aboard the *Endeavor* space shuttle in 1992.

* The only sculpture Michelangelo signed was *The Pietà*, completed in 1500.

The Congo is the only river that flows both north and south of the equator. It crosses the equator twice.

* In 1958, Zsa Zsa Gabor became the first and only recipient of a Golden Globe Award for 'Most Glamorous Actress'. The category was never announced again.

NATIONAL ANTHEM RECORDS:

Oldest words – Japan, from the ninth century

Oldest music – Netherlands, from the sixteenth century

Shortest – Uganda, with only nine bars of music

Longest lyrics – Greece, 158 verses

Longest tune – Uruguay, 105 bars of music

Shortest lived – Somaliland, five days

Only nation with no anthem – Cyprus

☆ BIZARRE AILMENTS ☆

Stendhal Syndrome – becoming ill in the presence of great works of art, named after the French writer who was overwhelmed to the point of sickness while looking at frescoes in Florence. According to one study, Michelangelo's statue of David, and Caravaggio's painting of Bacchus are especially disturbing to sufferers of the syndrome of which the symptoms include rapid heartbeat, dizziness and stomach trouble.

Alien-Hand Syndrome – caused by brain damage, this peculiar neurological illness causes a person's hand to rebel and act independently of its owner's intentions. Sufferers have been known to punch, pinch and slap themselves, and often the only way to control a rogue hand is to sit on it.

Foreign-Accent Syndrome – only 50 or so cases have been recorded of this intriguing affliction, where individuals suddenly adopt a new accent, usually after having suffered a stroke or injury. One of the oddest cases on record is that of a Norwegian woman who fell into a coma during an air raid in 1941. On waking, she found herself talking in a strong German accent. She soon lost most of her Norwegian friends ...

TOP-EARNING
DEAD CELEBRITIES

I.	Yves Saint Laurent	$350 million
II.	Rodgers & Hammerstein	$235 million
III.	Michael Jackson	$90 million
IV.	Elvis Presley	$55 million
V.	J. R. R. Tolkien	$50 million
VI.	Charles Schulz	$35 million
VII.	John Lennon	$15 million
VIII.	Dr Seuss	$15 million
IX.	Albert Einstein	$10 million
X.	Michael Crichton	$9 million
XI.	Aaron Spelling	$8 million
XII.	Jimi Hendrix	$8 million
XIII.	Andy Warhol	$6 million

Figures for 2009. Source: *Forbes* magazine.

☆ ★ INSECTS ★ ☆

* There are more insects in one square mile of rural land than there are human beings on the entire Earth.

* **There are more than 900,000 known species of insects in the world, and roughly 10,000,000,000,000,000,000 living today. One per cent of them are ants.**

* The combined weight of the world's insects exceeds that of all the humans that have ever lived – around 90 billion.

* **More people are killed each year by bees than by snakes.**

* The longest-living insect is the termite queen: they have been known to live for at least 50 years and some scientists believe they may live to 100.

* **Each year, insects eat one third of the Earth's food crops.**

* The colour of an adult head louse varies according to the hair colour of the person on which it is living.

* **Dragonflies have as many as 30,000 lenses in each eye.**

* The fastest runners are cockroaches, which can move almost a foot per second – about one mile an hour.

* **Mosquitoes avoid citronella because it irritates their feet.**

* The queen of a termite colony may lay 6,000–7,000 eggs per day, and may live from 15 to 50 years.

* Dragonflies fly at speeds of up to 30 miles per hour.

A male spider's reproductive organ is located on the end of one of his legs.

* A 1960s experiment on spiders showed that spiders fed flies injected with caffeine will spin 'nervous', badly organised webs.

Beetles taste like apples, wasps like pine nuts and worms like fried bacon.

* Worker ants can live for up to seven years.

Some worms will eat themselves if they can't find any food!

* For more than 3,000 years, Carpenter ants have been used to close wounds in India, Asia and South America.

A honey bee can lift 300 times its own weight – the equivalent of a person lifting 15 tons.

* Tarantulas survive for up to two years without eating.

Only full-grown male crickets can chirp.

* Locusts can eat their own weight in food in a day. A human being eats his own body weight in about half a year.

Monarch caterpillars shed their skin four times before they become a chrysalis, growing more than 2,700 times their original size.

* The praying mantis is the only insect that can turn its head.

✧ **Since the 1998 launch of space shuttle *Columbia* on mission STS-90 there have been more crickets in space than humans. The results of CRISP (Crickets In Space) revealed that the development of gravity-related behaviour in crickets was not affected by weightlessness.**

✳ Snails can sleep for three years without eating.

CURIOUS CONTESTS

In a good marriage? Prove it. Every four years happy couples descend on the village of Great Dunmow to persuade a panel of strangers – 'six maidens and six bachelors' that their relationship is not on the rocks. The Flitch Trials go back to the twelfth century, the prize being a 'flitch' of bacon – half a cured pig. Winning couples are paraded through the streets towards their winnings.

Playing chess make you want to punch someone? Try chess boxing. Two-minute rounds of boxing alternate with four-minute rounds of chess. 'Fighting is done in the ring. Wars are waged on the board' and competitions are held annually somewhere in the world.

Good at pulling faces? If so, gurning contests may be for you. An English tradition dating back to the thirteenth century, a gurning contest is held annually at the Egremont Crab Fair in Cumbria. Starting out in 1998, Peter Jackman became England's best-known gurner, and won the competition four times. He even had his teeth removed to make his job easier.

☆ ★ HUMANS ★ ☆

✳ Statistically we are more likely to divorce than change bank account.

✳ **People of ancient China believed that swinging the arms could cure a headache.**

✳ More than a third of Brits aged 25–34 have a tattoo.

✳ **It is estimated that 0.7 per cent of the world's population is drunk at any given time.**

✳ After spending hours working at a computer display, look at a blank piece of white paper. It will probably appear a little pink.

✳ Every time you lick a stamp, you're consuming one tenth of a calorie.

✳ **Around 2,000 left-handed people die annually due to improper use of equipment designed only for right-handed people.**

✳ If you are locked in a completely sealed room, you will die of carbon-dioxide poisoning before you will die of oxygen deprivation.

✳ **Eighty-five per cent of red lingerie is bought by men.**

✳ Ninety per cent of women turn right when they walk into a department store.

THE MAN WHO COULD EAT ANYTHING

Michel Lotito was a Frenchman whose tastes extended way beyond croissants. Known as 'Monsieur Mangetout', he began consuming indigestible objects from an early age. He had a healthy appetite for metal, glass and rubber, and considered a chopped-up bicycle or television a real treat. His biggest meal – a Cessna 150 aircraft – took him two years to polish off. He washed his metallic morsels down with mineral oil to keep his insides lubricated, and was able to consume up to a kilogram of material a day. Between 1959 and 1997, Lotito is estimated to have eaten a ton of metal. However, he couldn't stomach bananas or eggs.

☆ ★ SOME RATHER ★ ☆ PECULIAR WEBSITES

virtual-bubblewrap.com – Pop some plastic online

mycathatesyou.com – Terrifying felines

dogjudo.com – Canine martial arts

sillywalksgenerator.com – Create your own Pythonesque strut

guimp.com – World's tiniest website

dullmensclub.com – A paradise for bores and pedants

forkbend.com – For Uri Geller wannabes

paranoiamagazine.com – Put your mind at ease

monobrow.com – Celebrating the caterpillar-on-the-forehead look

davesweboflies.com – Made up 'facts'

isitnormal.com – Are you as weird as you think? Probably not

blackpeopleloveus.com – White people satirise themselves

nakednews.com – World events without garments

afterlifetelegrams.com – Pay per word send a message to a loved one

extremeironing.com – Household chore becomes dangerous sport

ihateclowns.com – The name says it all

trafficcone.com – Homepage of The Traffic Cone Preservation Society

marry-an-ugly-millionaire-online-dating-agency.com – Golddiggers unite

ladiesagainstfeminism.com – Popular with men, probably

MAGGIE THATCHER'S VARIOUS NICKNAMES

Attila the Hen – The Blessed Margaret – The Boss – Daggers – The Iron Lady – The Grocer's Daughter – The Lady with the Blowlamp – The Leaderine – Mother – The Plutonium Blonde – She Who Must Be Obeyed – TINA (acronym for There Is No Alternative).

☆ ★ KISSING ★ ☆

* Two thirds of people tip their head to the right when they kiss.

* **The charming expression 'kiss my arse' dates back at least to 1705.**

* Lips are 100 times more sensitive than the tips of the fingers, and more sensitive than the genitals too.

* **Kissing at the conclusion of a wedding ceremony can be traced to ancient Roman tradition, where a kiss was used to seal a legal contract.**

* The film with the most kisses is *Don Juan* (1926) in which John Barrymore and Mary Astor share 127 kisses. The film with the longest kiss is Andy Warhol's 1963 film *Kiss,* in which Rufus Collins and Naomi Levine embrace for 50 minutes – the full length of the movie. The 1961 film *Splendor in the Grass*, starring Natalie Wood and Warren Beatty, made history for containing Hollywood's first French kiss.

* **On 5 July 2005 a couple in London locked lips and remained that way for 31 hours 30 minutes and 30 seconds, making it the longest kiss ever recorded.**

* Leper kissing became fashionable among medieval ascetics and religious nobility during the twelfth and thirteenth centuries. It was deemed proof of humility.

❋ **French kissing involves all 34 muscles in the face. A pucker kiss involves only two.**

✳ 'French kiss' entered the English language in the early 1920s as a slur on the French, who were considered to be overly obsessed with sex. In France, this form of kissing is called a 'soul kiss' because, if done right, it feels as if two souls are merging.

❋ **The Romans categorised kissing in three ways. *Osculum* was a kiss on the cheek, *basium* a kiss on the lips, and *savolium* a deep, passionate kiss.**

✳ There's a reason men like sloppy kisses – an open mouth allows men to provide women with small amounts of libido-enhancing testosterone which is contained in their saliva.

❋ **To 'kiss and make up' has a biological function. The hormone oxytocin is released when we hug and kiss, and this helps to reduce levels of the stress hormone cortisol that courses through our veins during arguments.**

HIGHER (AND WIDER) EDUCATION

The University of Alaska stretches across four time zones. It spans a distance starting from a community college in Ketchikan (near Alaska's south-eastern border) to a tiny learning centre on the remote island of Adak in the Aleutian Islands. These two points are roughly as far apart as London and Moscow.

☆ CELEBRITY ☆ NAME CHANGES

AS WE KNOW THEM	ORIGINAL
50 Cent	Curtis Jackson
Adam Ant	Stuart Leslie Goddard
Alice Cooper	Vincent Damon Furnier
Anna Nicole Smith	Vickie Lynn Hogan
Axl Rose	William Bailey
Barbara Windsor	Barbara-Ann Deeks
Barry Manilow	Barry Alan Pinkus
Billy Idol	William Broad
Bob Dylan	Robert Allen Zimmerman
Bono	Paul Hewson
Boy George	George O'Dowd
Charlie Sheen	Carlos Irwin Estévez
Cher	Cherilyn Sarkisian
Cheryl Baker	Rita Crudgington
Cliff Richard	Harry Webb
David Bowie	David Robert Jones
David Copperfield	David Kotkin
David Tennant	David McDonald
David Walliams	David Williams
Diana Ross	Diane Earle
Dido	Florian Cloud de Bounevialle Armstrong
Elle Macpherson	Eleanor Gow
Elton John	Reginald Dwight
Elvis Costello	Declan MacManus
Frank Skinner	Chris Collins

Freddie Mercury	Farrokh Bulsara
Gene Wilder	Jerome Silberman
George Orwell	Eric Blair
Jennifer Aniston	Jennifer Anastassakis
John Cleese	John Cheese
Lulu	Marie Lawrie
Marilyn Manson	Brian Warner
Marilyn Monroe	Norma Jeane Baker
Meatloaf	Marvin Aday
Mel Gibson	Columcille Gibson
Natalie Portman	Natalie Hershlag
Nina Ricci	Maria Nielli
Nina Simone	Eunice Wayman
Ozzy Osbourne	John Osbourne
Pink	Alecia Moore
Ralph Lauren	Ralph Lipschitz
Shakin' Stevens	Michael Barratt
Snoop Doggy Dogg	Calvin Broadus
Sting	Gordon Sumner
Suggs	Graham McPherson
The Edge	David Evans
Tina Turner	Anna Mae Bullock
Vic Reeves	Jim Moir
Vin Diesel	Mark Vincent
Whoopi Goldberg	Caryn Johnson
Woody Allen	Allen Konigsberg

☆ SURPRISING SCIENCE ☆

Country Music and Suicide – A 2004 report by psychologists Steven Stack and Jim Grundlach entitled 'The Effect of Country Music on Suicide' showed that white men were more likely to commit suicide if exposed to country music on the radio. The phenomenon is thought to be related to the dark and melancholy themes in the music, which can push those already at risk of suicide to acting on their impulses.

Rollercoasters and Asthma – In 2010 Simon Rietveld of the University of Amsterdam, The Netherlands, and Ilja van Beest, of Tilburg University, provided evidence that riding on a rollercoaster can reduce the symptoms of asthma.

Coffee and Strange Feelings – A UK study of 200 coffee-drinking students proved that drinking seven or more cups of coffee a day makes you three times more likely to see or hear things that are not there. Coffee stimulates the stress hormone cortisol, and scientists think this may be responsible for the extra-sensory overload in heavy users. So next time you feel the presence of a dead man, keep walking when you get to Starbucks.

Teeth and Blindness – A man regained his sight when surgeons removed one of his teeth, placed a lens inside and sewed it into his eyeball. A tooth was chosen because, unlike a plastic equivalent, the body will not reject it.

Falling in Love and OCD – Biochemically, the emotions we experience when smitten are virtually indistinguishable from acute obsessive-compulsive disorder, according to Donatella

Marazziti of the University of Pisa. Can't stop thinking about someone? Perhaps you're ill.

Expensive Painkillers Are Best (even when fake) – In 2008 Rebecca Waber and Professor Dan Ariely completed a study showing how expensive placebos work better than cheap placebos. The bottom line is, you get what you pay for, even if it's all in your head.

WHAT'S WITH THE BAND NAME?

Ace of Base named after the band's first studio, located in the basement of a car repair shop. They considered themselves the 'aces' of the studio …

The Beautiful South the name sarcastically expressed singer Paul Heaton's dislike of southern England, and was also a cheeky way to force macho men to say the word 'beautiful'.

Bee Gees often said (falsely) to be a contraction of 'Brothers Gibb', the name is actually a reference to the initials of Bill Goode and disc jockey Bill Gates, who helped the group in their early days.

Coldplay originally called Starfish, the band asked to use the name when another band – named Coldplay – disbanded.

The Cure called Easy Cure at first (the name of an early song), then changed to The Cure because Robert Smith felt it sounded less American and 'hippyish'.

Duran Duran after playing at Barbarella's nightclub in Birmingham, the band named themselves after Dr Durand-Durand, villain of sci-fi film *Barbarella*.

Green Day originally called Sweet Children, the band changed its name to avoid confusion with another band named Sweet Children. The band got their new name from a song by Billie Joe Armstrong entitled 'Green Day', a slang term for a day spent smoking marijuana.

Joy Division originally Warsaw but, worried about being confused with punk band Warsaw Pakt, renamed as Joy Division in reference to the prostitution wing of a Nazi concentration camp in 1955 novel *The House of Dolls*.

Kaiser Chiefs after the South African Kaizer Chiefs Football Club.

Marillion originally Silmarillion, after the J. R. R. Tolkien novel of the same name, but soon shortened to avoid possible legal issues.

Oasis originally The Rain, but renamed when Liam Gallagher joined the band. Inspired by an Inspiral Carpets tour poster – one of the venues listed was the Oasis Leisure Centre in Swindon.

Pink Floyd Syd Barrett devised the name, which refers to two blues musicians, Pink Anderson and Floyd Council.

Radiohead the band's label did not like their first name – On A Friday – and gave them two weeks to come up with something better. The result is a reference to 'Radio Head', the 1986 Talking Heads song from the album *True Stories*.

Steely Dan named after a dildo in William S. Burroughs' novel *Naked Lunch*.

✩ ON AVERAGE ... ✩

* A hedgehog's heart beats 190 times a minute. Its heartbeat drops to 20 beats per minute during hibernation.

* **A beaver can cut down 200 trees a year.**

* An ear of corn has 800 kernels in 16 rows.

* **A cat will sleep for sixteen hours a day – more than any other mammal.**

* An average woman's uterus expands up to 500 times its normal size during pregnancy.

* **A human body has an average of 32 million bacteria on it.**

* A man will grow nine metres' worth of facial hair in his lifetime.

* **A couple marry in Las Vegas 150 times every day.**

* An elephant produces 22 kilograms of dung every day.

* **A lead pencil can draw a 35-mile-long line or write around 50,000 words in English.**

* A person will laugh nine times a day, go to the toilet six times and fall asleep in seven minutes.

* **A snail moves at approximately 0.000362005 miles per hour.**

* A typical Egyptian mummy is wrapped in 900 metres of linen bandage.

☆ **A raindrop falls from the sky at an average speed of 23 kilometres per hour.**

———◆◆◆◆———

☆ UNFORGETTABLE FOOD ☆

* Chewing gum while peeling onions will prevent you from crying.

☆ **Groucho Marx was 81 when he ate his first bagel.**

* If you put a raisin in a glass of champagne, it will sink then rise, sink then rise, sink then rise …

☆ **Sausages were nicknamed bangers during the Second World War. To save on meat, water was added to sausages and, when cooked, the steam often made them explode.**

* Americans munch through 18 acres of pizza every day.

☆ **Astronauts are not allowed to eat beans before takeoff, as passing wind damages their spacesuits.**

* 'Groaking' means to watch people eating in the hope they will offer you some.

☆ **More than 500 peanuts are used to make a jar of peanut butter.**

* Japan is the largest exporter of frogs' legs.

☆ **Orange juice helps the body absorb iron more easily when consumed with a meal.**

✳ Since 1978, at least 37 people have died as a result of shaking vending machines in an attempt to get free merchandise.

☆ **The dark meat on a turkey is higher in calories than the white.**

✳ Apple pips contain traces of cyanide.

A-Z

The A–Z was designed by portrait painter Phyllis Pearsall. After getting lost on her way to a party in Belgravia one night in 1935, and finding the 1919 Ordnance Survey Map particularly unhelpful, Phyllis decided to map London herself. Each morning, she set off from her bedsit on Horseferry Road, walking (and cataloguing) the 23,000 streets of the city, and clocking up 3,000 miles along the way. She kept her jottings in a shoebox under her bed. The good woman's working day was 18 hours long and she drew up the final map with the help of a single draughtsman, James Duncan. Unable to find a publisher, Phyllis founded the Geographer's Map Company in 1936, and printed 10,000 copies herself. Two hundred and fifty copies were delivered to W. H. Smith in a wheelbarrow, and more orders came flooding in soon after. All A–Z maps print a non-existent 'trap street' so that they can tell if a map has been illegally copied from theirs. Where a new, as yet unnamed street is being constructed, the A–Z map will include a made-up name. One such trap street was Bartlett Place, which was subsequently given its official name, Broadway Walk.

THE YO-YO

Second to the doll, the yo-yo is one of the oldest toys in history. The ancient Greeks decorated the two halves (made of wood, metal and terracotta) with depictions of the gods. Originally, the British referred to the yo-yo as the Bandalore, Quiz or the Prince of Wales, the French to *l'incroyable* or *l'émigrette*. *Yoyo* itself is a Filipino word from the Tagalog language, meaning 'come back' – the story goes that large, sharp-edged yo-yos were once used as weapons in the Philippines, but this may be an urban legend ...

☆

THE AMAZING FALLING BABY

In 1937, American street sweeper Joseph Figlock was going about his business in a Detroit alley when a baby fell from a fourth-storey window and struck him on the head. Joseph was slightly injured, but the baby was unharmed. A year later, while Joseph was clearing another alley, two-year-old David Thomas toppled from a fourth-floor window and crashed down upon Joseph. Once again, there were no serious injuries.

LAST WORDS ON THE MOON

We all know that the first words spoken on the moon were Neil Armstrong's 'One small step for man. One giant leap for mankind' in 1969. (As it happens, Neil Armstrong stepped on the moon with his left foot first.) Less well known are the *last* words to be uttered on the moon, as spoken by Commander Eugene Cernan, 'the last man on the moon' on the Apollo 17 mission in 1972: 'America's challenge of today has forged man's destiny of tomorrow.' Moon exploration involved six missions over three years, and 12 astronauts.

Spacecraft	Astronauts	Mission dates	Time spent moonwalking
Apollo 11	Neil Armstrong Edwin 'Buzz' Aldrin	16–24 July 1969	2 hrs 32 sec.
Apollo 12	Charles Conrad Jr Alan L. Bean	14–24 Nov. 1969	2 hrs 15 sec.
Apollo 14	Alan B. Shepard Edgar D. Mitchell	31 Jan.– 9 Feb. 1971	9 hrs 23 sec.
Apollo 15	David R. Scott James B. Irwin	26 July–7 Aug. 1971	19 hrs 8 sec.
Apollo 16	John W. Young Charles M. Duke Jr	16–27 April 1972	20 hrs 14 sec.
Apollo 17	Eugene A. Cernan Harrison H. Schmitt	7–19 Dec. 1972	22 hrs 4 sec.

PROVERB GAME

Can you recognise the proverb from the initials?

AAADKTDA	LBAF
ABITHIWTITB	LBYL
AFAHMASP	LSSM
AFILAW	LTPLM
AFINIAFI	MHWTSS
AMTHGF	MLNW
APSIAPH	OOSOOM
ASITSN	PMP
AWWIND	RDASS
BCBC	RWBIAD
BIITEOTB	TCTAC
BLTN	TEIHTFD
BSTS	TLNRS
ECHASL	TMCSTB
FSD	TNFLAOF
GMTA	TNPLH
HHNFLAWS	TWDMAR
HIWTHI	WNWN
HTGT	WTAWTAW
INRBIP	YCGBOOAS
LALL	

PROVERB GAME

———◦•×•◦———

Answers

An apple a day keeps the doctor away

A bird in the hand is worth two in the bush

A fool and his money are soon parted

All's fair in love and war

A friend in need is a friend indeed

Absence makes the heart grow fonder

A problem shared is a problem halved

A stitch in time saves nine

A woman's work is never done

Beggars can't be choosers

Beauty is in the eye of the beholder

Better late than never

Better safe than sorry

Every cloud has a silver lining

Fools seldom differ

Great minds think alike

Hell hath no fury like a woman scorned

Home is where the heart is

Here today, gone tomorrow

It never rains but it pours

Live and let live

Life begins at forty

Look before you leap

Least said soonest mended

Little things please little minds

Make hay while the sun shines

Make love not war

Out of sight, out of mind

Practice makes perfect

Rats desert a sinking ship

Rome wasn't built in a day

Two's company, three's a crowd

To err is human to forgive divine

True love never runs smooth

Too many cooks spoil the broth

There's no fool like an old fool

There's no place like home

Two wrongs don't make a right

Waste not, want not

Where there's a will, there's a way

You can't get blood out of a stone

☆ A PAGE OF POPCORN ☆

* Popcorn is the only type of corn that will pop.

☆ **The scientific name for popcorn is _Zea mays everta_.**

* 1948, 5,000-year-old popped kernels were discovered in caves in New Mexico.

FOR PERFECT POPCORN WITH NO BURNT KERNELS

3 tbsp canola, peanut or grapeseed oil

⅓ cup popcorn kernels

1 large covered saucepan

2 tbsp butter

Salt to taste

Method

Heat oil on medium high heat

Put 3 or 4 popcorn kernels into the oil and cover pan

When kernels pop, add remaining kernels in an even layer

Cover, remove from heat and count 30 seconds

Return the pan to the heat

Gently shake the pan by moving it back and forth while kernels pop

Keep the pan lid slightly open to let the steam from the popcorn release

Once the popping slows to several seconds between pops, remove the pan from the heat, remove the lid, and dump the popcorn immediately into a wide bowl

Salt to taste

✧ **Christopher Columbus introduced popcorn to the Europeans in the late fifteenth century. The first commercial popcorn machine was invented by Charles Cretors in Chicago in 1885.**

✳ Each kernel contains a small amount of moisture. As the kernel is heated, this water turns to steam. Popcorn differs from other grains in that the kernel's shell is not water-permeable, so the steam cannot escape and pressure builds up until the kernel finally explodes, turning inside out.

✧ **A kernel will pop when it reaches a temperature of around 175°Celsius.**

BAD LUCK OR URBAN MYTH?

In 1883, one Henry Ziegland broke up with his girlfriend, who consequently committed suicide. Enraged, the girl's brother vowed to hunt down Ziegland and shoot him dead. After shooting Ziegland, and believing him to be dead, the brother turned the gun on himself and died. As it turned out, Ziegland was injured but not killed – the bullet had merely grazed his face and lodged itself in a tree. What a lucky escape, thought Ziegland. Some years later Ziegland decided to cut down the tree, but due to its size felt that dynamite would serve him better than a saw. The ensuing explosion took the tree down, but it took Ziegland, too – the explosion sent the bullet, which had missed him some years earlier, flying straight into his head, and he died instantly.

SOME ACRONYMS USED IN HOSPITALS

NFN   Normal For Norfolk

PFO   Pissed and Fell Over

ADASTW   Arrived Dead And Stayed That Way

GROLIES Guardian Reader Of Limited Intelligence In Ethnic Skirt

TFBUNDY Totally Fucked But Unfortunately Not Dead Yet

WOFTAM   Waste Of Fucking Time And Money

TUBE   Totally Unnecessary Breast Examination

☆ NO SHIT, SHERLOCK ☆

* The phrase 'Elementary, my dear Watson' cannot be found in the Sherlock Holmes books.

Holmes' famous deerstalker cap was not created by Conan Doyle, but by the illustrator Sidney Paget.

* Most famous quote: 'When you have eliminated the impossible, whatever remains, however improbable, must be the truth.'

Watson's bullet wound in the shoulder is mentioned in *A Study in Scarlet*, but later in *The Sign of the Four* it had moved to the leg.

* In 1964, only the Bible sold more copies than Sherlock Holmes books.

☆ **Star of the 2009 film *Sherlock Holmes* Jude Law admitted he didn't know anything about the movie, the books or his character until shooting started.**

✳ Sherlock means blond, but two of the actors most famously associated with the role, Basil Rathbone and Jeremy Brett, both had dark hair.

☆ **On 8 July 1989, Leslie Bricusse's *Sherlock Holmes: The Musical* was staged at the Cambridge Theatre, London, but received such terrible reviews that it closed after just one performance. The show was revived four years later, in 1993, and made a successful tour of the UK.**

✳ Abbey National, which occupied the site of Holmes' address at 221B Baker Street from 1932 to 2002, employed a secretary to deal with the fan mail. Any correspondence is now delivered to the nearby Sherlock Holmes Museum.

THREE LITTLE QUESTIONS

1. Half of all Americans live within 50 miles of what?
2. If you were to spell out numbers, how far would you have to go until you would find the letter 'A' other than in the word 'and'?
3. What do bulletproof vests, fire escapes, windscreen wipers and laser printers all have in common?

1. Their birthplace.
2. One thousand.
3. All invented by women.

SOME CLASSIC FILM ☆ ★ MISTAKES ★ ☆

* In the 1991 remake of *Father of the Bride*, Annie and Bryan marry on 6 January, but the opening scenes of *Father of the Bride 2* contain a framed invitation of their wedding which gives 9 October as the date.

* **Near the end of *Forrest Gump*, Forrest says that his wife died on a Saturday. In the next scene Forrest visits her grave and headstone reads 22 March 1982 – a Monday.**

* John Travolta is not the man walking down the street at the start of *Saturday Night Fever*. The legs belong to his stand-in, Jeff Zinn.

* **Stanley Kubrick's *Full Metal Jacket* was filmed in England. A telltale sign is the moment the Marines are jogging around the training camp – the road they are jogging on shows British road markings.**

* In *Lord of the Rings: Return of the King*, Frodo has a scar on his face for part of the film, but its size and position keep changing. It even moves from one cheek to the other.

* **During the re-enactment of the Battle of Carthage in the Colosseum in *Gladiator*, a chariot is knocked on to its side and hits a wall. Just then, a blanket lifts up to reveal a gas cylinder in the back of the chariot ...**

* In *Pirates of the Caribbean: Curse of the Black Pearl*, Johnny Depp's Captain Jack Sparrow says, 'on deck, you scabrous dogs', and at that moment a member of the film crew can be seen decked out in T-shirt and sunglasses.

* **In 1980s classic *Teen Wolf*, an extra can be seen exposing himself in the final victory scene during the American football game between the Beavers and the Dragons. As Scott's dad comes out of the crowd to congratulate him, the fan behind him quickly slips his privates in and out of his trousers.**

* Hitchcock's *North by Northwest* contains a scene in the Mount Rushmore café. Just before gunfire is heard, a boy in the background puts his fingers firmly in his ears.

* **In the *Charlie's Angels* scene where they fight a strange assassin played by Crispin Glover, Drew Barrymore picks up Lucy Liu and spins her round to kick Crispin. However, Barrymore warns Lucy Liu what she is about to do by shouting 'Lucy', not Alex, the character's name.**

* *Top Gun* contains a fundamental error. In real life, aeroplane throttles are pushed forward to increase power, and back to reduce it. Unfortunately, Tom Cruise never fails to pull back when he wants to go faster and vice versa.

* **The *Titanic* scene in which Jack tells Rose of his ice fishing experiences in Lake Wissota, Wisconsin, is very lovely, but rather implausible – the artificial lake was created when a dam was built six years after the *Titanic* sank.**

WEIRD US LAWS THAT STILL EXIST

Place	Illegal to …
Washington State	… boast that one's parents are rich.
Maryland	… play Randy Newman's 'Short People' on the radio.
Alabama	… play dominoes on Sunday.
Minneapolis, Minnesota	… double-park (punishable by being put on a chain gang).
Kentucky	… push a wife out of bed when touched by her cold toes.
Willowdale, Oregon	… swear during sex.
Minnesota	… hang male and female underwear on the same washing line.
Tennessee	… shoot any game other than whales from a moving automobile.

☆ ✳ # THE LOWDOWN ON BARBIE ✳ ☆

✳ Barbie first appeared at the New York Toy Fair on 9 March 1959. Her full name is Barbie Millicent Roberts and her parents are Ruth and Elliot Handler. She has four sisters: Skipper (1964), Stacie (1992), Kelly (1995) and Krissy (1995). Barbie's boyfriend, Ken, came on the scene in 1961. After a solid 43-year relationship, they split up on Valentine's Day 2004.

☆ **An American girl aged between three and eleven has, on average, ten Barbie dolls in her toy box.**

✳ Every second, two Barbie dolls are sold somewhere in the world. Placed head to toe, the Barbie dolls and family members sold since 1959 would circle the Earth more than seven times.

Barbie has had more than 43 pets including 21 dogs, 12 horses, three ponies, six cats, a parrot, a chimpanzee, a panda, a lion cub, a giraffe and a zebra. The best-selling Barbie ever was Totally Hair Barbie. She had hair from the top of her head to her toes.

✳ Barbie's real-life statistics would be 39-23-33

Comedian Russell Brand once inserted a Barbie doll into his bottom while on stage.

—•+•+•—

☆ ✭ PIG FACTS ✭ ☆

✳ Pigs might not fly, but they can swim. In fact, swimming pigs are a tourist attraction in the clear waters of Big Major Spot Island in the Bahamas. Tourists flock to Pig Beach to swim with the happy family of brown and pink boars. A more questionable story of aquatic pigs exists: once upon a time, sailors kept pigs on board in case of shipwreck. It was believed that, should the boat sink, pigs would always swim toward the nearest shore. There is little evidence for this.

A domesticated pig has approximately 15,000 taste buds, more than any other mammal, including humans.

PIGS IN GEOGRAPHY

Boarhills, Scotland	Hog Point, Virginia
Hog Island, Florida	Hog Head, Ireland
Hog Island, Grenada	Pig Point, Virginia
Hog Island, Guyana	Bay of Pigs, Cuba
Hog Island, Michigan	Sow River, England
Hog Island, Virginia	

※ The pig is considered the fourth most intelligent animal.

※ **There are more than 180 species of pig and they are bred on every continent except Antarctica.**

※ A pig's orgasm lasts thirty minutes. Apparently.

※ **Pigs can't look up at the sky.**

※ In the early stages of development, a pig's embryo is similar to a human's.

※ **A pig squeals at a range from 100 to 115 decibels.**

※ Cuba's Bay of Pigs is named after fish, not pigs. *Cohino* means pig in Spanish, but is also the name of a fish common to the area.

※ **'Poke' is an old word for sack or bag, so to buy a 'pig in a poke' is to buy a pig before you've seen it. The expression dates from the Middle Ages, and serves as a warning to consumers not to purchase goods until you have examined them.**

Pigs are perceived as dirty, but actually keep themselves cleaner than most household pets. They lie in mud because they lack sweat glands and constantly need water or mud to cool off.

In Denmark, there are twice as many pigs as people.

SOME RANDOM FACTS AND FIGURES

One in ten people in the world live on an island.

The opposite sides of a dice cube always add up to seven.

If you count the seconds without stopping, it would take you eleven and a half days to reach one million, and 32 years to reach one billion.

In 1870, there were more Irish living in London than in Dublin, and more Catholics living in London than in Rome.

The chance of being born on leap day (29 February) is about 684 in a million, or one in 1,461.

Worldwide, fewer than five million people celebrate their birthday on leap day.

Each year, about 27 per cent of food in developed countries is thrown away.

☆ **Almost 1.2 billion people are undernourished – a similar number are obese.**

✳ Since 1972, around 64 million tons of aluminium cans (about three trillion cans) have been produced. Placed end to end, they would stretch to the moon a thousand times. Cans represent less than 1 per cent of solid waste material.

☆ **In Australia, sheep outnumber people five to one.**

✳ All the chemicals in a human body combined are estimated to be worth about 6.25 euros.

FAMOUSLY BISEXUAL

Alexander the Great

Hans Christian Andersen

Brett Anderson

Joan Baez

Amanda Barrie

Drew Barrymore

Simone de Beauvoir

Sarah Bernhardt

Leonard Bernstein

John Betjeman

Marlon Brando

Rupert Brooke

Julie Burchill

William S. Burroughs

Lord Byron

Caligula

Bruce Chatwin

Neneh Cherry

Montgomery Clift

Joan Crawford

Aleister Crowley

Dave Davies

Sammy Davis Jr

James Dean

King Edward VII

Marlene Dietrich

Amanda Donohoe

Carol Ann Duffy

Deborah Dyer

Bret Easton Ellis

William Empson

Kenny Everett

Fergie (of the Black Eyed Peas)

Megan Fox

Alan Freeman

Nelly Furtado

Lady Gaga

Greta Garbo

Julie Goodyear

Cary Grant

Peggy Guggenheim

Alec Guinness

Katharine Hepburn

Laurel Holloman

Angelina Jolie

Grace Jones

Janis Joplin

Frida Kahlo

Pat Kavanagh

Calvin Klein

Ronnie Kray

Christian Lacroix

Burt Lancaster

D. H. Lawrence

Lindsay Lohan

Rebecca Loos

Katherine Mansfield

Robert Mapplethorpe

Daphne du Maurier

George Melly

Herman Melville

Freddie Mercury

Lord Montagu of Beaulieu

Lord Louis Mountbatten

Nero

Anaïs Nin

Laurence Olivier

Joan Osborne	Pauline Réage	Kevin Sharkey	Rebecca Walker
Camille Paglia	Michael Redgrave	Anna Nicole Smith	Sylvia Townsend Warner
Peaches			
Édith Piaf	Arthur Rimbaud	Susan Sontag	Evelyn Waugh
Mimi Pollak	Martin Rossiter	Dusty Springfield	Rosemary West
Cole Porter	Renato Russo	Michael Stipe	Amy Winehouse
Dawn Porter	Françoise Sagan	Gore Vidal	Virginia Woolf
Dee Dee Ramone	Pam St Clement	Alice Walker	Aileen Wuornos

FRENCH KISSING

The French kiss was brought to England by First World War soldiers who had witnessed the decadent manner in which the French showed affection. In France, the tongue-kiss is known as *un baiser amoureux* (love kiss) or, more bizarrely, as a *patin* (ice-skating shoe). Internationally, there are many different expressions for French kissing:

Australia and New Zealand		Pashing or lashing
Belgium	*Iemand binnendoen*	(taking someone in)
Bosnia (often)	*Žvaka*	(bubblegum)
Brazil	*Beijo de lingual*	(tongue kiss)
China	*Shiwen*	(wet kiss)
Costa Rica	*Apretar*	(to squeeze)
Denmark	*Snave*	(snog)
Germany	*Zungenkuss*	(tongue kiss)
Greece	*Glosofilo*	(tongue kiss)
Iceland	*Fara í sleik'*	(go into licking)
Italy	*Limonare*	(to lemon)
Malta	*Tintreda*	(sucking)
Panama	*Arropar*	(to wrap with)
Portugal	*Linguado*	(sole fish)
Slovenia	*Zalizati*	(to lick someone)
South Africa	*Tong in die long*	(tongue in the lung)
Spain	*Morrear*	(to muzzle)

☆ KILLED BY THEIR ☆ OWN INVENTIONS

(OR WHEN NECESSITY IS THE MOTHER OF DEATH)

Franz Reichelt – the Austrian-born tailor most famous for inventing an overcoat designed to double as a parachute. In 1912, 'The Flying Tailor' gained permission to demonstrate his invention from the top of the Eiffel Tower – the only condition was that he used a dummy instead of himself. A large crowd of media and onlookers gathered to watch the dummy plummet like a stone. On closer inspection, it became apparent that this was no dummy – Franz had himself jumped, and died instantly on impact.

Thomas Midgley – the American chemist who gave us leaded petrol and CFCs, and was dubbed the one person who 'had more impact on the atmosphere than any other single organism in Earth's history'. Neither of these inventions killed him, however – not directly, anyway. In 1940, at the age of 51, Midgley was bedbound with lead poisoning and polio, so he designed a complicated system of strings and pulleys to help lift him from his bed. Four years later he strangled himself, having become entangled in the device.

Alexander Bogdanov – the physician, economist, sci-fi writer and founder of Bolshevism was also a pioneer of blood transfusion. He set up the first institution to explore the possibilities of the practice, and undertook 11 transfusions himself. Bogdanov reported better eyesight and less hair loss before going back for some more blood. Unfortunately, in 1928 he swapped his blood for that of a student with tuberculosis and malaria. Bye-bye, Alexander.

William Bullock – the American who revolutionised the printing industry by inventing the rotary printing press in 1863. While he was tinkering with one of his presses, his leg became trapped in the machinery. Bullock was badly injured and contracted gangrene. The only solution was to amputate the leg, but Bullock died during the operation.

Henry Winstanley – the English engineer who lost two of his ships on the treacherous Eddystone Rocks of the south-west corner of Devon, and decided to build a lighthouse to protect his property. The first Eddystone lighthouse was lit in 1698, and Winstanley proudly declared his desire to be inside should 'the greatest storm that ever there was' strike. His wish came true on 26 November 1703, when a hurricane tore at the coast and swept away the lighthouse, and Henry Winstanley with it.

Marie Curie – the pioneer in the field of radioactivity and two times Nobel Prize winner (Physics and Chemistry), who discovered polonium and radium died of aplastic anaemia on 4 July 1934. This was a result of radiation exposure during her experiments. Back then, the dangers of exposure were not known. Due to their radioactivity levels, Curie's original scientific papers and even her cookbook are thought too dangerous to be handled without protective clothing.

☆

☆ FELINE FACTOIDS ☆

* If a male cat is both orange and black it will probably be sterile. To have both the orange and the black coat colours, the male cat must have all or part of both female X chromosomes.

* **Cats are born unable to see or hear; it is the vibration of the mother's purr that attracts them to start feeding.**

* Cats have more than one hundred vocal sounds, while dogs have only about ten.

* **In a lifetime, the average house cat spends approximately 10,950 hours purring.**

* Chocolate is poisonous to cats.

* **There are more homeless cats in Rome than anywhere else in the world.**

* Catgut comes from sheep, not cats.

* **Lions can sleep as long as 20 hours in one day.**

* Domestic cats are the only feline species that can hold their tails upright while walking.

* **Cats bury their faeces to cover their trail from predators.**

* Ancient Egyptians shaved off their eyebrows to mourn the deaths of their cats.

☆ **Lion, leopards, tigers and jaguars are the only cats that can roar. They cannot purr, however.**

✳ There were no cat species in Australia until they were imported.

☆ **When not sleeping, cats spend nearly a third of their lives grooming themselves.**

✳ Isaac Newton invented the first cat flap made out of felt for his laboratory door to save his light experiments being ruined by his cat wandering in and out.

☆ ✳  ✳ ☆

✳ David Beckham once picked up empty pint glasses at Walthamstow dog track for £10 a night.

☆ **The expression 'dog days' (meaning very hot days) has been around since Roman times. *Canculares* days were, in the eyes of the ancients, the result of Sirius – the Dog Star – rising with the sun, combining to create the hottest days of summer.**

✳ Approximate number of facial expressions dogs can make: 100.

☆ **A sled dog running in Alaska's annual Iditarod race will burn 10,000 calories a day.**

✳ In Norman, Oklahoma, it is illegal to make an ugly face at a dog.

✧ 'When I go to restaurants, the waiters always ask me if I want a doggy bag. I'm tired of that. All you waiters, stop asking me if I want a mother******* doggy bag' – Snoop Dogg.

✱ Know an ugly dog? Then perhaps you should enter it in the World's Ugliest Dog Contest. Held annually in Petaluma, California, the competition attracts mutts from all over the world. With prize money of $1,000 and a guaranteed publicity tour for dog and owner, competition is stiff.

✧ During the classic torture scene in *Reservoir Dogs* (accompanied by the song 'Stuck in the Middle with You'), police officer Marvin Nash's hands are handcuffed, but throughout the scene the position of his hands changes. One second his hands are in front of him, and the next they are behind his back.

✱ *Knitting with Dog Hair*, by Kendall Crolius and Anne Montgomery, is essential reading for anyone who wants a scarf made from their pooch.

✧ Comedian Harry Hill can sing 'How Much Is That Doggie in the Window?' backwards.

✱ Dogs have been known to allow other species such as cats to suckle from them.

✧ The last wolf in the British Isles was killed in Scotland in 1743.

✱ 'Woof woof' in Japanese is 'wan wan'.

✧ A dog's sense of smell is 20 times stronger than ours.

TASTE

Butterflies taste with their back legs.

Humans can taste only when food is mixed with saliva.

On average a human has approximately 9,000 taste buds.

Salt is 100 per cent taste and 0 per cent smell,
a rare characteristic for a condiment.

Fried spiders taste nutty.

Our ability to taste fades with age.

When humans consume a food, the texture and temperature of the
food are connected to the flavour. Because their textures are so
similar, eating an apple, potato or an onion with your nose plugged
makes them indistinguishable.

AFTER DEATH

* Elephants have been reported to remain standing for some time after they have died.

* **Galileo's middle finger was severed from his corpse in the sixteenth century and placed on display in a glass case in Florence, Italy.**

* The living do not outnumber the dead. Since time began, it is estimated that 60 billion people have died.

☆ **The Malagasy people of Madagascar have an annual funerary tradition called famadihana. The bones of loved ones are exhumed, dressed in new clothing and danced with around the tomb.**

✳ A body will take about ten days to disintegrate in the sun, leaving only the skeleton.

☆ **Charlie Chaplin was stolen from his own grave and his body held for a ransom of 600,000 francs.**

✳ A US company will take your remains and turn them into a diamond which can be worn by your loved ones. LifeGem uses the cremated remains of you or a pet to create synthetic diamonds which range in weight and price. A full human body can provide sufficient carbon to make up to 50 one-carat diamonds (which cost around £10,000 each). In 2007, strands of hair from Ludwig van Beethoven were used to produce a diamond which raised $202,700 for charity on eBay.

☆ **Light-bulb inventor Thomas Edison was friends with Henry Ford. As Edison lay dying, Ford told his son, Charles, to capture Edison's dying breath in a bottle. Charles bottled some of the air in the room. Today it stands on display at the Henry Ford Museum.**

✳ Memorial Space Flights launch cremated remains into outer space, but at a price. Loved ones get to watch the rocket take off, and once the deceased is in orbit, their whereabouts can be logged on the internet. Handy.

☆ **The Victorians photographed the dead since it was cheaper than taking photos while the subject was alive. Photography was in its infancy, and it was very expensive and time-consuming. A person's death warranted the cost of a photo, since it was something to remember them by.**

✳ Queen Victoria insisted on being buried with the bathrobe of her long-dead husband, Prince Albert, and a plaster cast of his hand.

☆ **Tibetan Buddhists cut and beat a dead body (including the bones) to a pulp and leave the results for vultures to eat.**

✳ English philosopher Francis Bacon, a founder of the scientific method, died in 1626 of pneumonia after stuffing a chicken with snow to see if cold would preserve it.

THE REAL FAGIN

Isaac 'Ikey' Solomon is the man who, in Victorian times, was thought to have inspired Charles Dickens' character from *Oliver Twist*. He was a notorious leader of a gang of young pickpockets. Artfully, he dodged arrest, but was eventually captured and tried at the Old Bailey in 1830. Escaping the death sentence, he received a sentence of 14 years' transportation. A fate, some might argue, worse than death.

☆ ★ BAD ARTS AND ★ ☆ ENTERTAINMENT PREDICTIONS

'Who the hell wants to hear actors talk?' – H. M. Warner, co-founder of Warner Brothers, 1927.

'Reagan doesn't have that presidential look' – United Artists Executive, rejecting Ronald Reagan as lead in 1964 film *The Best Man*.

'We don't like their sound, and guitar music is on the way out' – Decca Recording Co. rejecting the Beatles, 1962.

'I'm just glad it'll be Clark Gable who's falling on his face and not Gary Cooper' – Gary Cooper on his decision not to take the leading role in *Gone with the Wind*.

'The wireless music box has no imaginable commercial value. Who would pay for a message sent to nobody in particular?' – David Sarnoff's associates in response to his urgings for investment in the radio in the 1920s.

'Television won't last because people will soon get tired of staring at a plywood box every night' – Darryl Zanuck, movie producer, 20th Century Fox, 1946.

'Can't act. Slightly bald. Can dance a little' – memo written by the MGM testing director after Fred Astaire's first screen test in 1933. Astaire got the memo and hung it over his fireplace.

'Overwhelmingly nauseating, even to an enlightened Freudian ... the whole thing is an unsure cross between hideous reality and improbable fantasy. It often becomes a wild neurotic daydream ... I recommend that it be buried under a stone for a thousand years' – publisher on Vladimir Nabokov's *Lolita*.

'I'm sorry, Mr Kipling, but you just don't know how to use the English language' – editor of the *San Francisco Examiner* to Rudyard Kipling.

AIDS CONSPIRACY

S ad but true: there are people who believe that the CIA created the AIDS virus in an attempt to wipe out the gay community along with African Americans. This insane notion dates to 1981, when the Centers for Disease Control and Prevention first reported the epidemic. Even now, a number of high-profile public figures have faith in the idea of a CIA plot. South African President Thabo Mbeki has touted the theory and refuted the rather more plausible scientific explanation that the virus originated from African monkeys in the 1930s. Rather, Mr Mbeki accused the US government of manufacturing the disease in military labs. On winning the Nobel Peace Prize, Kenyan ecologist Wangari Maathai announced to the world that she, too, believed the conspiratorial hype. Others are convinced that the government merely injected the virus into gay men in 1978 while conducting hepatitis B experiments in New York, San Francisco and Los Angeles. Some camps blame Richard Nixon for authorising the scheme when he combined the US Army's bio-warfare department with the National Cancer Institute in 1971.

INTERNATIONAL PIZZA TOPPINGS

Americans consume around 350 slices of pizza a second, or 21,000 a minute, or 1,260,000 an hour. It all adds up to over 100 acres a day. While pepperoni is firm favourite in the US, other countries have different ideas of the perfect topping.

Country	Popular toppings
India	Pickled ginger, minced mutton, paneer (a type of cottage cheese)
Russia	Mockba (a mixture of sardines, tuna, mackerel, salmon, onions and red herring)
Brazil	Green peas
Japan	Eel, squid, Mayo Jaga (mayonnaise, potato, bacon)
France	Flambée (bacon, onion and fresh cream)
Costa Rica	Coconut
Korea	Potato pizza – potato, onions, bacon, mushrooms, cheese and mayonnaise
Switzerland	Tex-Mex – onions, double beef, fresh tomatoes and jalapeño peppers
Greece	Hellenic – pepperoni, onion, green pepper, fresh tomato, Greek olive, feta cheese and oregano

INTERNATIONAL TOPPINGS FOR CHIPS

Cheese, carne asada, sour cream, and guacamole (US)

Curry sauce (Ireland)

Cheese curds and gravy (Canada)

Garlic (US)

Cheese powder (Philippines)

Lemon (Mexico)

Chopped raw onions (Netherlands)

Malt vinegar (UK)

Mint coriander sauce (Pakistan)

Mustard (Norway)

Oregano (Greece)

Peanut sauce (Netherlands)

Remoulade sauce (Denmark)

Sugar and butter (Vietnam)

Turkey stuffing, peas, cheese and gravy (Canada)

White vinegar (Canada)

VICTORIAN CRIMES PUNISHABLE BY DEATH

By 1815 there were more than 200 offences that would send your neck straight to the hangman's noose. Fittingly, the penal system was dubbed the 'Bloody Code'. Though sentences were very harsh by today's standards, the acquittal rate of 25 per cent was fairly close to the current levels of around 20 per cent. That said, the list below proves it didn't take much to send oneself to an early grave:

Being in the company of gypsies for a month.

Damaging Westminster Bridge.

Cutting down trees.

Stealing livestock, or anything worth more than five shillings (£30 today).

Pickpocketing.

General poaching.

Stealing from a shipwreck.

Going out at night with a blackened face (and therefore looking like a burglar).

EVIL MEN'S MUSICAL TASTES

Evil man	Leader of …	Preferred music
Osama bin Laden (dec.)	Al-Qaeda	B-52s and Whitney Houston
Robert Mugabe	Zimbabwe	Cliff Richard
Colonel Gaddafi	Libya	Lionel Richie
Kim Jong-il	North Korea	Eric Clapton
King Mswati III	Swaziland	Michael Jackson, Eric Clapton
Mahmoud Ahmadinejad	Iran	Chris de Burgh

FANTASTIC HOAX 1 – THE TURK

The Turk was an 'automaton chess player' famed in eighteenth-century courts of Europe and shown around the world for over 80 years. The model figure was built by Wolfgang von Kempelen in 1770, and rumoured to operate using an 'ingenious' mechanical combination of cogs and cranks combined with a touch of magic. While touring the world to play some of the finest chess experts in the world, the Turk caused credulous wonder among the educated classes of Paris, London and New York, famously taking on and checkmating Benjamin Franklin and Napoleon Bonaparte. The mysterious mechanical master caused much fascination and speculation, and Edgar Allan Poe wrote a magazine article pondering how the machine might operate. Eventually, the Turk was destroyed by fire in a museum, and only then was its secret revealed: the cogs and cranks were an illusion. All along, a human chess master had been hidden inside a compartment below the board and moved the pieces using magnets.

TIPS OF THE SLUNG ☆
(SOME AMUSING SPOONERISMS)

The spoonerism (where consonants and vowels are swapped in speech) is named after the Reverend William Archibald Spooner, a nineteenth-century warden of New College, Oxford. The Reverend was prone to getting his words mixed up, and many a spoonerism has been attributed to him.

We must drink a toast to the queer old dean [dear old queen].

We'll have the hags flung out [the flags hung out].

It is kisstomary to cuss the bride [customary to kiss].

Cattle ships and bruisers [battle ships and cruisers].

A blushing crow [crushing blow].

A well-boiled icicle [well-oiled bicycle].

The Lord is a shoving leopard [a loving shepherd].

You were fighting a liar in the quadrangle [lighting a fire].

Is the bean dizzy [dean busy]?

BONES

Humans are born with 300 bones in their bodies, but the only bone fully grown at birth is located in the ear. When a person reaches adulthood he or she only has 206 bones in total because some bones fuse together as we grow. The feet contain a quarter of the bones in the body. One in 20 people have an extra rib. The strongest bone is the femur, or thighbone, which is hollow. The only jointless bone in a human being is the hyoid bone in the throat. A flute carved from a bird's wing bone more than 9,000 years ago is the oldest playable musical instrument in the world. Skull and Bones is a secret society at Yale University. Informally, the society is known as 'Bones', and its members are called 'bonesmen'. Their emblem is a skull and crossbones over the number 322. Several American politicians, including George W. Bush, his father and Senator John Kerry, are members. The society has achieved a certain notoriety for stealing, or 'crooking', from university buildings, and has been accused of stealing the skulls of Martin Van Buren (eighth President of the United States), Geronimo (nineteenth-century Native American leader) and Pancho Villa (Mexican revolutionary general).

☆ ★ 'ONLYS' IN THE ★ ☆ ENGLISH LANGUAGE

✳ Only four words ending in 'dous': tremendous, horrendous, stupendous and hazardous.

✴ **Only word pronounced the same way when last four letters are removed: queue.**

✳ Only planet not named after a god: Earth.

✴ **Only three world capitals beginning with letter O: Ottawa, Canada; Oslo, Norway; Ouagadougou, Burkina Faso.**

✳ Only six words containing 'uu': Muumuu, vacuum, continuum, duumvirate, duumvir and residuum.

✴ **Only word beginning and ending in 'und': underground.**

✳ Only five words ending in 'mt': daydreamt, dreamt, outdreamt, redreamt, undreamt.

✴ **Only word that, when capitalised, changes from noun or verb to a nationality: polish.**

NOVELTY BETS

Also known as exotic betting, novelty bets are wagers on non-sporting events. They've been around for years. During the Renaissance, travelling carnivals allowed punters to gamble on 'shin kicking'. Competitors would kick each other's shins until one wimped out from the pain. In the eighteenth and nineteenth centuries, 'pedestrianism' was popular. Bets were placed on how long it would take to walk, run or hop a certain distance. In 1789, an Irishman bagged £20,000 after walking from Britain to Constantinople (Istanbul) and back in less than a year. Jules Verne's *Around the World in Eighty Days* was inspired by the craze for distance bets.

In 1989, a 40-year-old night-shift worker from Newport bet £30 that in the year 2000 Cliff Richard would have been knighted, U2 would still be going, *EastEnders* would still be a BBC soap opera along with *Neighbours* and *Home and Away*. All five predictions came true, netting a whopping £194,370 at 6,479-1 odds.

FAILED TO IMPERSONATE
☆ THEMSELVES ... ☆

Elvis Presley – came third in an Elvis lookalike contest. Towards the end of his life, Elvis ate hamburgers at an obscure diner. The owners knew who he was, but respected his desire to remain incognito when he lost the competition.

Alistair Cooke – the presenter of *Letter from America*, came third in an 'impersonate Alistair Cooke' competition on the Radio 4 show *Broadcasting House*.

US TV newsreader David Brinkley – was once told that a record producer was looking for someone who could imitate his voice for a comedy record. Brinkley rang the producer and said, 'A lot of people tell me I sound like David Brinkley.' The producer told David he sounded nothing like himself, and hung up.

Dolly Parton – once failed to win a Dolly Parton lookalike contest. 'I got beaten by some drag queen,' said Dolly.

Charlie Chaplin – entered a Chaplin contest in San Francisco and failed to make the finals. He informed a reporter that he was 'tempted to give lessons in the Chaplin walk, out of pity as well as the desire to see the thing done properly'.

David Bowie – came third in a David Bowie lookalike contest.

THE MOONS OF URANUS ...

... are all named after characters from English literature, namely from the works of William Shakespeare and Alexander Pope.

MOONS FROM SHAKESPEARE PLAYS:

Miranda, Caliban, Sycorax, Prospero, Setebos, Stephano, Trinculo, Francisco, Ferdinand	*The Tempest*
Titania, Oberon, Puck	*A Midsummer Night's Dream*
Cordelia	*King Lear*
Ophelia	*Hamlet*
Bianca	*The Taming of the Shrew*
Cressida	*Troilus and Cressida*
Desdemona	*Othello*
Juliet, Mab	*Romeo and Juliet*
Portia	*The Merchant of Venice*
Rosalind	*As You Like It*
Margaret	*Much Ado About Nothing*
Perdita	*The Winter's Tale*
Cupid	*Timon of Athens*

MOONS FROM ALEXANDER POPE:

Ariel, Umbriel, Belinda	*The Rape of the Lock*

USELESS TV FACTS

✳ Presenter Judy Finnigan had elocution lessons to disguise her Mancunian accent.

✳ **Harry Hill's favourite television soap is *EastEnders*.**

✳ Terry Wogan was a virgin when he got married.

✳ **Comedian and presenter Alan Carr debuted as the Milky Bar Kid aged eight.**

✳ Presenter and writer Stephen Fry had gained nine O levels by the age of thirteen. When he was eighteen he was jailed for credit card fraud.

✳ **Jamie Oliver rebuffed Nestlé and Coca-Cola, both of whom asked him to pose naked for an ad campaign.**

✳ US actress/TV hostess Oprah Winfrey should have been called Orpah, after the biblical figure but the midwife spelled the name wrong on the birth certificate. Her production company, Harpo, is Oprah spelled backwards. She is a distant cousin of Elvis Presley.

✳ **Simon Cowell dropped out of school at the age of 16 and one of his first jobs was as a mail boy. In 2007, Cowell was offered £1 million to become the face of Viagra. Insulted by the offer, he turned it down. He featured in *Scary Movie 3* where he played a judge of a rap competition. He is a vegetarian.**

* Matt Lucas lost all of his hair when he was six, and went to Weight Watchers in his teens. The *Little Britain* star supports Arsenal FC.

☆ *The Simpsons* **creator Matt Groening managed to incorporate his own initials into the animated Homer. M is his hair and G is his ear.**

* TV cook Nigella Lawson failed her eleven-plus exam because she refused to take the maths paper.

☆ **Ulrika Jonsson has a devil tattooed on her bottom.**

☆ SUGGESTIVE PLACES ☆

Arsoli (Lazio, Italy)

Bastard (Norway)

Beaver (Oklahoma, USA)

Beaver Head (Idaho, USA)

Brown Willy (Cornwall, England)

Chinaman's Knob (Australia)

Climax (Colorado, USA)

Cunt (Spain)

Cunter (Switzerland)

Dikshit (India)

Dildo (Newfoundland, Canada)

Dong Rack (Thailand–Cambodia border)

Dongo (Democratic Republic of the Congo)

Effin (Limerick, Ireland)

Fukue (Honshu, Japan)

Fukui (Honshu, Japan)

Fukum (Yemen)

Hold With Hope (Greenland)

Intercourse (Pennsylvania, USA)

Lickey End (West Midlands, England)

Little Dix Village (West Indies)

Lord Berkeley's Knob (Sutherland, Scotland)

Middle Intercourse Island (Australia)

Muff (Northern Ireland)

Nobber (Donegal, Ireland)

Pis Pis River (Nicaragua)

Sexmoan (Luzon, Philippines)

Seymen (Turkey)

Shafter (California, USA)

Shag Island (Indian Ocean)

Shitlingthorpe (Yorkshire, England)

Tittybong (Australia)

Tong Fuk (Japan)

Turdo (Romania)

Twatt (Orkney, Scotland)

Wank (Germany)

Wankendorf (Schleswig-Holstein, Germany)

Wankener (India)

Wankie (Zimbabwe)

Wankie Colliery (Zimbabwe)

Wanks River (Nicaragua)

Wankum (Germany)

Wet Beaver Creek (Australia)

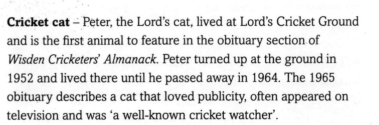

CAT FEATS

Cricket cat – Peter, the Lord's cat, lived at Lord's Cricket Ground and is the first animal to feature in the obituary section of *Wisden Cricketers' Almanack*. Peter turned up at the ground in 1952 and lived there until he passed away in 1964. The 1965 obituary describes a cat that loved publicity, often appeared on television and was 'a well-known cricket watcher'.

Royal cat – King Charles I owned a black cat named Luck. The King became convinced that any ill fortune experienced by his pet would be passed on to him, so arranged armed guards to protect the feline 24 hours a day. All was well until Luck became ill and died. The following day, Charles was arrested for treason and subsequently beheaded.

Literary cat – When Thomas Hardy died in 1928, his wife faced a dilemma. The authorities wanted to bury him in Poets' Corner at Westminster Abbey, but Hardy's wishes were that he be buried at Stinsford, Dorset. Eventually it was decided that the poet's ashes would be buried at Westminster, but that his heart be interred at Stinsford. A doctor was called to remove the heart but, at the end of the operation, was called away on urgent business. On returning, the doctor was horrified to discover that his cat had eaten half of it. As punishment the cat was killed and buried with Hardy's heart.

Ship cat – Trim the cat was rather an adventurer. Born aboard HMS *Reliance* in 1799, he fell overboard when just a kitten, but deftly swam back to the ship and scaled a rope to climb back on board. Explorer Matthew Flinders was impressed by Trim's fighting spirit, and from then on Trim was always at his side. The black and white cat accompanied Flinders aboard HMS *Investigator* on a two-year voyage to circumnavigate and map the coastline of Australia. Later he shared a Mauritian prison cell with Flinders, whom the French had accused of spying. During the incarceration, Trim inexplicably disappeared. Flinders was convinced his beloved cat had been stolen and eaten by famished slaves. In a tribute to Trim, the captain called him 'one of the finest animals I ever saw'. Today, a bronze statue of Trim sits on a window ledge in Sydney's Mitchell Library. In front of the same ledge stands a statue of his owner.

Many cats – Jack and Donna Wright of Kingston, Ontario, made their way into the *Guinness Book of Records* for having the highest number of cats. According to the book they have 689 cats, many descended from a tabby called Midnight. In 1888, an Egyptian peasant discovered an estimated 300,000 mummified cats in Beni Hassan, Egypt. Many of the cats were stolen once the find was made public, but the remaining mummified cats were shipped to Great Britain and used as agricultural fertiliser.

ON HUMAN CANNONBALLS

The practice of being shot from a cannon has been around since the 1870s. The subject achieves flight with the help of a spring, or compressed air pushing a cylinder within the cannon. Firecrackers and gunpowder are used *outside* the cannon to complete the illusion. A net or a body of water is used for the landing. The first human cannonball was a young girl called Zazel. In 1877, the fourteen-year-old shot to fame at the Royal Aquarium in London. Afterwards, she joined P. T. Barnum's circus. Zazel's spring cannon was invented by 'The Great Farini' – Canadian William Leonard Hunt. In 1983, David 'Cannonball' Smith flew over 50 metres to break the world record, achieving a speed of 70 miles per hour. Many human cannonballs black out in flight. Circus historian A. H. Coxe says that of 50 famous human cannonballs more than 30 have been killed, mostly by falling outside the net.

WEIRD EBAY ITEMS
(LOT 1)

A LIFE – Ian Usher had had enough, so put his life up for sale. For £200,000, the winning bidder received Ian's house, car, job and introductions to his friends in Perth, Australia.

VIRGINITY – Eighteen-year-old English girl Cary put her virginity up for auction. She wanted to pay her university fees. A businessman gave her $10,000, but did not take Cary up on her offer.

A BABY – A couple put their baby up for sale for one euro. They were only joking, and soon took down the auction. The child was removed from their custody until authorities were satisfied the couple were not child traffickers.

A VOTE IN THE 2008 US ELECTION – A University of Minnesota student attempted to auction his vote and received charges of bribery, treating and soliciting under an 1893 law banning the sale of votes.

REVENGE KNICKERS – A jilted wife sold the oversize knickers of her husband's mistress and a 'small-sized' condom wrapper she'd found in their bed.

SERIAL KILLER'S FINGERNAILS – In 1979, Roy Norris and Lawrence Bittaker went on a five-victim killing spree in California. Many years later, Norris sold his fingernail clippings on eBay for $9.99. One of the creepiest auctions ever.

HAUNTED RUBBER DUCK – In 2004, a man sold a rubber duck he considered 'haunted'. His two-year-old son had told stories of the duck's fights, and the father claimed the child had been bitten by the duck. Bizarrely, it sold for $107.50.

VIRGIN MARY SANDWICH – Diane Duyser's grilled cheese sandwich looked too much like the Virgin Mary to be eaten, so she auctioned it and received $28,000 from an online casino.

☆ FIRST THINGS FIRST ☆
(THE 2ND)

✳ Will Smith's first ever day of acting was the first episode of *The Fresh Prince of Bel-Air*.

✳ **Keira Knightley spent her first ever pay packet on a doll's house. Her first nude scene was in *The Hole*, at the age of sixteen.**

✳ Jim Morrison was the first ever rock star to be arrested on stage. He had exposed himself in front of the crowd and used profane language.

✳ **Denzel Washington found his first job sweeping hair at a barbershop, aged 11. He feels the position primed him for a career in acting because the best liars hang out at barbershops.**

✳ Comedian Russell Brand's first stage appearance was in *Bugsy Malone*. He played Fat Sam.

☆ **Over 25 million viewers watched Barbara Windsor in her first episode of *EastEnders*.**

✳ When Kylie Minogue first appeared in *Neighbours*, she only had a one-week contract. The word *kylie* is Aborigine for boomerang.

☆ **The first time Madonna was a guest on David Letterman's US chat show, she was bleeped twelve times for foul language.**

✳ J. K. Rowling wrote her first story, 'Rabbit', at the age of five.

☆ **David Blaine's first meal after spending 44 days fasting in a plastic box was chicken satay.**

IN CASE YOU WERE WONDERING

☆ ✳ ✳ ☆

✳ Farmers today plant their crops up to three weeks earlier than they did 15 years ago. In the 1960s, temperatures from January to March averaged 4.2°C; they rose to 5.6°C in the 1990s.

☆ **Brussels sprouts contain three times as much vitamin C as oranges.**

✳ The heat generated by a laptop, and the knees-together pose needed to balance it, can damage a man's fertility.

Brazilians are the nationality most likely to read spam.

Some pigeons follow roads and turn off at motorway junctions when navigating.

'A spectre is haunting Europe – the spectre of Communism' – the first sentence of Marx and Engels' *Communist Manifesto* of 1848 was initially translated into English by Helen Macfarlane as 'A frightful hobgoblin stalks through Europe'.

There are 75 withdrawals from cash machines every second in the UK.

The collective noun for rhinos is a 'crash'.

Osama bin Laden referred to 9/11 as 'Manhattan'.

The word 'electricity' was first used in English in about 1600 by Elizabeth I's physician.

George W. Bush got the highest number of votes for president of any candidate in US history, in November 2004.

Half of Britons have a collection of more than 20 carrier bags at home. One in ten people has up to 80.

The word 'celeb' is not a recent invention – it was used in a letter to Woodrow Wilson in 1913.

The Sydney Harbour Bridge contains just 16 nuts and bolts. The rest is held together by rivets, because it doesn't need to be dismantled.

Herrings break wind to communicate and keep the school together.

☆ **Bob Dylan originally planned to use his first two given names, Robert Allen, as his stage name, because it sounded like the name of a Scottish king. After he read some Dylan Thomas poems, he chose Dylan as his new surname instead.**

☆

DO BEEFEATERS EAT BEEF?

Beefeaters are the guards at the Tower of London. Their official title is 'Yeomen Warders of Her Majesty's Royal Palace and Fortress the Tower of London, and Members of the Sovereign's Body Guard of the Yeoman Guard Extraordinary'. Golly.

King Henry VII formed the Body Guard in 1485 to uphold the dignity and grandeur of the English Crown for all time. A Yeoman was a 'man of the district', and yeomen were in a class of their own, wedged between the upper class and labourers and recognised by the state in the fourteenth and fifteenth centuries. They lived well and didn't have to starve in winter, like their poorer neighbours.

But why are they called Beefeaters? Count Cosmo, the Grand Duke of Tuscany, noted on his travels in England in the seventeenth century that they were 'Eaters-of-Beef, of which a considerable portion is allowed them daily by the Court'. If you want to become a Beefeater you must be retired from the armed forces after at least 22 years of service, and be prepared to work from home – yeomen and their families live in the Tower of London. You don't have to eat beef, but it surely can't do any harm.

LEADERS

According to North Korea's official biography of Kim Jong-il, the Dear Leader learned to walk by the age of three weeks, talk by eight weeks, and he wrote his first manifesto on the future of the Korean people by the age of two.

Attila the Hun died not in battle, but of a nosebleed after sex.

George Washington's false teeth were made from hippo ivory and cow teeth, held together by metal springs.

Boudicca was queen of the Iceni tribe of East Anglia, and joined up with the Trinovantes of Essex to rebel against the Roman treatment of her people. They attacked Roman settlements at Colchester, St Albans and London, burning the city down in AD 60. The passionate leader is also rumoured to be buried under platform 10 of King's Cross Station in London.

Queen Christina of Sweden was petrified of fleas. So extreme was the seventeenth-century queen's phobia that she commissioned a miniature cannon with which to exterminate her jumpy enemies. Christina kept the weapon in her bedroom and spent an unhealthy amount of time trying to use it.

Hitler's handwriting was impeccable. When psychologist Carl Jung saw Hitler's script in 1937, he remarked: 'Behind this handwriting I recognise the typical characteristics of a man with essentially feminine instinct.'

ABSOLUTE NONSENSE?*

☆ ☆

* A species of oyster in the Caribbean can actually climb trees.

* **The increased electricity used by modern appliances is causing a shift in the Earth's magnetic field. By the year 2327, the North Pole will be located in mid-Kansas, while the South Pole will be just off the coast of East Africa.**

* Male rhesus monkeys often hang from tree branches by their amazing prehensile penises.

* **Legislation passed in Britain during the First World War making it illegal to say 'gesundheit' to a sneezer was never repealed.**

* Manatees possess vocal cords that give them the ability to speak like humans, but don't do so because they have no ears with which to hear the sound.

* **Catfish are the only animals that naturally have an odd number of whiskers.**

* Replying more than 100 times to the same piece of spam e-mail will overwhelm the sender's system and interfere with their ability to send any more spam.

* **Polar bears can eat as many as 86 penguins in a single sitting.**

* You can get blood from a stone, but only if it contains at least 17 per cent bauxite.

✴ **In 1843, a Parisian street mime artist got stuck in his imaginary box and consequently died of starvation.**

✴ Touch-tone telephone keypads were originally planned to have buttons for police and fire departments, but they were replaced with * and # when the project was cancelled when the 999 system was developed.

✴ **Watching an hour-long soap opera burns more calories than watching a two-hour football match.**

✴ Until 1978, Camel cigarettes contained minute particles of real camels.

✴ **Urine from the male Cape water buffalo is so flammable that some tribes use it as lantern fuel.**

✴ If you part your hair on the right side, you were born to be carnivorous. If you part it on the left, your physical and psychological make-up is that of a vegetarian.

✴ **In ancient Greece, children of wealthy families were dipped in olive oil at birth to keep them hairless throughout their lives.**

✴ The Venezuelan brown bat can detect and dodge individual raindrops in mid-flight, arriving safely back at its cave completely dry.

❋
Yes, all of it.

☆ GASTROKNOWLEDGE ☆

* There are more nutrients in the cornflakes packet than there are in the actual cornflakes.

A typical American eats 28 pigs in his/her lifetime.

* Large doses of coffee can be lethal. Ten grams, or 100 cups over four hours, can kill the average human.

Per capita, the Irish eat more chocolate than Americans, Swedes, Danes, French and Italians all together.

* The Swiss eat more chocolate per capita than any other nation.

The vintage date on a bottle of wine indicates the year the grapes were picked, not the year of bottling.

* Cream does not weigh as much as milk.

Iceland consumes more Coca-Cola per capita than any other nation.

* Weekend drinkers in Dublin drink 9,800 pints an hour between 5.30 p.m. on Friday and 3 a.m on Monday.

Within two hours of standing in daylight, milk loses between a half and two-thirds of its vitamin B content.

* Place a T-bone steak in a bowl of Coke and it will be gone in two days.

The peach was the first fruit eaten on the moon.

* The Romans ate fried canaries, the ancient equivalent of our full-English fry-up.

* **Heat a grape in a microwave and it will explode.**

* The first soup was made of hippopotamus.

* **Worcestershire Sauce contains anchovies.**

LAWN-MOWER RACING

Dreamed up by Irish racing man Jim Gavin in reaction to the increasing costliness of motorsport, The British Lawn Mower Racing Association (BLMRA) was founded in 1973 at the Cricketers Arms in Wisborough Green, West Sussex. Its aims were simple – no sponsorship, no commercialism, no cash prizes and no modifying of engines, thus keeping costs down. The 250-member-strong group meet every year for twelve races including the British Championship, the World Championship, the British Grand Prix and a 12-Hour Endurance race. Famous racers include Sir Stirling Moss (winner of the British Grand Prix and the 12-Hour race), Le Mans legend Derek Bell (twice winner of the 12-Hour race) and actor Oliver Reed.

☆ COCKROACHES ... ☆

Madonna once compared herself to a cockroach: 'I am a survivor. I am like a cockroach, you just can't get rid of me.'

Cockroaches exist in over 3,500 varieties, and can be as small as half a centimetre and as large as ten centimetres.

They love eating all things human, including dead skin cells, eyelashes, eyebrows, toe- and fingernails, sweat, skin oils and sock dust. They will also happily eat paper, soap, glue and leather.

Cockroaches will not eat cucumbers.

In parts of Asia, cockroaches fried with garlic are used for curing indigestion. In some regions, they are dried, powdered and consumed to help with urinary tract infections.

Cockroaches fart every 15 minutes, can survive for a month without eating but will die within nine days without water. Roaches can survive headless for nine days, too.

Cockroaches can survive underwater for up to 15 minutes.

☆

ANIMAL TOP SPEEDS ☆

(MILES PER HOUR)

Cheetah	70	Giraffe	32
Pronghorn antelope	61	White-tailed deer	30
Wildebeest	50	Warthog	30
Lion	50	Grizzly bear	30
Thomson's gazelle	50	Cat (domestic)	30
Horse	47.5	Human	27.89
Elk	45	Elephant	25
Cape hunting dog	45	Black mamba snake	20
Coyote	43	Six-lined racerunner	18
Gray fox	42	Wild turkey	15
Hyena	40	Squirrel	12
Zebra	40	Pig (domestic)	11
Mongolian wild ass	40	Chicken	9
Greyhound	39.35	Mouse	7.5
Whippet	35.5	Common house spider	
Rabbit (domestic)	35	(*Tegenaria atrica*)	1.17
Mule deer	35	Giant tortoise	0.17
Jackal	35	Three-toed sloth	0.15
Reindeer	32	Garden snail	0.03

SOME HISTORICAL CURIOSITIES

In medieval castles, spiral staircases ran clockwise (when looking upwards from the bottom) so that defending knights coming down the stairs or reversing up them could swing their swords freely, while the attacking knights' right arms would be blocked by the wall. Left-handed men were never knighted, as it was believed they were descended from the devil.

Pirates wore earrings in the belief that it improved their eyesight

Colonel Pierrepoint installed the world's first traffic island outside his London club. He was killed crossing over to it.

The Grand Canyon was not seen by a white man until after the American Civil War. It was first observed on 29 May 1869 by geologist John Wesley Powell.

Peter the Great (1672–1728) introduced a tax on beards in an effort to modernise Russia. On his return from his 1698 Grand Tour of the West (where beards had fallen out of fashion), Peter shaved off his advisers' beards and insisted those who defied the law pay an annual beard tax of 100 roubles.

During the marriage ceremony of ancient Incas of Peru, the couple were considered officially wed when they took off their sandals and handed them to each other.

'The memoirs of Catherine II inform us that at St Petersburg, scarcely a hundred years since, whenever the czar or czarina was displeased with a Russian prince, he was forced to squat down in the great ante-chamber of the palace, and to remain in that posture a certain number of days, mewing like a cat, or clucking like a sitting hen, and pecking his food from the floor' – Victor Hugo, *The Man Who Laughs* (1869).

Sex workers in Roman times charged the equivalent price of eight glasses of red wine.

The Hundred Years War waged between the House of Valois and the House of Plantagenet for the French throne lasted 116 years, from 1337 to 1453.

Alexander Graham Bell may have invented the telephone, but his wife and mother had little use for it – they were both deaf.

In the late 1800s, fashionable Parisian women never went out in windy weather unless they had a lightning rod attached to their hats. This was after Benjamin Franklin, who invented the lightning rod, became a celebrity figure when he lived in Paris as America's first Ambassador to France.

During the American Revolutionary War (1775–83) some brides wore red to symbolise the colonies' independence from England.

Studies indicate that half of Stone Age people were left-handed.

Stone Age implements discovered seem equally divided between left and right and studies of cave drawings have indicated a preference for the left hand. When tools became more sophisticated, a clear hand preference emerged. Today, 95 per cent of people are right-handed.

SOME ELECTRIFYING
FACTS

* If your hair stands on end during a storm, it could mean that positive charges are rising through you, reaching towards the negatively charged part of the storm. This is a bad sign. Go indoors immediately.

* **Most people injured by lightning while inside their homes are talking on the telephone during the strike.**

* Each second there are 50 to 100 cloud-to-ground lightning strikes to the Earth worldwide.

✦ **Most lightning strikes average two to three miles long and carry a current of 10,000 amps at 100 million volts.**

✳ A 'positive giant' hits the ground up to 20 miles away from the storm. Because it appears to strike from a clear sky, such lightning is known as 'a bolt from the blue'.

LIGHTNING STRIKES

Lightning kills around five people a year in the UK, and the odds of being struck are around one in three million. Long odds indeed, but not long enough for some. Park ranger Roy C. Sullivan holds the record for the person to have survived the most lightning strikes. Between 1942 and 1983, Roy was struck by lightning seven times and became known as 'The Human Lightning Rod'. Strike one hit when Roy was up a lookout tower in 1942; the lightning bolt shot through his leg and knocked his big toenail off. Strike two took Roy by surprise on a mountain road in 1969; he was knocked unconscious and woke up to find his eyebrows had burned off. Only a year later, in 1970, Roy 'The Rod' was crossing his garden to fetch his post when – pow! – strike three took his breath away and seared his left shoulder. After a strike-free 1971, 1972 brought more pain for Roy – this time the lighting set his hair on fire. Roy grew his locks back only to have them singed off again in 1973 when a bolt shot a hole in his hat, threw him off his truck, knocked his shoe off and burned his legs. The sixth strike came in 1976 – this time injuring his ankle – with the seventh and final bolt hot on Roy's heels while he was fishing in 1977. This time around chest and stomach burns landed the poor fellow in hospital. Roy was never hit again, but eventually shot himself dead in 1983, aged 71, reportedly over unrequited love for a woman.

PECULIAR MUSEUMS

Sulabh International Museum of Toilets . . . . New Delhi, India
The Paris Sewer Museum . . . . Paris, France
Museum of Medieval Torture Instruments . . . . Prague, Czech Republic
Icelandic Phallological Museum . . . . Husavik, Iceland
Goreme UFO Museum . . . . Goreme, Turkey
The Museum of Questionable Medical Devices . . . . Minneapolis, USA
The Museum of Witchcraft . . . . Boscastle, UK
The Meguro Parasite Museum . . . . Tokyo, Japan
Banana Museum . . . . Auburn, USA
British Lawnmower Museum . . . . Southport, UK
Dog Collar Museum . . . . Leeds Castle, Kent, UK

☆ REPUTED DISTANCE ☆ ORIGINS

Foot – the length of French emperor Charlemagne's foot. (Modified in 1305 to 36 barleycorns laid end to end. Now 12 inches.)

Inch – the width across the knuckle on Saxon King Edgar's thumb (or three barleycorns). Now 0.83 feet.

Yard – the reach from King Henry I's nose to his fingertips. Now 3 feet.

Cubit – the length of the arm from elbow to fingertip.

Mile – originally 1,000 double steps of a Roman legionary. Later, Elizabeth I added more feet so that the mile would equal eight furlongs. Now 5,280 feet, or 1,760 yards.

Furlong – the length of a furrow a team of oxen could plough before resting.

Acre – the amount of land a yoke of oxen could plough in one day.

Fathom – the span of a seaman's outstretched arms; 880 fathoms make a mile.

☆ LETTERS IN FOOTBALL ☆

Hull City is the only British football league team without any letters in its name that one could colour in with a pen.

The names of only four teams out of the 92 in England (Premiership, Championship and Divisions 1 and 2) start with the same letter that they end with: Liverpool, Aston Villa, Charlton Athletic, Northampton Town.

St Johnstone is the only team out of the four divisions in England and the four divisions in Scotland that has a 'J' in its name.

The names of only two teams in the leagues of England and Scotland each contain the letters A, B, C, D and E: Wycombe Wanderers and Cowdenbeath.

Hartlepool United, Torquay United, Rotherham United and Rushden and Diamonds are the only four teams in the English leagues whose names contain all five vowels.

Swindon Town is the only team name to contain none of the letters in the word mackerel.

●━━●━●━●━●

☆ A LOAD OF BALLS ☆

* An octopus's testicles are in its head.

* **To 'testify' was based on men in the Roman court swearing to a statement made by swearing on their testicles. So the story goes, anyway. There is a link between the word testicle and testify, because the Romans understood the Latin *testis* to mean a reliable third party in an argument, and sometimes figuratively in reference to their testicles. But the connection ends there. The Old Testament contains references to swearing on the King's private parts, so perhaps the confusion arose from this.**

* A man's testicles increase in size by 50 per cent when he is aroused.

* **The left testicle usually hangs lower than the right for right-handed men. The opposite is true for lefties.**

* Hitler and Napoleon each had only one testicle.

* **Avocado comes from the Aztec word *ahuacatl'*, meaning testicle.**

☆ WEIRD WORDS FOR ☆ HUMAN TRAITS

Agelast	A person who never laughs
Apodyopsis	To mentally undress someone
Autotonsorialist	Person who cuts his or her own hair
Batrachophagous	Feeding on frogs
Borborygmus	The rumbling noise produced by gas moving through the intestines
Cagamosis	An unhappy marriage
Callipygean	Having beautifully proportioned buttocks
Colposinquanonia	Estimating a woman's beauty based on her chest
Ecdysiast	A striptease artist
Exsibilation	The hissing of a disapproving audience
Jumentous	Smelling like horse urine
Krukolibidinous	Staring at someone's crotch
Lalochezia	Emotional relief gained from the use of foul or abusive language
Lygerastia	Tendency to become sexually aroused only when the lights are out
Matronolagnia	An attraction to older women, especially those with children
Misocapnist	One who hates the smell of tobacco smoke
Oculoplania	Letting one's eyes wander while assessing someone's charms
Qualtagh	The first person you see after leaving your house
Skoptsy	Self-castration
Tatterdemalion	A shabbily dressed person
Tiromancy	The art of predicting the future using cheese
Uxorious	Extremely submissive to one's wife
Wuncation	Weeding

✫ MATHEMATICAL CURIOS ✫

✳ 1089 x 9 = 9801. It has reversed itself.

✫ **19 = 1 x 9 + 1 + 9 and 29 = 2 x 9 + 2 + 9. Same goes for 39, 49, 59, 69, 79, 89 and 99.**

✳ Two is the only number that gives the same result added to itself as it does multiplied by itself

✫ **Multiply 21,978 x 4. The answer is the same number backwards.**

✳ Forty is the only number that has all its letters in alphabetical order.

✫ **1 ÷ 37 = 0.027027027 … and 1 ÷ 27 = 0.037037037 …**

✳ 1/1089 = 0·00091827364554637281 … (And the numbers in the nine-times table are 9,18,27,36 …)

✫ **One is the only number in the English language with its letters in reverse alphabetical order.**

✳ The number four is the only number in the English language that is spelled with the same number of letters as the number itself.

✫ **1 x 9 + 2 = 11. 12 x 9 +3 = 111. 123 x 9 + 4 = 1111. And so it goes on.**

✳ To add all the numbers from 1 to 10, simply divide the 10 by two then write the answer out twice – 55. This works for 1–100, 1–1,000, 1–10,000 and so on.

✳ **Eight is the only cube that is one less than a square.**

'THE CUSTOM OF THE SEA' AND THE EDGAR ALLAN POE INCIDENCE

A age-old phrase used to describe a set of principles adhered to by ship and boat crews, the Custom of the Sea is distinct from Maritime Law in that its rules are unofficial, passed down by word of mouth. One such custom is that, should a vessel be in danger – or, indeed, sinking – the captain must be the last person to disembark. A more macabre example was the rule whereby cannibalism was permitted in extreme cases of life or death. If a ship was stranded, survivors drew straws to determine who would be killed and eaten. The shortest straw determined the victim, while the second shortest pointed to the executioner. For his 1837 novel *The Narrative of Arthur Gordon Pym of Nantucket*, Edgar Allan Poe drew on several historical accounts of such cannibalism to weave the story of a castaway ship on which the fictional Richard Parker draws the short straw. Fifty years later fact and fiction collided most chillingly. Two real-life survivors of the shipwrecked *Mignonette* were charged with murder after killing and eating members of their crew, having drawn lots in accordance with the Custom of the Sea. The men were eventually sentenced to death, and the *Regina* v *Dudley and Stephens* case outlawed the Custom and set a legal precedent that necessity is no defence against murder. And the connection to Poe's novel? The man eaten by Dudley and Stephens was called Richard Parker, as was the man in Edgar Allan's story.

☆

CREATURES

* It is often said that, for reasons unknown, a duck's quack does not echo. This is pure scientific myth – duck quacks were shown to echo for the British Association Festival of Science in 2003.

* **If a cat falls off the seventh floor of a building, it has about a 30 per cent less chance of surviving than a cat that falls off the twentieth floor. The theory goes that it takes about eight floors for the cat to realise what is occurring, relax and prepare itself for landing.**

* Primates like porn. An experiment conducted at Duke University, Durham, North Carolina, showed that male rhesus monkeys were content to accept less fruit juice every day in exchange for video footage of female monkeys parading their bodies.

* **The koala bear does not need to drink liquids; it can obtain all of its liquids from eucalyptus leaves, which are 50 per cent water.**

* Giraffes and humans have the same number of bones in their necks: seven.

* **If a female ferret goes into heat but cannot find a mate, she will die. If a female ferret remains on heat too long, her elevated oestrogen levels will eventually cause her bone marrow to stop producing red blood cells.**

✳ The pistol shrimp's claw snaps shut so forcefully that it rivals the sperm whale as one of the loudest sea creatures. When it 'fires a shot', it creates an air bubble which implodes to momentarily produce a temperature as high as the sun's. The shock of its sonic boom kills nearby sea creatures, which the shrimp then eats.

GOOD FACTS COME IN THREES

1. 'A man a plan a canal panama' reads the same backwards, which makes it a palindrome.

2. 'Indivisibility' has only one vowel, which occurs six times.

3. An anagram of 'twelve plus one' is 'eleven plus two'.

☆ ✦ BRITISH TELLY ✦ ☆

✳ *Inspector Morse* creator Colin Dexter was an extra in every episode of the show.

✩ Anne Robinson began winking on TV as an act of rebellion. While presenting *Points of View*, a director told her not to wink. From that moment on, she winked at the end of every episode.

✳ The original concept for Andrex adverts included a little girl running through her house trailing a roll of Andrex behind her, but it was blocked by television regulators who believed it would encourage children to be wasteful. Instead, the girl was replaced by a puppy. Hundreds of Labrador retrievers have appeared in the adverts since the 1970s. During filming, several puppies from the same litter are used for each advert to stop the pups from becoming tired.

J. K. Rowling once turned down the opportunity to write an episode of *Dr Who*.

Bosses at the BBC once felt David Attenborough should not work in television because his teeth were too big.

Each recording of *Antiques Roadshow* attracts around 2,000 antique-bearing hopefuls, but the average value of their items is usually around £50.

When Anna Ford was 30 years old, she was told she was too old to become a newsreader. That was in 1974.

RANDOM MUSIC PARAGRAPH

To win a gold disc, an album must sell 100,000 copies in Britain, and 500,000 in the United States. The first pop video was 'Bohemian Rhapsody' by Queen, released in 1975. Melba toast was named after Australian opera singer Dame Nellie Melba (1861–1931). Ninety per cent of all music downloads are illegal – around 40 billion songs a year. Klezmer music gets its name from two Hebrew words, *clay* and *zimmer*, meaning 'vessel of music'. The LP was invented by Paul Goldmark in 1948, and even today more than 10 million are sold every year. 'We've Only Just Begun', the hit song by The Carpenters, was originally featured in a television commercial for a California bank. Karen Carpenter had a doorbell that chimed the start of the same song.

☆ AMERICAN TRIVIA ☆

* One-third of all Americans flush the toilet while they are still sitting on it.

* **The US flag displays 13 stripes – representing the original 13 states.**

* The US nickname Uncle Sam was derived from Uncle Sam Wilson, a meat inspector in Troy, New York.

* **The electric chair was invented by a dentist.**

* Forty thousand Americans are injured by toilets each year.

* **In 1996, President Clinton passed a law on toilet paper, taxing each roll six cents and increasing the price of the product to 30 cents per roll.**

* When the divorce rate goes up, toy makers report that the sales of toys also rise.

* **Every bearded president has been a member of the Republican Party.**

* Theodore Roosevelt's wife and mother died on the same day.

* **You can see five states from the top of the Empire State Building: New York, New Jersey, Connecticut, Massachusetts and Pennsylvania.**

* It is estimated that a new lawsuit is filed every 30 seconds in the USA.

✴ **There are more cars than people in Los Angeles.**

✴ Each year, Americans eat enough peanuts to fill ten 85-storey buildings.

✴ **There are approximately 500,000 detectable seismic tremors in California annually.**

✴ Twenty-seven per cent of Americans believe we never landed on the moon, while 33 per cent believe God has spoken to them directly.

✴ **Alaska is the state with the highest percentage of people who walk to work.**

✴ The chances of a white Christmas in New York are roughly one in four.

✴ **The term 'The Big Apple' was coined by touring jazz musicians of the 1930s who used the slang expression 'apple' for any town or city. To play New York City was to play the big time – hence The Big Apple.**

✴ There are more plastic flamingos in the US than real ones.

✴ **In 2002, the year after 9/11, the most popular boat name in the US was *Liberty*.**

✴ Percentage of American men who say they would marry the same woman if they had to do it all over again: 80 per cent.

✴ **A monkey was once tried and convicted for smoking a cigarette in South Bend, Indiana.**

✴ It costs about three cents to make a $1 bill.

LOVELY WORDS

An international poll by the British Council asked people to nominate the English words they found the most beautiful. The top 70 were published to mark the Council's seventieth anniversary:

1. Mother 2. Passion 3. Smile 4. Love 5. Eternity 6. Fantastic
7. Destiny 8. Freedom 9. Liberty 10. Tranquility 11. Peace 12. Blossom
13. Sunshine 14. Sweetheart 15. Gorgeous 16. Cherish 17. Enthusiasm
18. Hope 19. Grace 20. Rainbow 21. Blue 22. Sunflower 23. Twinkle
24. Serendipity 25. Bliss 26. Lullaby 27. Sophisticated 28. Renaissance
29. Cute 30. Cosy 31. Butterfly 32. Galaxy 33. Hilarious 34. Moment
35. Extravaganza 36. Aqua 37. Sentiment 38. Cosmopolitan 39. Bubble
40. Pumpkin 41. Banana 42. Lollipop 43. If 44. Bumblebee 45. Giggle
46. Paradox 47. Delicacy 48. Peekaboo 49. Umbrella 50. Kangaroo
51. Flabbergasted 52. Hippopotamus 53. Gothic 54. Coconut
55. Smashing 56. Whoops 57. Tickle 58. Loquacious 59. Flip-flop
60. Smithereens 61. Oi 62. Gazebo 63. Hiccup 64. Hodgepodge
65. Shipshape 66. Explosion 67. Fuselage 68. Zing 69. Gum 70. Hen night.

☆ GREET THE LOCALS ☆

New Zealand – the traditional Maori welcome is the *hongi* – the rubbing of noses when meeting someone. Often referred to as the 'ha', or 'breath of life'.

Tibet – poking your tongue out is good manners here. Dating back to the ninth century, this way of welcoming people stems from an old Tibetan fear of Lang Darma – a nasty king with a black tongue. To prove you're not Lang reincarnated, stick out your normal pink tongue and you'll be OK.

Tuvalu – press your face to your host's cheek and take a deep sniff – that's the traditional welcome on this little island.

Mongolia – Mongols will often present new guests with a piece of silk or cotton known as a *hada*. Receive it graciously by holding it gently with both hands. Then bow slightly to signify mutual respect.

Japan – the bow is *de rigueur* here, from a little nod of the head to deep, right-angle bend at the waist – the longer the bow, the deeper the respect. Most young people use the nodding version these days.

Kenya – the Masai warriors traditionally greet guests with a welcoming dance called the *adamu*, or jumping dance. Don't worry: you're not expected to reciprocate, but you may be offered a drink of cow's milk mixed with blood …

Greenland – the Inuit people greet friends and family with the *kunik* – one person's nose and top lip is pressed against another person's skin for a few breaths. If you are greeted in this way, consider yourself one of the family.

China – to carry off the *kowtow* greeting, fold your hands together and bow and, if you're a woman, then move the hands down to your sides.

Thailand – the *wai* is easy to master. Make a slight bow of the body and head with palms pressed together in a prayer-like fashion and say *Sawaddee* (meaning 'hello'). The higher the hands, the greater the respect. This tradition was first used to prove oneself free of weapons, but now it's just a way of being nice.

Philippines – if greeting someone older than yourself, take their right hand with your right hand, say *Mano Po* (*mano* for hand, *po* for respect) and they will gently guide your knuckles to their forehead. A younger person may expect you to do the same for them.

SOME OF THE ODDEST BOOK TITLES
AVAILABLE ON AMAZON.COM

How to Shit in the Woods, by Kathleen Meyer

How to Cook Roadkill, by Richard Marcou

People Who Don't Know They're Dead, by Gary Leon Hill

How to Succeed in Business Without a Penis, by Karen Salmansohn

The Big Book of Lesbian Horse Stories, by Alisa Surkis and Monika Nolan

How to Avoid Huge Ships, by Captain John W. Trimmer

Old Tractors and the Men Who Love Them, by Roger Welsch

Whose Bottom Is This?, by M. Butterfield and C. J. Church (children's title)

Bombproof Your Horse, by Sgt Rick Pelicano

Scouts in Bondage, by Michael Bell

Reusing Old Graves, by Douglas Davies and Alastair Shaw

How to Write a How to Write Book, by Brian Piddock

English as a Second F*cking Language, by Sterling Johnson

Are Women Human? by Catharine A. MacKinnon

I Was Tortured by the Pygmy Love Queen, by Jasper McCutcheon

Cheese Problems Solved, edited by P. L. H McSweeney

Lightweight Sandwich Construction, by J.M. Davies

Sodomy and the Pirate Tradition, by Barry R. Burg

Hitler: Neither Vegetarian nor Animal Lover, by Rynn Berry

Living with Crazy Buttocks, by Kaz Cooke

A LITTLE BIT OF
☆ ✦ ENGLAND ✦ ☆

* Britain is still paying off debts that pre-date the Napoleonic Wars because it's cheaper to do so than buy back the bonds on which they are based.

* **Allotment plots come in the standard measure of ten poles – a pole is the length from the back of the plough to the nose of the ox.**

* Metal detector enthusiasts are referred to as 'detectorists'; there are about 30,000 in the UK.

* **There are 2.5 million rodent-owning households in Britain, according to the Pet Food Manufacturers' Association.**

* Flushing a toilet costs, on average, 1.5p.

* **Just 20 words make up a third of teenagers' everyday speech.**

* Around six months of the average driver's lifetime are spent waiting at traffic lights.

IF YOU HAPPEN TO BE IN SPACE

Your spinal column expands without gravity around and you will grow taller by up to eight centimetres. This may give you backache and nerve issues. Lack of gravity is also likely to render you severely disorientated at first. Many cosmic explorers report feeling suddenly 'upside down' and experience a strange inability to locate their arms and legs – a phenomenon known as Space Adaptation Syndrome. It's also highly likely you will throw up regularly. When you can keep your food down, you'll have to do without salt and pepper, as sprinkling it is impractical and dangerous – it won't end up on your plate, but may end up damaging vital equipment. Don't worry too much if you experience bizarre flashes of light that feel as if they are inside your eyeballs – it's only a bit of space radiation (subatomic particles whizzing through your head) – but don't be surprised if you develop cataracts later on. The good news is that you are unlikely to keep your fellow astronauts awake by snoring – gravity contributes to problem snoring, so without it you should sleep silently. If you stay away for more than 438 days, you'll be a record holder, as nobody has remained in space longer than Russian Valeri Polyakov did in 1994–5. Once you are back on solid ground, it will take you a while to get used to gravity again. A number of astronauts forget they are back on Earth, and absent-mindedly let go of objects in mid-air with amusing results.

UNFORTUNATE ALLERGIES

Sun – Many people are allergic to the sun in one way or another, but there is a particular sun allergy – solar urticaria – that is very rare. Exposure to UV radiation induces a hives that can appear in both covered and uncovered areas of the skin.

Water – Known as aquagenic urticaria, this condition affects only one in 23 million people, but wreaks biological havoc on an unlucky few. Contact with the world's most plentiful substance results in painful hives, welts, lesions and rashes on the body that crop up quickly and can last for several hours. Most sufferers are confined to their homes, and it is believed that they are hypersensitive to the ions found in non-distilled water, as well as other additives.

Kissing – Kissing itself will not provoke an allergic reaction but, if you have a strong allergy to a medication or food, kissing a partner who has recently consumed your 'poison' can have disastrous results. In the worst cases, lovers have died after kissing, but fortunately most reactions to kissing involve nothing worse than sickness.

Wood – They are rare, but sufferers must go through life without touching paper or furniture or coming into contact with sawdust. Most wood allergies cause coughing, sneezing and rashes, but people have been known to react so badly that their skin turns black as if it has been burned.

SPORE MOONERISMS TO PONDER (NOT ATTRIBUTED TO MR SPOONER)

Know your blows, go and shake a tower, tease my ears, nicking your pose, you have very mad banners, lack of pies, it's roaring with pain, sealing the hick, go help me sod, pit nicking, bowel feast, I'm a damp stealer, this is the pun fart, bedding wells, I must mend the sail, cop porn, bat flattery, belly jeans, fight in your race, cack of pards.

☆ ★ PAY ATTENTION ★ ☆ MR WHIPPY!

The English 'Code of Practice on Noise from Ice-Cream Van Chimes' of 1982 states that it is illegal to sound ice-cream van chimes 'so as to cause annoyance'. Chimes must not ...

- ... be sounded for any longer than four seconds at a time.
- ... be used more often than once in every three minutes.
- ... be sounded when a vehicle is stationary.
- ... be used when they are in sight of other ice-cream vans which are trading nearby.
- ... sound when they are within 50 metres of a school, any places of worship, or hospitals.
- ... sound more than once every two hours in the same street.

MUZAK

The term we all use to refer to dull and uninspired background music was once the name of a music company. In the early 1920s, General George Squier devised the name by combining 'music' with 'Kodak', a company he admired, and the company began producing music for hotels, restaurants and workplaces. At first, records were played on phonographs down electrical lines, and the company enjoyed great success for many years. By the late 1980s it was estimated that around 80 million people encountered muzak on a daily basis, but it also attracted the scorn of many a musician. In 1989, American rock star Ted Nugent famously made a $10 million bid to buy the company with the intention of closing it down. He failed.

☆ SAVE YOUR BREATH ☆

- WORDS YOU NEEDN'T USE

Pleonasm is the use of redundant words, and tautology is the repetition of meaning. Look with your own eyes at this and spot which is which, either or both ...

Added bonus	Couture fashion
Add up	Descend down
Advance planning	Doctorate degree
Advance preview	Downward descent
Advance reservation	Each and every
Advance warning	Eliminate altogether
Affluent rich	Empty hole
Aid and abet	Empty space
Alternative choice	End result
Ascend up	Entirely eliminating
ATM machine	Essential necessity
Attach together	Exact replica
Basic fundamentals	Exact same
Boat marina	Existing condition
Boiling hot	Experiment carried out
Close proximity	Favourable approval
Combined together	Fellow colleague
Commuting back and forth	Final end
Completely annihilated	Final showdown
Completely expired	First conceived
Completely full	Foreign imports
Component parts	Former graduate
Continuing on	Forward planning

Free gift

Freezing cold

Frozen ice

Good benefit

Grateful thanks

Growing greater

Hard rock

Hear with one's own ears

HIV virus

Hot fire

Hot-water heater

Individual person

Invited guests

Joint collaboration

Join together

Killed dead

Knowledgeable experts

Lesbian women

Literate readers

Long litany

Many frequent

Marital spouse

Mental thought

Merge together

Mutual cooperation

Necessary essentials

Never ever

New discovery

New recruit

Nostalgia for the past

Not sufficient enough

Null and void

Old adage

Original founder

Original source

Outside in the garden

Overused cliché

Pair of twins

Past experience

Past history

Personal friend

PIN number

Postponed until later

Pre-planning

Refer back

Repeat again

Resulting effects

Return back

Revert back

Rise up

Round circle

Round wheels

Safe haven

Serious danger

Small speck

Specific examples

Successful achievement

Sudden impulse

Sum total

Surrounded on all sides

Tiny speck

True facts

Tuna fish

Twelve midnight

Unexpected surprise

Unsolved mystery

Usual custom

PEOPLE WHO HAVE SUFFERED FROM DEPRESSION

Buzz Aldrin

Woody Allen

Hans Christian Andersen

Adam Ant

Richard Ashcroft

Charles Baudelaire

Ingmar Bergman

William Blake

Anthony Callea

Drew Carey

Jim Carrey

Raymond Chandler

Agatha Christie

Winston Churchill

Kurt Cobain

Leonard Cohen

Joseph Conrad

Catherine Cookson

Billy Corgan

Ian Curtis

Rodney Dangerfield

John Denver

Charles Dickens

Fyodor Dostoyevsky

Kirsten Dunst

T. S. Eliot

James Ellroy

William Faulkner

Harrison Ford

Stephen Fry

Nelly Furtado

Paul Getty

Vincent van Gogh

Francisco Goya

Graham Greene

Tony Hancock

Anne Hathaway

Friedrich August Hayek

Ernest Hemingway

Michael Hutchence

Natalie Imbruglia

Janet Jackson

Henry James

Billy Joel

Samuel Johnson

John Keats

Beyoncé Knowles

Hugh Laurie

Heath Ledger

John Lennon

Abraham Lincoln

Gustav Mahler

Henri Matisse

Ewan McGregor

Paul Merton

Michelangelo

Spike Milligan

Morrissey

Wolfgang Amadeus Mozart

Isaac Newton

Friedrich Nietzsche

Bill Oddie

Marie Osmond

Ronnie O'Sullivan

Gwyneth Paltrow

Sylvia Plath

Edgar Allan Poe

Jackson Pollock

J. K. Rowling

Robert Schumann

Will Self

Brian Sewell

Brooke Shields

Britney Spears

Amy Tan

Catherine Tate

Pyotr Ilyich Tchaikovsky

Leo Tolstoy

Lars Von Trier

Mark Twain

Jeff Tweedy

Kurt Vonnegut

Evelyn Waugh

Walt Whitman

Robbie Williams

Tennessee Williams

Brian Wilson

Owen Wilson

Virginia Woolf

Thom Yorke

☆ UGLEY AND MUFF ☆

Ugley – Ugley in Essex is anything but; it sits between Saffron Walden and Bishop's Stortford, in prime commuterland. The name probably means 'Woodland clearing of a man named Ugga'. The Ugley Women's Institute grew so tired of the juvenile jibes that it changed its name to the Women's Institute of Ugley, a rebranding exercise not yet repeated by the Ugley Farmers' Market.

Muff – Muff – from the Irish word *magh* – is a village in County Donegal, on the border between the Republic and Northern Ireland. Over the last decade, Muff has seen a huge growth in population, with people from Northern Ireland moving across the border. The first week in August sees the Muff Festival – and there's a diving club in the village called, yes, the Muff Diving Club.

NAKED SOLDIERS

The nickname 'The Skins' was allegedly originated at Maida in Italy when a naked bathing party the Irish Inniskilling regiment abandoned their swim and prepared to meet French cavalry with little more than their muskets. But it was at the final battle of the Napoleonic Wars that the Inniskillings had their greatest day when, according to the Duke of Wellington, they saved the centre of his line at Waterloo on 18 June 1815 and thus contributed significantly to the Allied victory.

A BRIEF HISTORY OF CHEWING GUM

The world's oldest piece of chewing gum is 9,000 years old. It was discovered in 1993 by Swedish archaeologists, who found three wads of honey-sweetened birch resin in the floor of a hut used by ancient hunters. The teeth imprints indicated that the chewer was in possession of a wonderful set of choppers, so may have been a teenager. Chewing gum started with the Greeks. They chewed resin from the mastic tree to keep their teeth clean and breath fresh ('mastic' most likely is derived from the Greek *mastichon*, meaning 'to chew', and is the root of the English verb 'to masticate'). In the early 1800s, settlers in New England observed Native Americans chewing the gummy resin from spruce trees. Before long, spruce gum was being sold commercially. By the 1850s, spruce gum was old news – everybody was chewing sweetened paraffin wax instead. It was dentist Thomas Adams who invented gum as we know it. Hoping to devise a new type of rubber, Adam brought chicle (juice from the Central American sapodilla tree) to the United States in the 1860s. He ended up selling flavoured chicle in a sweet shop. Before long William Wrigley bought the idea from Adams, and started giving away packs of gum with sales of his baking powder.

☆ ★ FACEBOOK ★ ☆

* Was originally launched as TheFacebook.

Founder Mark Zuckerberg called himself 'Founder, Master and Commander and Enemy of the State'.

✳ Seventy per cent of users are outside the United States.

✳ **The site has more than 500 million active users.**

✳ Fifty per cent of active users log on to Facebook on any given day.

✳ **The average user has 130 friends.**

✳ Lamebook.com regularly reposts funny Facebook posts.

✳ **People spend over 700 billion minutes per month on Facebook.**

✳ There are over 900 million objects that people interact with (pages, groups, events and community pages).

✳ **While stressing that correlation does not equal causation, a recent poll suggested that Facebook users have lower overall grades than non-users.**

✳ The average user is connected to 80 community pages, groups and events.

✳ **The average user creates 90 pieces of content each month.**

✳ In January 2009, an advertising campaign for Burger King titled 'WHOPPER Sacrifice' rewarded Facebook users with a free 'Angry Whopper' for publicly deleting ten friends, who then received a message informing them that they had been deleted for a free burger.

✳ **More than 30 billion pieces of content (web links, news stories, blog posts, notes, photo albums, etc) are shared each month.**

* There are more than 200 million active users currently accessing Facebook through their mobile devices.

* **A 20-year-old IBM employee in Canada lost sick-leave benefits from her insurer because her Facebook page showed 'cheerful' photos while she was on paid leave for depression.**

* People who use Facebook on their mobile devices are twice as active on Facebook than non-mobile users.

A LITTLE CHINESE WISDOM

* To extend your life by a year take one less bite each meal.

* **If one eats less, one will taste more.**

* Count not what is lost, but what is left.

* **Wisdom is attained by learning when to hold one's tongue.**

* Cowards have dreams, brave men have visions.

* **Wise men may not be learned; learned men may not be wise.**

* Sow melon, reap melon; sow beans, reap beans.

* **The old horse will know the way.**

* Learning is like the horizon; there is no limit.

⚝ **Eloquence provides only persuasion, but truth buys loyalty.**

✳ Do not kill the hen for her eggs.

☆ **Be not afraid of growing slowly, be afraid only of standing still.**

✳ Deep doubts, deep wisdom; small doubts, little wisdom.

☆ **A clever person turns great troubles into little ones and little ones into none at all.**

✳ A book tightly shut is but a block of paper.

☆ ★  FLAGS ★ ☆

✳ The Italian flag was designed by Napoleon Bonaparte.

☆ **Denmark's national flag is the oldest in the world.**

✳ The British flag is only called the Union Jack on a ship out at sea.

☆ **The expression 'show one's true colours' is flag-related. 'Colours' used to mean 'flag'. Warships often carried the flags of several countries on board so that they could deceive the enemy into thinking they were friendly. When close enough to engage in battle, a ship would raise its 'true colours' (its national flag) and open fire. Thus, to show one's true colours is to reveal oneself for what or who one really is.**

✳ The tomato-based pizza, resembling the popular pizza we eat today, reportedly derived from Queen Margarita's visit to Naples in 1889. To mark her arrival a local pizza chef spread layers of tomato, mozzarella and basil on flatbread to symbolise the three colours of the Italian flag and named it in the queen's honour.

☆ **Ohio is the only US state without a rectangular flag. Its flag is a pennant.**

✳ Until the Canadian two-dollar bill was discontinued in 1996, many people mistook the flag flying over the Parliament Building on the note for an American flag.

THE WORLD'S FUNNIEST JOKE ...

A scientist once set out to discover the one joke that most tickled the world's funny bone. In 2002, the University of Hertfordshire's Prof. Richard Wiseman and The British Association for the Advancement of Science asked people to send in their favourite jokes and to rate the gags submitted by others. The project received worldwide publicity and (40,000 jokes and 1.5 million ratings later) the results were published. The winning joke turned out to be based on a 1951 joke by Spike Milligan, written for *The Goon Show*:

Two hunters are out in the woods when one of them collapses. He doesn't seem to be breathing and his eyes are glazed. The other guy whips out his mobile and calls the emergency services. He gasps, 'My friend is dead! What can I do?' The operator says 'Calm down. I can help. First, let's make sure he's dead.' There is a silence, then a shot is heard. Back on the phone, the guy says, 'OK, now what?'

And the runner-up:

Sherlock Holmes and Dr Watson were going camping. They pitched their tent under the stars and went to sleep. Some time in the middle of the night Holmes woke Watson and said: 'Watson, look up at the stars, and tell me what you see.' Watson replied: 'I see millions and millions of stars.' Holmes said: 'And what do you deduce from that?' Watson replied: 'Well, if there are millions of stars, and if even a few of those have planets, it's quite likely there are some planets like Earth out there. And if there are a few planets like Earth out there, there might also be life.' And Holmes said: 'Watson, you idiot, it means that somebody's stolen our tent.'

☆ ★ **CRICKET** ★ ☆

* Actor Russell Crowe's two cousins are former New Zealand cricketers Martin and Jeff Crowe.

* **The history of the Ashes urn dates back to 1882 and England's first ever defeat by Australia, at The Oval. A mock obituary at the time lamented the death of English cricket and quipped 'the body will be cremated and the ashes taken to Australia'. On the next 1882–3 tour – 'the quest to regain the Ashes of English cricket' – England captain Ivo Bligh was presented with the urn, said to contain the ashes of a burned pair of bails. In 2006, the last time the Ashes were taken from England to Australia, the urn was afforded three security guards and a business-class seat on a Virgin Atlantic flight.**

✳ J. W. H. T. Douglas is the only England captain to have four initials.

There are ten ways in which a batsman can get out in cricket: caught, bowled, leg before wicket, run out, stumped, handling the ball, obstructing the field, hit the ball twice, hitting wicket, timed out.

✳ The 1939 Test match between England and South Africa was drawn on day ten because the England team had a boat to catch.

Shepherds – who originated the game – used to bat in front of a tree stump, hence the term 'stumps'. As the game progressed it was often played in front of a wicket-gate, which led to the term 'wickets'.

✳ In the first ever Test match in 1877, Australia beat England by 45 runs. One hundred years later – in the Centenary Test – the margin was exactly the same.

Health and Safety regulations hit Harrogate Cricket Club hard in 2008 – players were banned from hitting sixes. Any sixes hit counted only as fours.

✳ W. G. Grace was nine years old when he first took to the field for West Gloucestershire.

Geoffrey Boycott faced the first ever ball in one-day cricket. Graham McKenzie was the bowler.

✳ On the 1974 tour of England, Indian opener Sudhir Naik was accused of stealing a pair of socks from Marks & Spencer.

John Thayer was the only first-class cricketer on board the *Titanic*.

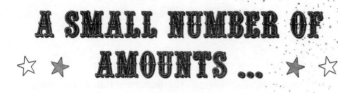

A SMALL NUMBER OF
☆ ★ AMOUNTS ... ★ ☆

Dentists recommend that toothbrushes be kept six feet away from a toilet to avoid airborne particles resulting from flushing.

Divide the Great Pyramid's perimeter by two times its height and you get pi to the fifteenth digit.

A cubic mile of fog consists of less than a gallon of water.

A jiffy is the unit of time for one-hundredth of a second. Hence 'I'll be there in a jiffy'.

A lightning bolt generates temperatures five times hotter than the sun's surface.

A rainbow can occur only when the sun is 40 degrees or less above the horizon.

Toss a penny 10,000 times and it will not come up heads 5,000 times. The head picture is heavier, so it ends up on the bottom more frequently. Heads will come up around 4,950 times.

Apollo 11 had only 20 seconds' worth of fuel left when it landed.

☆

☆ ★ WAYS TO GO ★ ☆

* Felix Lloyd Powell wrote the music to the war song 'Pack Up Your Troubles in Your Old Kitbag And Smile, Smile, Smile!'. He also committed suicide.

* **Mark Twain was born when Halley's comet appeared in 1835 and died on the day it next appeared, in 1910.**

* Ivan the Terrible died while playing chess.

* **In 1471, Pope Paul II died while being sodomised by a pageboy.**

* Alexander the Great dropped dead in the middle of a drinking contest at the age of 32.

* **Harry Houdini died when he dared a man to punch him in the stomach – the blow caused an internal rupture.**

* Pope Alexander VI passed away after accidentally drinking poison intended for his cardinals.

* **Pope John XIII was having sex with a married woman when he was caught and murdered by her irate husband.**

* In 1899, French president Félix Faure died during sex with a prostitute in a Paris brothel. The prostitute went into shock, and the president's penis had to be surgically removed.

* **George II's wife died laughing. Queen Caroline was hysterically amused when a candle set her doctor's wig on fire while he sat at her bedside.**

* Both Marc Bolan and Bing Crosby died within weeks of recording TV shows with David Bowie.

☆ **Keith Moon, drummer of The Who, died in the same London flat as singer Mama Cass Elliot of The Mamas and the Papas.**

* Terry Kath, lead singer of Chicago, died in 1978 while playing Russian roulette. His last words were 'Don't worry, it's not loaded'.

☆ **Olympic gold medallist Stella Walsh died in 1980 when she was shot during an armed robbery. During the autopsy it was revealed that she was in fact a man.**

* US horror actor Bela Lugosi was buried in his Dracula cloak.

☆ **James Brown, Dean Martin, Charlie Chaplin and W. C. Fields all died on Christmas Day.**

☆ ★ A LITTLE ★ ☆
ENTERTAINMENT

* Disneyworld covers 47 square miles (121.7 square kilometres), making it bigger than each of the world's five smallest countries – Vatican City – 0.17 square miles (0.44 square kilometres), Monaco – 0.8 square miles (1.96 square kilometres), Nauru 8 square miles (21 square kilometres); Tuvalu nine square miles (26 square kilometres) and San Marino – 24 square miles (61 square kilometres).

☆ **The top three most popular luxuries chosen by castaways on *Desert Island Discs:* 1. A piano 2. Writing materials 3. A bed.**

☀ Dire Straits got their name from the suggestion of a friend who observed the band's worrying financial situation.

☆ **After his first concert performance, Elvis Presley was advised to become a truck driver.**

☀ In 1976 Rodrigo's 'Concierto de Aranjuez' (for classical guitar) was No. 1 in the UK for only three hours because of a computer error.

☆ **Beethoven's Fifth was the first symphony to include trombones.**

☀ EMI stands for ' Electrical and Musical Instruments'.

☆ **At age 22, Jerry Lee Lewis married for the third time. His bride? His 13-year-old cousin.**

☀ The film *Lawrence of Arabia* has no female speaking parts.

☆ **The mask used by Michael Myers in the original *Halloween* was a William Shatner Captain Kirk mask painted white.**

☀ ABBA were originally called The Engaged Couples.

☆ **PAC-MAN was originally going to be called PUCK-MAN, but the name was changed when executives saw the potential for vandals to scratch out part of the letter P in promotional material for the game.**

WHAT'S WITH THE
☆ ★ BRAND NAME? ★ ☆

Accenture – from 'Accent on the future'.

AMSTRAD – formed by Lord Alan Sugar and a contraction of Alan Michael Sugar Trading.

ASDA – abbreviation of Asquith and Dairies; the name originated in 1965 after the merger of the Asquith chain of supermarkets and Associated Dairies.

BMW – Bayerische Motoren Werke, or Bavarian Motor Works.

Google – initially a misspelling of 'googol', the company settled on its name because google.com was an unregistered domain.

Haribo – from Hans Riegel (company founder's name) and Bonn (the company's home town).

Hovis – dreamed up in 1890 by Herbert Grime as part of a competition to find a name for S. Fitton and Sons' flour. Herbert derived the name from *hominis vis*, latin for 'the strength of man', and received £25 for his trouble.

IKEA – Ingvar Kamprad Elmtaryd Agunnaryd. From the first letters in founder Ingvar Kamprad's name, the farm on which he grew up and the small nearby village.

Lego – from the Danish *leg godt*, meaning 'play well'.

Nabisco – formerly The National Biscuit Company, changed in 1971 to Nabisco.

Nikon – originally Nippon Kogaku, meaning 'Japanese Optical'.

Qantas – from its original name, Queensland and Northern Territory Aerial Services.

Reebok – alternative spelling of *rhebok* (*Pelea capreolus*), an African antelope.

Ryvita – from the word 'rye' and *vita*, the Latin for life.

Samsonite – after the biblical character Samson, known for his great strength.

Sharp – named from its first product, an ever-sharp pencil.

Skype – originally conceived as Sky-Peer-to-Peer, then Skyper and, finally, Skype.

Sony – from the Latin *sonus* (sound) and 'sonny', American slang for a bright youngster.

Starbucks – after Starbuck, a strong and steady ship's mate in Herman Melville's novel *Moby-Dick*.

Virgin – when Richard Branson was about to start selling records, one of his assistants said, 'What about Virgin? We're complete virgins at business.'

☆ AMUSING HEADLINES ☆

Safety Experts Say School Bus Passengers Should Be Belted

Drunk Gets Nine Months in Violin Case

Survivor of Siamese Twins Joins Parents

Farmer Bill Dies in House

Iraqi Head Seeks Arms

British Left Waffles on Falkland Islands

Lung Cancer in Women Mushrooms

Eye Drops Off Shelf

Teacher Strikes Idle Kids

Enraged Cow Injures Farmer with Axe

Plane Too Close to Ground, Crash Probe Told

Miners Refuse to Work after Death

Juvenile Court to Try Shooting Defendant

Stolen Painting Found by Tree

Two Soviet Ships Collide, One Dies

Killer Sentenced to Die for Second Time in 10 Years

Drunken Drivers Paid $1000 in '84

War Dims Hope for Peace

If Strike Isn't Settled Quickly, It May Last a While

Cold Wave Linked to Temperatures

Red Tape Holds Up New Bridge

Deer Kill 17,000

Typhoon Rips Through Cemetery; Hundreds Dead

Man Struck by Lightning Faces Battery Charge

New Study of Obesity Looks for Larger Test Group

Astronaut Takes Blame for Gas in Spacecraft

Kids Make Nutritious Snacks

Chef Throws His Heart into Helping Feed Needy

Arson Suspect Is Held in Massachusetts Fire

British Union Finds Dwarfs in Short Supply

Ban On Soliciting Dead in Trotwood

Lansing Residents Can Drop Off Trees

Local High School Dropouts Cut in Half

New Vaccine May Contain Rabies

Man Minus Ear Waives Hearing

Deaf College Opens Doors to Hearing

Air Head Fired

Steals Clock, Faces Time

Old School Pillars Are Replaced by Alumni

Bank Drive-in Window Blocked by Board

Hospitals are Sued by 7 Foot Doctors

Include Your Children When Baking Cookies

Students Cook and Serve Grandparents.

SEXUALITY AND BLINKING

Men and women blink differently when startled, but research has shown that lesbians blink like heterosexual men. This suggests that the part of the brain responsible for this reflex has been 'masculinised' in the womb. We all blink when startled, but men blink less vigorously than women. This led Qazi Rahman of the University of East London to test the responses of homosexuals. When presented with a single sound, or a soft sound followed by a loud sound (both intended to startle the subjects), straight men's blinks were 40 per cent less vigorous in response to the soft-then-loud sound. Straight women dropped 13 per cent, and lesbians dropped 33 per cent. This made the lesbians statistically closer to straight men than to straight women. Other research has given some evidence for male characteristics in lesbians – they are better and more accurate throwers of objects than straight women and, on average, their ring fingers are longer than their index fingers (like men and unlike heterosexual women).

THREE WATER-RELATED STORIES – SPOT THE URBAN LEGEND

Every year in Honduras, the Festival de la Lluvia de Peces (Rain of Fish Festival) takes place in the city of Yoro. The phenomenon of raining fish has long existed in Honduran folklore, with witnesses describing a dark cloud followed by lightning and heavy rain. Once the weather subsides, thousands of living fish can be found on the ground. To this day, the Rain of Fish is said to occur annually some time between May and July.

Twice a year, a great mass of Atlantic water makes its way up the Amazon River in Brazil. The result is the longest wave on the planet. Known as the Pororoca (from the indigenous Tupi language, meaning 'great destructive noise'), this 'tidal bore' generates waves up to 12 feet in height that travel 13 kilometres inland. Since 1999, an annual surfing championship has been held in São Domingos do Capim, where those brave enough attempt to ride the wave for as long as possible. In 2003, a surfer stayed on his board for 37 minutes, travelling 12.5 kilometres.

In 1995, the crew of a Japanese fishing trawler were rescued off the coast of Japan. They claimed that a cow had fallen out of the sky and struck the boat, which then sank. What seemed a very tall story landed them in jail, as it was believed the crew had faked the incident and passed their fish on to another vessel to reap the profits for themselves rather than for their employer. A couple of weeks later, the Russian air force informed Japanese authorities that the crew of one of its cargo planes had had no choice but to push an angry and violently thrashing cow from the plane to save the aircraft and themselves. At about 30,000 feet, the crew let the cow out of the cargo hold as they were flying over the Sea of Japan.

☆ **VALENTINE'S FACTS** ☆

* On Valentine's Day in 1989, the Ayatollah Khomeini went on Radio Tehran to read out the fatwa that sentenced Salman Rushdie to death for writing *The Satanic Verses*.

☆ **Fifteen per cent of American women send themselves flowers on Valentine's Day.**

✳ According to superstition, if a woman sees a robin on Valentine's Day, she'll marry a sailor; if she sees a sparrow, she'll marry a poor man and be happy; and if she sees a goldfinch, she'll marry a millionaire and be very happy.

☆ **The Welsh used to give each other wooden spoons on 14 February.**

✳ Valentine's Day is not really recognised in Finland. Instead, the Finns celebrate Friendship Day by being nice to each other.

☆ **Al Capone wiped out his rivals in the Valentine's Day Massacre.**

FOR THE SAKE OF NEW
☆ ★ YEAR'S EVE ★ ☆

Does your memory fail you when midnight strikes? Chances are you never learned the words of the traditional song in the first place! Here's your chance to put things right. Incidentally 'Auld lang syne' translates as 'long long ago'.

☆

Robert Burns' original Scots verse

Should auld acquaintance be forgot,
And never brought to mind?
Should auld acquaintance be forgot,
And auld lang syne?

CHORUS:
For auld lang syne, my jo,
For auld lang syne,
We'll tak a cup o' kindness yet,
For auld lang syne.

And surely ye'll be your pint-stowp!
And surely I'll be mine!
And we'll tak a cup o' kindness yet,
For auld lang syne.

(CHORUS)

We twa hae run about the braes,
And pu'd the gowans fine,
But we've wander'd mony a weary fit,
Sin' auld lang syne.

(CHORUS)

We twa hae paidl'd i' the burn,
Frae morning sun till dine,
But seas between us braid hae roar'd
Sin auld lang syne.

(CHORUS)

And there's a hand, my trusty fiere,
And gie's a hand o' thine,
And we'll tak a right gude-willy waught,
For auld lang syne.

(CHORUS)

English translation

Should old acquaintance be forgot,
And never brought to mind?
Should old acquaintance be forgot,
And old lang syne?

CHORUS:
For auld lang syne, my dear,
For auld lang syne,
We'll take a cup of kindness yet,
For auld lang syne.

And surely you'll buy your pint cup,
And surely I'll buy mine,
And we'll take a cup o' kindness yet,
For auld lang syne.

(CHORUS)

We two have run about the slopes,
And picked the daisies fine,
But we've wandered many a weary foot,
Since auld lang syne.

(CHORUS)

We two have paddled in the stream,
From morning sun till dine;
But seas between us broad have roared
Since auld lang syne.

(CHORUS)

And there's a hand my trusty friend,
And give us a hand o' thine,
And we'll take a right good-will draught,
For auld lang syne.

(CHORUS)

HUGH WOULD BELIEVE IT?

On 5 December 1664, a ship sank in the Menai Strait off the coast of Wales. Of its 81 passengers, the sole survivor was a lucky man named Hugh Williams. On 5 December 1785, another ship sank in the Menai Strait. All on board perished but one. His name was Hugh Williams. On 5 August 1820, 35 years later, a small 25-passenger vessel went down in the Menai Strait. Once again, there was only one survivor. And once again, his name was Hugh Williams.

ALIVE WHEN REPORTED DEAD

Most people don't get to read their own obituaries. Mistakes happen, however. In April 2003, news site CNN.com got into hot water when it emerged that draft obituaries for a number of public figures appeared on the development area of their website. These included Fidel Castro, Dick Cheney, Bob Hope, Gerald Ford and Ronald Reagan. Some had been based on Queen Elizabeth II and the Queen Mother's pre-written tributes. The problem was they were unfinished – Dick Cheney was noted as the 'UK's favourite grandmother', while Pope John Paul II was celebrated for his 'love of racing'.

Many prominent figures have been reported dead before their time (though not by CNN): Sharon Osbourne, Alice Cooper, Arthur C. Clarke, Will Ferrell, Ian Dury, Zach Braff, Miley Cyrus, Paul McCartney, Norman Wisdom, Ernest Hemingway, George W. Bush, Alfred Nobel, Rudyard Kipling, Russell Crowe, Kanye West, Mark Twain, Margaret Thatcher, Britney Spears, Jimmy Savile, Bertrand Russell, Harold Pinter, Nelson Mandela, Madonna, Steve Jobs, Jeff Goldblum.

INTERNATIONAL
APPETITES

✳ In Mexico, tortillas are sometimes made with red and white agave worms. Their popularity stems from the belief that they are an aphrodisiac.

In some parts of Indonesia, bats are grilled or deep fried. Fruit bats are skinned and the head and wings removed. The body is cut into cubes and stewed, while the wings are served in coconut milk.

✳ In North Africa and the Middle East, nomadic tribes feast on roasted camel. Thanks to their North African empire, the French developed a taste for camel, too, though in France the preferred dish is camel's foot.

The puffer fish is a delicacy in Japan, but it can only be prepared by licensed chefs, since a mouthful of its liver can be fatal. Around 20 people die from eating it in Japan every year. Symptoms of poisoning occur within ten minutes; death follows in 30.

✳ South Koreans are known to eat live baby octopuses dipped in oil. This practice is rumoured to kill around six people a year.

In Colombia roasted black ants are served in cinemas. They have a smoky flavour and are rather good for you.

BUTTERFLY BODYGUARDS

Large Blue butterflies receive protection from red ants. Caterpillars make their way into the ants' nests and hibernate inside tunnels. To 'fit in' – and appear less of an intruder – the caterpillar imitates both the sound and scent of the ants, as well as providing a gift of honeydew for the ants to feast on. Three weeks later, it will emerge as a butterfly and often be escorted from the nest by a multitude of ants. Amazingly, they take the butterfly to a safe place for it to find a mate. The butterfly is still delicate at this stage, so the ants hang around for a few days to ward off predators while the butterfly finds its feet.

☆ UNUSUAL BEQUESTS ☆

Harry Houdini – the magician died in 1926 and left his wife ten random words. Harry's will instructed her to hold a séance every Halloween so that he could use those words to communicate with her. After ten years of séances, Houdini had still not made contact and his wife gave up.

John Porter Bowman – a nineteenth-century tanner from Vermont, Bowman lost his wife and two daughters early on, but believed the family would be reincarnated when he died. Accordingly, his will set aside $50,000 for the maintenance of his mansion, and left several specific instructions. The most bizarre was Bowman's insistence that a full dinner be prepared and laid out on the table every night in case the family came back hungry.

Napoleon Bonaparte – when he died in 1821, the emperor's will directed that his head be shaved and his hair shared out between his friends.

Gene Roddenberry – the *Star Trek* creator died in 1991 and requested that his ashes be launched into space in a capsule. He was carried away on a Spanish satellite in 1997, and his wife joined him in space after her death around ten years later.

Mark Gruenwald – the author who wrote *Spider Man* and *Captain America* for Marvel Comics died in 1996 and, in accordance with his wishes, his ashes were mixed with the ink used to print the first *Squadron Supreme*, a compilation of comics.

Fred Baur – the inventor of Pringles died in 2008 and his will instructed that his ashes be buried in a Pringles can.

Robert Louis Stevenson – the author of *Treasure Island* and *The Strange Case of Dr Jekyll and Mr Hyde* passed away in 1894 and left his birthday – 13 November – to friend Annie H. Ide. Annie had often complained to Stevenson about feeling cheated out of her own birthday, which fell on Christmas Day.

Philip Grundy – a dentist who died in 1974, Mr Grundy left dental nurse Amelia White £181,000 on condition that she not go out with men or wear make-up or jewellery for five years.

Samuel Bratt – Bratt's wife forbade him to smoke, so when he died in 1960 he left her £330,000 on condition that she smoke five cigars a day.

Heinrich Heine – the poet died in 1856 and left his estate to his wife on condition that she remarry so 'there will be at least one man to regret my death'.

George Bernard Shaw – the playwright left money in trust for research on a 'Proposed British Alphabet' of at least 40 letters. Nothing came of his request.

☆ ★ TRIVIAL ★ ☆ APPROXIMATIONS

* A penguin swims at a speed of approximately 15 miles per hour.

* **A person uses approximately 57 sheets of toilet paper each day.**

* Approximately 25,000 workers died during the building of the Panama Canal, and approximately 20,000 of them contracted malaria or yellow fever.

* **An adult porcupine has approximately 30,000 quills on its body.**

* Approximately 20 per cent of Americans own a passport.

* **A baby's eyes cannot produce tears until it is approximately six to eight weeks old.**

* In New York City, approximately 1,600 people are bitten by other humans every year.

* **At the age of 35, a human being will start to lose approximately 7,000 brain cells a day. They will never be replaced.**

* Our galaxy has approximately 250 billion stars.

* **Sea water is approximately 3.5 per cent salt.**

* The Eiffel Tower is painted approximately once every seven years and requires nearly 50 tons of paint each time.

* **The Empire State Building in New York City weighs approximately 365,000 tons.**

* A human eyeball weighs approximately 28 grams.

* **There are approximately 45 billion fat cells in an average adult, 7,000 feathers on an eagle, 75,000,000 horses in the world and 9,000 taste buds on the human tongue.**

☆ BETWEEN THE SHEETS ☆

---

* Approximately 100 million acts of sexual intercourse take place each day.

* **An orgasm can cure hiccups.**

* Kissing can help to reduce tooth decay. This is because the extra saliva produced helps to keep the mouth clean. Kissing for one minute can also burn 26 calories.

* **A Durex World Sex Survey concluded that, globally, we are each having sex 103 times per year, or 1.98 times per week, or 0.28 times per day.**

✳ Food thought to boost the sex drive: lean meat, grains, watermelon, pumpkin seeds, almonds, bananas, strawberries, mango, avocado, chilli, basil, cardamom, figs, pepper, oysters, chocolate, truffles, caviar.

✩ **Impotence is grounds for divorce in 26 US states.**

✳ A hour of sex can burn about 70–120 calories for a 60-kilogram woman, and 77–155 calories for an 80-kilogram man.

✩ **Americans and Greeks have the most sex. Each year, they get down to it on average 124 and 117 times respectively. Indians get cosy only 76 times, while the Japanese only manage 36 nights of passion per annum.**

✳ A man's beard grows fastest when he is anticipating sex.

✩ **Sleep studies show that men have about nine erections during a night's sleep – regardless of what they dream about.**

✳ The most common month for a male to lose his virginity is June.

✩ **It takes a sperm approximately one hour to swim six inches.**

✳ In 2004 pornographic actor Lisa Sparxxx set a new world record – she had sex with 919 men in 24 hours.

☆ ANIMAL COLLECTIVES ☆

A shrewdness of apes

A troop of baboons

A cete of badgers

A sloth of bears

A sounder of boar

An obstinacy of buffalo

A quiver of cobras

An intrusion of cockroaches

A float of crocodiles

A murder of crows

A dule of doves

A pace of donkeys

A gang of elks

A mob of emus

A business of ferrets

A skulk of foxes

A tower of giraffes

A troubling of goldfish

A bloat of hippopotamuses

A parcel of hogs

A smack of jellyfish

A murder of magpies

A mischief of mice

A labour of moles

A romp of otters

An ostentation of peacocks

A string of ponies

A rhumba of rattlesnakes

An unkindness of ravens

A sleuth of sloths

A murmuration of starlings

A swift of tigers

A hover of trout

A bale of turtles

A pitying of turtledoves

BAD AMERICAN SANTAS

In 2004, a man dressed as Santa attacked a 74-year-old woman with a 2 × 4 inch wooden board at a shopping mall in Atlanta. Elkin Donnie Clarke told police he knocked the woman unconscious because she had taken 29 boxes of Hershey's chocolates from him.

In 2007, a cunning Santa and two of his helpers robbed a perfume shop, a garage and a clothes shop in three different Swedish towns. They escaped in a different Volvo after each robbery.

In 2009, a Nashville, Tennessee, Santa entered a bank wearing sunglasses. When asked to remove them, he pulled out a 9mm gun and asked for money 'to pay his elves'. Witnesses described the robber as 'jovial'.

In 2009, a jolly Santa from Wisconsin had a few too many sherries before walking down the street, hugging random children and demanding they tell him 'where his reindeer had gone'. He was eventually arrested and charged with possessing liquor in public.

RUDEICONS

Assicons		Boobicons	
Regular	(_!_)	Regular	(o)(o)
Fat	(__!__)	Big	(O)(O)
Tight	(!)	Perky	(')(')
Dumb ass	(_?_)	Saggy	(,)(,)
Smart ass	(_E=mc²_)	Silicon	($)($)

SILLY MONEY – SOME VERY COSTLY ITEMS

Mobile phone – Goldstriker's iPhone 3GS Supreme costs $3.2 million. A 271-gram solid 22-kilogram gold case, a screen trimmed with 53 one-carat diamonds and a home button covered with a single 7.1-carat diamond.

Coffee – The most expensive coffee in the world comes from Indonesia. Kopi Luwak is made from coffee beans eaten, partly digested and then excreted by the common palm civet, a weasel-like animal. *Kopi* is Indonesian for coffee, and *luwak* is the local name for the civet, which digests the soft outer part of the coffee cherry, but does not digest the inner beans. In April 2008 the brasserie at London's Peter Jones department store began selling a blend of Kopi Luwak and Blue Mountain coffee for £50 a cup.

Dog – Tibetan Mastiffs can grow to 30 inches and often weigh around 140 pounds. The dogs can be black, grey, brown or, rarely, completely white. They are odour-free, thanks to their odour-shedding coats, and come at a price that's not to be … sniffed at – around £500–£700. The world's most expensive dog is a black Tibetan Mastiff named Yangtze River Number 2. His owner, a Chinese millionaire named only as Ms Wang, forked out $582,000 for the beast.

Jeans – Manufacture of Dussault Apparel's Trashed Denim line of handmade men's jeans involves thirteen washes, with dying and painting performed between each washing to add 'depth'. Each pair features 16 one-carat rubies, 26 .05-carat rubies, 8 .05-carat diamonds and 1,080 grams of 18-kilogram white or rose gold. The result? A buyer $250,000 out of pocket.

Water – Bling H_2O costs from $40 to $2,600 a pop, depending on how many hand-applied Swarovski crystals are on the bottle. Bottled in Dandridge, Tennessee, this American water was the brainchild of Hollywood writer and producer Kevin G. Boyd. Needless to say, there are people in the world prepared to pay for it. Celebrities, too.

☆

PLAYING CARDS WHO'S WHO

JACK

Spades	Ogier the Dane. Legendary hero of *Chansons de Geste*, eleventh-century French epic poems.
Hearts	*La hire*. French military commander during the Hundred Years War.
Diamonds	Hector. Trojan warrior and mythological hero of *The Iliad*.
Clubs	Lancelot. Knight of the Round Table in Arthurian legend.

QUEEN

Spades	Athena. Greek goddess of wisdom, war, justice and arts and crafts.
Hearts	Judith. Biblical widow from the Book of Judith.
Diamonds	Rachel. Biblical wife of Jacob and mother of Joseph.
Clubs	Argine. Anagram of *regina*, Latin for queen.

KING

Spades	David. Biblical Hebrew King of Israel.
Hearts	Charlemagne. King of the Franks from 768 to 814.
Diamonds	Caesar. Julius.
Clubs	Alexander the Great, King of Macedonia.

THE ACE OF SPADES IS DIFFERENT

In most packs of cards, the Ace of Spades symbol is larger than that of other aces. In England, taxes on playing cards were raised in 1588, 1628 and several times thereafter, and a duty stamp was made on the face of each pack's Ace of Spades (as the ace was normally at the top if held face-up). In 1765, the tax office began printing its own aces to be inserted by manufacturers, and forging Aces of Spades became a capital offence. The government spade pips were larger than most card designs. After the government stopped taxing cards in 1960, manufacturers continued to print a larger Ace of Spades, and the tradition endures to this day.

Aces of Spades were used as a psychological weapon in the fight against the Viet Cong during the Vietnam War. Believing (falsely, as it turned out) that the Vietnamese considered the spade a symbol of death, American troops left Aces of Spades on dead bodies and dispersed hundreds of cards throughout the jungle. The practice was perceived as being good for US soldiers' morale, and effective in scaring the Viet Cong. The United States Playing Card Company was commissioned to supply thousands of packs containing only Aces of Spades.

☆ OLD BRITISH SITCOMS ☆

Blackadder – in the *Blackadder Goes Forth* episode 'Corporal Punishment', Corporal Jones was named after the *Dad's Army* character played by Clive Dunn.

Dad's Army – John Laurie was the only cast member to have served in the Home Guard.

Fawlty Towers – George Bush reportedly relaxed by watching episodes during the 1991 Gulf War.

The Good Life – at an after-show party, Penelope Keith made a chilli for the cast and crew which caused everybody toilet trouble. Penelope had neglected to soak the beans before cooking them – soaking removes the toxins and makes the beans more digestible.

One Foot in the Grave – in the final episode, Victor Meldrew was run over and killed outside Shawford railway station in Hampshire. The day after it was screened, fans laid flowers outside the station.

Only Fools and Horses – close contenders for the part of Del Boy, played by David Jason, were Jim Broadbent, Enn Reitel, Robin Nedwell and Billy Murray. Anthony Hopkins is a big fan.

Porridge – the show began life as a pilot called *Prisoner and Escort*, part of a series called *Seven of One*. This series also spawned *Open All Hours*. The Slade prison gate was that of St Albans prison, which is now the headquarters of a mineral water company.

Yes Minister – the favourite sitcom of Margaret Thatcher, Tony Benn and Armando Iannucci.

☆ ★ SUPERSTITIONS ★ ☆

Event	Consequence	Remedy
Breaking a mirror	Seven years' bad luck	Throw broken mirror into a river
Walking under a ladder	Imminent death in the family	Don't speak until you see a four-legged creature
A black cat crossing your path	Harbinger of evil	Take four steps backwards
The sight of a single magpie	Evil entering one's life	Salute magpie
Spilling salt	Each grain represents a tear to be shed later	Throw some spilled salt over left shoulder

☆ ★ SOME ARCHITECTURAL TERMS ★ ☆

Acanthus – Depiction of leaves or plants at the top of a column

Barbican – Fortified gateway or outer defence of a city or castle

Campanile – A bell tower, usually detached

Capital – The top of a column

Console – Slightly projecting ornamental bracket

Dado – Lower part of room wall when painted or decorated differently from the rest of a wall

Hypocaust – Underground room in Roman architecture which contained a furnace used for central heating.

Mullion – The vertical bar in a window

Spandrel – Triangular space under a staircase

Transom – The horizontal bar in a window

BORN ON CHRISTMAS DAY

Dido (1971), Helena Christensen (1968), Shane McGowan (1957), Annie Lennox (1954), Sissy Spacek (1949), Kenny Everett (1945), Humphrey Bogart (1899), Sir Isaac Newton (1642).

☆ ★ BATS ★ ☆

* Bats always turn left when they leave their caves.

☆ **A single little brown bat can eat up to 1,000 mosquitoes in an hour, and, with a lifespan of nearly 40 years, is one of the world's longest-living mammals.**

* An anticoagulant derived from vampire-bat saliva is used to treat human stroke victims.

☆ **Many bats can see nearly as well as human beings.**

* The 20-million-strong Mexican free-tail bats from Bracken Cave, Texas, eat approximately 200 tons of insects nightly.

☆ **Thailand's bumblebee bat is the world's smallest mammal, and weighs less than a penny.**

✳ Vampire bats don't suck blood. They use their sharp teeth to make a tiny incision in the skin of a sleeping animal before feeding on the blood-flow. Vampire-bat saliva contains a chemical that prevents the blood from clotting.

☆ **The largest bats are flying foxes. They live in Indonesia, Australia and on islands off the east coast of Africa, and have wingspans of up to two metres.**

ANTHONY HOPKINS - WHAT ARE THE CHANCES?

In 1973, Anthony Hopkins landed a role in *The Girl from Petrovka*, a film based on the novel by George Feifer. In preparation, Hopkins set out to buy a copy of the book, but to no avail. After trudging around many of London's bookshops, he was astonished when, at Leicester Square tube station, he glanced down and discovered a copy lying on a bench. But the coincidence didn't end there; one year later, Hopkins met the author on the film set in Vienna. Not long into their conversation, George Feifer lamented the fact that he had lent his one and only annotated copy of the book to a friend, who had lost it. It turned out that the copy found on the bench by Anthony Hopkins belonged to George Feifer.

☆

MONEY WORDS

£1	Quid, bar, squid, nicker
£2	Bottle, deuce, pair of nickers
£3	Tray/trey
£4	French loaf, rofe
£5	Beehive, deep-sea diver, handful
£6	Tom/Tom Mix
£7	Neves
£8	Garden/garden gate
£10	Big Ben, tenner, Ayrton Senna, brick, Tony Benn
£15	Commodore
£20	Score
£25	Pony, macaroni
£50	McGarrett, bull's eye
£100	Oner, ton
£500	Monkey
£1,000	Bag of sand, grand
£2,000	Archer
£1 million	Marigold

TWO BOGEYMEN

Spring-Heeled Jack, a fiend with an ability to jump extraordinarily high, was claimed to exist during the Victorian era. After the first 'sighting' in London 1837, Spring-Heeled Jack began popping up all over the country, with reports flooding in from London, Sheffield, Liverpool, the Midlands and Scotland. Witnesses to his presence described a terrifying sight – a tall, thin, devilish gentleman with clawed hands, a tight, white oilskin outfit and eyes like 'red balls of fire'. Not the kind of fellow the average Victorian wanted jumping around in front of him, not least because he was said to breathe fire. The first report of Jack came from a London businessman who had been shocked late at night by a strange creature with pointed ears and nose jumping easily over a high cemetery wall and landing in his path. The second account was more disturbing still – Jack leaped out in front of a servant girl named Mary Stevens as she walked through Battersea Park, grabbed her arms with hands 'cold and clammy as a corpse', and tried to kiss her. The following day, several witnesses claimed to have seen the same man leaping over a nine-foot wall and cackling, and rumours began spreading like wildfire among the servant girls of London. Soon enough, letters containing eyewitness accounts were pouring into the Lord Mayor's office, and *The Times* reported what would become the most famous incident. One night, teenage Londoner Jane Alsop answered the door to a man claiming to be a policeman in need of a light because he had caught Spring-Heeled Jack in the lane. But when she opened the door, the man proceeded to tear at Jane's dress and hair until family members came to her rescue. She told the police that the attacker had vomited blue and white flame from his mouth. Shortly after the incident, a man named Thomas Millbank was apprehended for claiming to be Spring-Heeled Jack. Millbank was arrested and tried but escaped conviction because he could not breathe fire. Whether or not Jack ever existed, his name was a contemporary legend in London, and featured in many penny dreadfuls (cheap fiction magazines aimed at the poor) and plays including the 1840 *Spring-Heeled Jack, The Terror of London*, by John Thomas Haines. Nearly a century on, in 1950, *Spring-Heeled Jack, The Terror of Epping Forest*, opened at the Theatre Royal in Stratford. More recently, Jack appeared in the 2009 spoof film, *Sherlock Holmes*.

The Owlman was supposedly sighted in the 1970s in Mawnan Smith, on the south coast of Cornwall. At the time the area was well known as a place for UFO sightings and bizarre animal behaviour – huge numbers of dog attacks and stories of human beings being taken hostage by cats abounded. But on 17 April 1976, the strangest claim yet was made. Two girls on holiday – 12-year-old June Melling and her nine-year-old sister, Vicky – were walking in the woods when they saw a huge owl-like creature flying above Mawnan church tower. Terrified, they ran away and told to their father, who called the sighting to the attention of Tony 'Doc' Shields, a local paranormal investigator. 'The Doc' visited the family and took away with him a drawing of the creature made by one of the girls, and the Melling family cut their holiday short and went back to Lancashire. Two months later, two other teenage girls were on a camping trip near the church. Fourteen-year old Sally Chapman and her friend were standing by their tent when they heard a hissing sound. Turning, they were met by a silvery-grey, man-sized owl with pointed ears and red eyes. Thinking it was a man in fancy dress, they started to laugh. Their amusement ceased when, suddenly, the creature spread its wings, took flight and revealed its black claws. Several more sightings were reported the following day, and later that year. All the sightings were near the church. Under police investigation, the girls were isolated and drew separate images of the creature. Both pictures were similar, but different enough to eliminate the possibility of conspiracy. Furthermore, the images matched the earlier picture drawn by June Melling. A string of sightings followed in 1989, 1995 and 2009, and a legend was born.

BAD SCIENCE AND
☆ ★ TECHNOLOGY ★ ☆
PREDICTIONS

'Everything that can be invented has been invented' –
Charles H. Duell, an official at the US Patent Office, 1899.

**'Ours has been the first [expedition], and doubtless [will] be
the last, to visit this profitless locality'** – Lt Joseph Ives, after
visiting the Grand Canyon in 1861.

**'Such startling announcements as these should be deprecated
as being unworthy of science and mischievous to its true
progress'** – Sir William Siemens, on Edison's light bulb, 1880.

**'The horse is here to stay but the automobile is only a
novelty, a fad'** – the president of the Michigan Savings Bank
advising Henry Ford's lawyer not to invest in the Ford Motor
Co., 1903.

'Airplanes are interesting toys but of no military value'
– Maréchal Ferdinand Foch, Professor of Strategy, École
Supérieure de Guerre, 1904.

**'Nuclear-powered vacuum cleaners will probably be a
reality in 10 years'** – Alex Lewyt, president of vacuum cleaner
company Lewyt Corp., in the *New York Times* in 1955.

**'The bomb will never go off. I speak as an expert in
explosives'** – Admiral William Leahy (1875–1959), US Atomic
Bomb Project.

'Atomic energy might be as good as our present-day explosives, but it is unlikely to produce anything very much more dangerous' – Winston Churchill, British Prime Minister, 1939.

'Rail travel at high speed is not possible, because passengers, unable to breathe, would die of asphyxia' – Dr Dionysius Lardner (1793–1859), Professor of Natural Philosophy and Astronomy, University College London.

'The world potential market for copying machines is 5,000 at most' – IBM, to the eventual founders of Xerox, saying the photocopier had no market large enough to justify production, 1959.

'There is no reason anyone would want a computer in their home' – Ken Olson, president, chairman and founder of Digital Equipment Corp., 1977.

'This "telephone" has too many shortcomings to be seriously considered as a means of communication. The device is inherently of no value to us' – Western Union internal memo, 1876.

'Man will never reach the moon regardless of all future scientific advances' – Dr Lee De Forest (1873–1961), inventor of the vacuum tube and father of television.

'Louis Pasteur's theory of germs is ridiculous fiction' – Pierre Pachet, Professor of Physiology at Toulouse, 1872.

'Submarine will do nothing' – H. G. Wells (1866–1946).

'The Americans have need of the telephone, but we do not. We have plenty of messenger boys' – Sir William Preece, chief engineer of the British Post Office, 1876.

'Radio has no future. Heavier-than-air flying machines are impossible. X-rays will prove to be a hoax' – William Thomson, Lord Kelvin, British scientist, 1899.

'There is not the slightest indication that nuclear energy will ever be obtainable. It would mean that the atom would have to be shattered at will' – Albert Einstein, 1932.

'The abdomen, the chest, and the brain will forever be shut from the intrusion of the wise and humane surgeon' – Sir John Eric Ericksen, British surgeon, appointed Surgeon-Extraordinary to Queen Victoria 1873.

CLASSIC RIDDLE #2

Three people check into a hotel. The room is £30 so they pay £10 each. Once the guests are in their rooms, the receptionist notices that the bill should only have been £25. He gives £5 to the bellboy and tells him to return the money to the guests. Since the £5 can't be split evenly between the three guests, the bellboy keeps £2 for himself and then gives the remaining £3 to the guests. With their money back, each of the guests has paid £9, making a total of £27, and the bellboy has pocketed £2. So there is £27 + £2 = £29 accounted for. Yet the guests originally paid £30. What happened to the missing pound?

ANSWER TO CLASSIC RIDDLE #2

This riddle is simply an example of misdirection. It is nonsensical to add £27 + £2, because the £27 that has been paid includes the £2 the bellboy made. The correct way to think about it is that the guests paid £27, and the bellboy took £2, which, if given back to the guests, would bring them to their correct payment of £27 – £2 = £25 with £5 in change.

AMUSING AND CONFUSING SENTENCES

Time flies like an arrow. Fruit flies like a banana.

Buffalo buffalo Buffalo buffalo buffalo buffalo Buffalo buffalo.

Rose rose to put rose roes on her rows of roses.

James, while John had had 'had', had had 'had had'. 'Had had' had had a better effect on the teacher.

That that is, is. That that is not, is not. Is that it? It is.

If the police police police police, who polices the police police? Police police police police police police.

But and and, and, and and and, and, and and so, are pairs of conjunctions.

It was 'and', I said, not 'are', and 'and' and 'are' are different.

☆ USELESS ACTRESS FACTS ☆

* Christina Ricci loves gambling and has no formal acting training.

☆ **Sandra Bullock uses haemorrhoid cream on her face and is allergic to horses.**

* Rachel Weisz's father invented the artificial respirator and also machines that sense landmines.

☆ **Demi Moore was born cross-eyed.**

✳ Angelina Jolie dropped out of acting classes when she was 14 because she wanted to become a funeral director. Her uncle, Chip Taylor, wrote the song 'Wild Thing'.

☆ *Buffy the Vampire Slayer* **star Sarah Michelle Gellar is afraid of cemeteries. She was once ranked third for figure skating in New York State.**

✳ Nicole Kidman used to pray she would be turned into a witch because she was in love with hit sixties US TV comedy *Bewitched*. Years later, she would star in the film of the series.

☆ **As a comedienne, Whoopi Goldberg's stage name was Whoopee Cushion.**

✳ When Vivien Leigh was making *Gone With the Wind* she complained that she did not like kissing Clark Gable because he had bad breath.

☆ **Katharine Hepburn had a phobia about dirty hair. When on set she would sniff everybody's hair to check if it had been washed.**

✳ When she gets nervous, Julia Roberts' left eye fills with tears.

☆ **Bette Midler once worked as a pineapple chunker in a cannery in Hawaii.**

✳ Sharon Stone has an IQ of 150 and is a member of Mensa.

☆ **Helena Bonham Carter owns a £2 million mansion previously owned by former British Prime Minister Herbert Asquith, her great-grandfather.**

✳ Kate Winslet gave birth to her son Joe to the music of Rufus Wainwright.

✳ **Sophia Loren was initially considered for the role of Alexis in *Dynasty* before Joan Collins got the part.**

✳ Joan Crawford changed every toilet seat in her house whenever she got a new husband.

☆

DIRTY MONEY

Research has revealed that most US banknotes bear traces of cocaine. This is in part due to bills being rolled up for consumption of the drug, and drug smugglers and dealers handling cash with cocaine-polluted hands. Interestingly, though, ATMs (Automatic Teller Machines, or cashpoints) play a role in distributing the drug – minute amounts cling to the machines' brushes and rollers and are passed on to previously clean bills.

But narcotics are by no means the only note-polluting substance. Faecal matter is present on 94 per cent of bills, and when tested paper money has been shown to carry a wider variety of germs that the average household toilet. While many viruses and bacteria can live on most exposed surfaces for no more than a couple of days, paper money can hold on to a flu virus for just over two weeks. Charming.

☆

☆ ★ TRIVIAL WORDS ★ ☆

* The word Blighty comes from *bilayti*, the Urdu for homeland.

* **Stewardesses is the longest word typed with only the left hand.**

* The name of each continent ends with the same letter it begins with.

* **The word 'monosyllable' has five syllables.**

* 'Typewriter' is the longest word that can be typed using the top row of the keyboard.

* **Stressed is desserts spelled backwards.**

* Mouth the word 'colourful' to a friend – they will think you're saying 'I love you'.

* **The dot on the letter 'i' is called a tittle.**

* 'Lethologica' describes the state of not being able to remember the word you desire.

* **'Xmas' comes from the Greek word *Xristos*, meaning Christ. During the sixteenth century, Christians started using the letter 'x' as an abbreviation for the saviour's names.**

* 'The quick brown fox jumps over the lazy dog' uses every letter in the English language.

* **The Albanians have no word for headache.**

* 'Q' is the only letter that doesn't appear in the names of any of the fifty states of the US.

* **The hash symbol (#) on a telephone is called an octothorpe.**

* The longest word in the English language, according to the *Oxford English Dictionary*, is pneumonoultramicroscopicsilicovolcanoconiosis.

* **The letters KGB stand for *Komitet gosudarstvennoy bezopasnosti*.**

* The word 'therein' contains thirteen words spelled with consecutive letters: the, he, her, er, here, I, there, ere, rein, re, in, therein and herein.

* **The six official languages of the United Nations are: English, French, Arabic, Chinese, Russian and Spanish.**

* Courtney Cox was the first person to say the word 'period' on American television. She was featured on a Tampax advert.

* **'Facetious' and 'abstemious' contain all the vowels in the correct order. So does 'arsenious', which means containing arsenic.**

* The word 'moose' comes from the Algonquian Indian word meaning 'twig eater'.

CELEBRITY BODY PART
☆ ★ INSURANCE ★ ☆

Keith Richards' third finger of his left hand is insured for $1.5 million.

Dolly Parton's breasts are insured for $600,000.

David Beckham's legs are insured for $70 million.

Bette Davis's waistline was insured for $28,000.

Jamie Lee Curtis insured her legs for $2 million.

Rod Stewart's voice is insured for $6 million.

Bruce Springsteen's voice is insured for $6 million.

Actress and singer Angie Dickinson insured her legs for $1 million.

America Ferrera insured her smile for $10 million.

Mariah Carey insured her legs for $1 billion.

Tom Jones's chest hair is insured for $7 million.

Heidi Klum's legs are insured for $2.2 million.

Tina Turner's legs are insured for $3.2 million.

Ken Dodd's teeth are insured for $7.4 million.

BEES AND HONEY

Bees are quite something. They are the only insects that produce food we like to eat, they are born fully grown and they never sleep. A bumblebee uses 21 muscles to sting, and a honeybee only dies after using its stinger on a mammal or a bird – it can safely sting other bees and insects without fear of death. In 1962, Johannes Relleke was stung 2,443 times (the stings were removed and counted) in Zimbabwe (then Rhodesia). She survived. Napoleon Bonaparte III used the bee as a symbol of immortality and resurrection during the Second Empire period (1852–70) and had bees printed on his red cape. Honey is the only food that does not spoil, because of its unique chemical composition – a combination of low water content and relatively high acidic level gives it a low pH (3.2–4.5), which makes it difficult for bacteria or other micro-organisms to grow. Legend has it that a group of archaeologists found 2,000-year-old jars of honey in Egyptian tombs and proclaimed it delicious. A queen bee can live from two to five years. The drone (male bee) lives 40–50 days. The workers are females, and live for between one and four months. A worker makes the honey, producing on average only one-twelfth of a teaspoon of honey in its lifetime. To make one kilogram of honey, bees must visit nearly five million flowers and fly the equivalent of four times around the world.

PET PERCENTAGES

According to a University of Bristol poll, people who own a cat are more likely to have a university degree than those with a pet dog. 47.2 per cent of households with a cat had at least one person educated to degree level, compared with 38.4 per cent of homes with dogs. The dog population in the UK is estimated at around eight million (75 per cent pedigree, 11 per cent cross breed, 14 per cent mixed breeds). The UK cat population is also around eight million (92 per cent moggies/non-pedigree, 8 per cent pedigree). Almost one in two households owns a pet, with the percentages as follows:

Dogs	23	Domestic fowl	0.8
Cats	19	Horses/ponies	0.5
Indoor fish	10	Tortoises/turtles	0.9
Outdoor fish	6	Gerbils	0.3
Rabbits	2.6	Snakes	0.4
Indoor birds	2.5	Lizards	0.5
Guinea pigs	1.6	Rats	0.3
Hamsters	1.1		

☆ ★ HANDY INSULTS ★ ☆

Deep down, she's shallow.

He's going through a nonentity crisis.

The sharpest thing about her is her tongue.

He's seen it all, done it all, forgotten it all.

I've seen her face on a milk carton.

Ordinary people live and learn. He just lives.

He's so egotistical he calls out his own name during sex.

I've seen nicer faces on a pirate flag.

He lives in fear of not being misunderstood.

She's thinks she's out of this world – and everyone wishes she were.

He sounds so much better with his mouth closed.

She's so stupid she needs watering twice a week.

If he did some soul-searching, maybe he'd find one.

She suffers from migraines – her halo's on too tight.

The strongest thing about him is his breath.

When a thought crosses her mind, it's a long and lonely journey.

He's as popular as a French kiss at a family reunion.

The only thing she ever gives away is secrets.

He's the sort of man you could lose in a crowd of two.

She'd steal the straw from her mother's kennel.

One day he stopped to think, and forgot to start again.

She has delusions of adequacy.

He'll double-cross that bridge when he comes to it.

She has a highly developed sense of rumour.

Even the Samaritans hang up on him.

She's been seen tossing breadcrumbs to helicopters.

Give him a big hand … across the mouth.

She has no equals, only superiors.

He has a big heart and a stomach to match.

She has a great voice – if you happen to hate music.

He's always lost in thought – it's unfamiliar territory.

Some figures stop traffic. Hers just blocks it.

I've seen wounds better dressed than him.

If good looks are a curse, she's blessed.

ARTHUR CONAN DOYLE HOAX?

Conan Doyle's name has been linked to the Piltdown Man hoax of 1912. A human skull fragment, an orang-utan's jaw and chimpanzees' teeth were combined and stained to achieve an ancient look, and for four decades the scientific community was fooled into believing it had an early human fossil on its hands. Many considered the Piltdown Man to be the missing link, and more than 250 scientific papers were written on the subject. The hoax was exposed in 1953, and thus began the quest to find the hoaxers. Conan Doyle was named as a suspect in the 1980s. He had lived near the East Sussex village of Pilton, and was a zealous spiritualist, embittered by the exposure and prosecution of Henry Slade, one of his favourite psychics. It was argued that Conan Doyle was motivated by a desire to discredit the scientific establishment by persuading them to believe in a false artefact. He was also an amateur bone hunter, participated briefly in the digs and loved hoaxes. His classic dinosaur adventure *The Lost World* is said to contain clues that he was responsible for the Piltdown Man hoax – one character, for example, says 'if you are clever and you know your business you can fake a bone as easily as you can a photograph'.

QUEEN OF NOTES

Queen Elizabeth II's face has appeared on the currencies of 33 different countries, making her the most 'noteworthy' person in the world. She first appeared in 1935 on Canadian $20 notes when still a princess at the age of nine. Over time, 26 different images of her have been used in the UK and its various current and former colonies, dominions and territories. Most of the portraits were commissioned expressly for the purpose, but some counties, including Rhodesia, Malta and Fiji, used existing depictions of Her Majesty. The majority of countries change their notes as the Queen ages, but some like to keep her young. In 1980, Belize overhauled the design of it currency, but chose a portrait from the early 1960s.

THE REAL RAIN MAN

Raymond Babbit, the character played by Dustin Hoffman in *Rain Man*, was inspired by American mega-savant Kim Peek, a man with an astonishing photographic memory. But while Babbit was autistic, Peek had FG syndrome, which causes low muscle tone and abnormally large head size. Kim was born with a brain abnormality whereby the nerves connecting the two sides of the brain were absent, and it is theorised that his neurons were connected in such a way that he developed astonishing memory function. Kim could read children's books when he was 16 months old, and at three was observed using a dictionary to look up the meaning of 'confidential'. At the age of six, he had memorised the Bible. Using a technique that involved reading the left page of a book with his left eye, and the right page with his right eye, Kim could read two pages at once (about ten seconds per page), and devour an average-length tome in an hour, remembering virtually its entirety. He could recall the contents of more than 12,000 books, including the complete works of Shakespeare and every story in every volume of *Reader's Digest*. Screenwriter Barry Morrow discovered Peek in Texas in 1984 while attending the National Conference of the Association of Retarded Citizens. After spending time with him, Morrow approached his father, Fran, to ask him if he was aware his son could recall every postcode, area code and road number in every American state. He urged Fran to share Kim with the world, but Fran only agreed to let Kim into the limelight two years later, when he was presented with the film script. Dustin Hoffman spent time with Kim in preparation for his part in *Rain Man,* and the film turned Kim into something of a celebrity. The famous scene in which Raymond goes to a casino and beats the house with his mental dexterity never took place – yet Morrow did give Kim a book on gambling to read before accompanying him to a casino. However, Kim refused to go in: he felt it would be morally wrong to use his skills in such a way. Following the success of the film, Morrow presented Kim with his Oscar, and Kim carried it with him to various public appearances – it has been dubbed the 'Most Loved Oscar Statue' because it has been held by more people than any other.

BIBLE NUMBER CRUNCH

On average, 50 bibles are sold every minute, making it the world's bestselling book. It is also the most shoplifted book. The word 'Christian' appears only three times in the Bible: in Acts 11:26; 26:28; 1 Peter 4:16. Dogs are mentioned 14 times, and lions 55 times but domestic cats are not mentioned at all. Pigs are mentioned twice, sheep are mentioned 45 times and goats 88 times. The 66 books (King James Version) are divided into 1,189 chapters consisting of 31,173 verses. The Old Testament has 929 chapters, the New Testament 260. The King James Old Testament has 592,439 words (2,728,100 letters) and the New Testament has 181,253 words (838,380 letters). The longest word in the Bible is 'Maher-shalal-hash-baz': in Isaiah 8:1. The shortest verse in the New International Version of the Bible is John 11:35: 'Jesus wept'. The word 'Lord' appears 1,855 times, while 'God' appears in every book except Esther and Song of Solomon. 'Grandmother' appears only once (2 Timothy 1:5), as does 'eternity' (Isaiah 57:15). Three wise men are not mentioned once – Matthew 2:1 only says: 'Magi from the east came to Jerusalem'. Almonds and pistachios are the only nuts mentioned in the text. The oldest manuscript of the Bible is the *Codex Vaticanus,* dating from the fourth century, now located in the Vatican Library. The last word in the Bible? Amen.

☆ ★ FILM FACTOIDS ★ ☆

* Arnold Schwarzenegger was paid $15 million for *Terminator 2: Judgment Day,* meaning the 700 words he spoke cost $21,429 per word. Therefore, 'Hasta la vista, baby' cost a cool $85,716.

* **The Cure for Insomnia is the longest film in the world. Directed by John Henry Timmis IV, and released in 1987, its running time is 5,220 minutes (87 hours).**

* *Star Trek's* Captain James T. Kirk's middle name is Tiberius.

* **The Walt Disney Company was founded in 1923. Four years later Walt dreamed up the idea of an animated mouse named Mortimer Mouse. His wife Lillian wasn't impressed, suggesting Mickey Mouse instead.**

* Clint Eastwood wrote the theme tunes for *Unforgiven, Absolute Power, A Perfect World* and *The Bridges of Madison County.*

* **Alfred Hitchcock never won an Oscar for directing. He did, however, direct *Blackmail* in 1931 – the first ever talking film made in England.**

* Actor Jeff Bridges was considered for the part of Travis Bickle in *Taxi Driver.* In *The Big Lebowski,* Bridges' character the Dude's shirt with oriental characters and an Asian holding a baseball bat is the same shirt worn by the actor in part of *The Fisher King.*

* **Mel Blanc was allergic to carrots. He was also the voice of Bugs Bunny.**

EXTRA EXTRAS

Russian film *War and Peace* (1967) required 120,000 extras, and in the same year South Korean monster *Wang-magwi* used 157,000. German film *Kolberg* (1945) recruited 187,000. But *Gandhi* (1982) stands alone as the film with the highest number of extras, featuring a staggering 300,000.

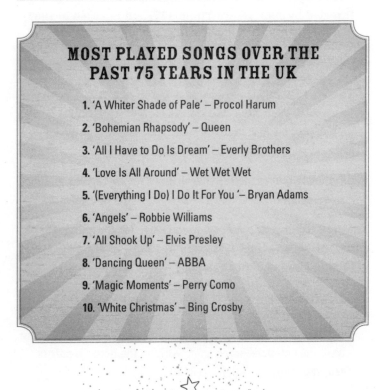

MOST PLAYED SONGS OVER THE PAST 75 YEARS IN THE UK

1. 'A Whiter Shade of Pale' – Procol Harum

2. 'Bohemian Rhapsody' – Queen

3. 'All I Have to Do Is Dream' – Everly Brothers

4. 'Love Is All Around' – Wet Wet Wet

5. '(Everything I Do) I Do It For You '– Bryan Adams

6. 'Angels' – Robbie Williams

7. 'All Shook Up' – Elvis Presley

8. 'Dancing Queen' – ABBA

9. 'Magic Moments' – Perry Como

10. 'White Christmas' – Bing Crosby

☆ NATIONAL ANTHEMS ☆

'My Country 'Tis of Thee' was the first US national anthem in 1832, and had the same melody as Britain's 'God Save the Queen', written by John Bull in 1619. Bull's melody has been used in national anthems more than any other. 'The Star-Spangled Banner' has been the US anthem only since 1931.

In 1909, while King Edward VII dressed, a German band played 'God Save The Queen' 17 times, a record for the number of times one anthem has been performed in a single sitting.

England uses 'God Save the Queen' at international football and rugby union matches, but not at Test cricket matches. Since 2003, 'Jerusalem' has been the song of choice. At the Common-wealth Games, 'Land of Hope and Glory' is the victory anthem. At international lacrosse matches, the England men's team sing 'God Save the Queen', the women's 'Jerusalem'. The Olympics Games has its own anthem, the 'Olympic Hymn', whose words were written by Greece's national poet, Costis Palamas, and set to music by Spirou Samara for the 1896 games in Athens. Since its first outing, the song has been played when the Olympic flag is raised during the opening ceremony. Anthematology is the study of national anthems.

BARKING

While roaming the Ecuadorian Andes in 1998, ornithologist Robert S. Ridgley came across a bird that resembled a duck, but with long, stilt-like legs. It certainly didn't sound like a duck, however. In fact, the song of *Antpitta avis canis Ridgley* bears no resemblance to that of any other bird. Rather, the bird barks like a dog. It is one of the largest birds to have been discovered in the last 50 years.

While there are no dogs that sing like birds, there are a number that do not bark, most notably the Basenji. When this small dog from Africa opens its mouth, the sound emitted is more akin to a yodel. The African wild dog also does not bark, but it does not yodel either.

In English slang, 'barking' is short for 'barking mad'. The English town of Barking is often associated with the origin of the phrase. The story goes that, in medieval times, an insane asylum was attached to Barking Abbey. Those within it were 'mad', hence the birth of an expression. The only problem is that there is no record of the phrase existing before the twentieth century. Chances are that the phrase is merely a comparison between the mentally unstable and barking dogs.

The barking spider is a species of tarantula that can be found along the coast of Queensland, Australia. Its name is misleading though. It does not bark, but hisses when provoked.

The Barking Dog Atlas is a website devoted to the most annoying of our canine companions. Disgruntled neighbours from all over the world can log on and add the precise location of noisy pooches to the database. If you want to move to a peaceful neighbourhood, check here first.

☆ ★ ARTY-FACTS ★ ☆

✳ In 1961, Matisse's *Le Bateau* (*The Boat*) hung upside down for two months in New York's Museum of Modern Art. The error went unnoticed by 116,000 visitors.

✳ **Picasso learned to draw before he could walk and his first word was 'Piz', short for *lapiz* the Spanish word for pencil. Later in life, when asked which of his paintings he liked the best, he replied 'the next one'.**

✳ In 1994, Chicago artist Dwight Kalb sent David Letterman a statue of Madonna, made of 180 pounds of ham.

✳ **In his last days, the painter Auguste Renoir was so crippled with arthritis that his brushes were tied to his arms so that he could continue to paint.**

✳ The Maesa Elephant Camp in Thailand supervised eight elephants spreading paint around a huge canvas in 2005. It fetched £20,000 at auction.

✳ ***The Discus Thrower*** **by the fifth-century BC sculptor Myron, one of the most famous of all Greek statues, is not Greek at all. The various versions of the statue around the world are all assembled from pieces of a Roman copy of the Greek original.**

✳ The *Mona Lisa* used to hang on the wall of Napoleon's bedroom. X-ray technology has shown there are three different versions of the *Mona Lisa* under the visible one.

✫ **And look closely at the *Mona Lisa* – there is a bridge in the background.**

✳ Congo the chimpanzee took up painting under the supervision of Dr Desmond Morris in the 1950s. His pieces were show at London's Institute of Contemporary Art in 1957. Picasso and Miró were fans, and owned several of the chimp's works. In 2005, three of Congo's finest compositions went for the grand total of £14,400 at auction.

✫ **When first exhibited in 1878, Auguste Rodin's statue *The Bronze Period* was considered so lifelike that onlookers suspected the sculptor had sacrificed a model to make the cast. He hadn't. In 1917, Rodin died of frostbite – even though his statues were kept safely in warm museums, the French government had refused the artist financial help for a place to live.**

✳ Vincent Van Gogh sold just one painting in his lifetime. *Red Vineyard at Arles* went to his brother Theo, an art dealer. Vincent also cut his left ear off, yet his *Self-Portrait with a Bandaged Ear* depicts the right ear as injured. The reason? He was painting his mirror image.

☆ USELESS ACTOR FACTS ☆

✳ Russell Crowe was once a pompadoured singer named Russ Le Roq. His first single was 'I Want to Be Like Marlon Brando' ... even though he'd never seen a Brando movie when he wrote the song.

☆ **In 2004, Orlando Bloom committed himself to Buddhism in an hour-long ceremony in Britain. He fell off his horse and broke a rib while filming *Lord of the Rings*. His friends call him O. B. or Orli for short. His first job was as a clay pigeon trapper at a shooting range, he speaks French and he has a dog called Maude.**

✳ Colin Farrell likes to check into hotels under the moniker Tom Foolery. He once auditioned to become a member of Boyzone.

☆ **David Schwimmer's *Friends* character, Ross, had a monkey but it was fired for vomiting up worms during filming.**

✳ Hugh Grant was once an assistant groundsman at Fulham Football Club.

☆ **The teenage Kevin Costner appeared in a soft-porn film about three young women and their love lives. *Sizzle Beach* was shot in 1974. Costner has been second choice to Harrison Ford for the role in two films: *JFK* and *Dragonfly*.**

✳ James Stewart had it written into each of his film contracts that he was able to choose the hats he wore on screen.

☆ **A childhood virus left Rob Lowe deaf in his right ear. 'No stereo for me,' he says. 'It's a mono world.'**

✳ Sean Connery was a bricklayer, lifeguard, and coffin polisher before he was famous. His hobby of bodybuilding culminated in a bid for the 1950 Mr Universe title. He came third.

☆ **John Travolta was cast in *Pulp Fiction* only because Michael Madsen, who had a major role in Tarantino's previous film, *Reservoir Dogs*, turned it down. Travolta is** famous for turning down two plum roles – in *An Officer and a Gentleman* and *American Gigolo* – in both of which Richard Gere starred.

* Christopher Walken manages to insert a little dance number into nearly all of his roles, no matter how small.

* **Christopher Lee is a Tolkien expert and the only member of the cast of *Lord of the Rings* who has met Tolkien himself.**

* George Clooney sometimes sleeps in the walk-in closet of his LA mansion because, he says, 'all the bedrooms are too light'. He defines his perfect woman as one who has the laughter of Nicole Kidman, the personality of Julia Roberts, the 'quintessence of beauty' of Michelle Pfeiffer and the ambition of Jennifer Lopez. He is one of only two men to have graced the cover of American *Vogue* magazine. The other was Richard Gere.

UK PLACE NAMES TO TITTER AT ☆ ★ ★ ☆

Asick Bottom	Bottom Head	Crapstone
Backside	Bummers Hill	Dead
Badger	Burpham	Dogdyke
Bell End	Buttock Point	Droop
Bitchfield	Cockermouth	Dyke
Blubberhouses	Cocking	Fatfield
Bogend	Cocklick End	Fingringhoe

Foul End
Gaywood
Great Fryupdale
Great Snoring
Happy Bottom
Hetton-le-Hole
Horsey Windpump
Land of Nod
Leatherhead
Lickey End
Loose
Lover
Lower Slaughter
Muff
Muffworthy
Nasty
Nether Wallop
Nobber
No Place
Once Brewed

Outcast
Pant
Penistone
Peover Superior
Piddle
Pity Me
Plucks Gutter
Plush
Pratts Bottom
Quaking Houses
Ramsbottom
Rashy Height
Shaggie Burn
Skinners Bottom
Slack
Slaggyford
Snodland
Spital-in-the-
    Street
Splatt

Splott Street
The Hard
Thong
Thrashbush
Three Cocks
Titsey
Titty Hill
Toe Head
Tongue
Tumby Woodside
Twatt
Twydall
Ugley
Upper Dicker
Upper Thong
Wetwang
Wideopen
Willey
Wormegay
Wyre Piddle

☆ ★ ★ ☆

CHESS

* The number of chess move combinations far exceeds the number of electrons in the universe – there are ten (to the 79) electrons and ten (to the 120) possible chess games. That's a thousand trillion, trillion, trillion, trillion, trillion, trillion, trillion, trillion, trillion games.

☆ **Chess was traditionally played by nobility, which explains why it is called the game of kings.**

✳ The oldest chess set was discovered on the Isle of Lewis. The pieces are made from walrus tusks and depict characters in a range of moods from irritation to anger to depression.

✳ **The rook's name derives from the Arabic word *rukh*, meaning chariot. Accordingly, it can only move quickly in straight lines. When chariots fell from use in the Middle Ages, the rook was modified to resemble a castle turret.**

✳ 'Checkmate' comes from a Persian phrase – *shah mat* – meaning 'the king is defeated'.

✳ **Lewis Carroll's *Through the Looking Glass* was based on a game of chess, with Alice representing a pawn. The idea of a huge chessboard came from Carroll's time in Oxmoor, where his lodgings looked over a moor divided up neatly into square fields.**

✳ The idea for a folding chessboard came to a priest in the early twelfth century. Chess was banned by the Church, so he made a chessboard that appeared to be one book lying on top of the other.

☆ ★ COFFEE ★ ☆

✳ The story goes that Ethiopian shepherds became interested in coffee when they noticed their goats becoming lively after eating coffee berries.

✳ **The Japanese bathe in coffee grounds mixed with pineapple pulp to improve their skin and reduce wrinkles.**

* Athletes who test positive for more than 12 micrograms of caffeine per millilitre of urine may be banned from the Olympic Games. This level can be reached after drinking around five cups of coffee.

Turkish grooms were once made to swear they would always provide their new wives with coffee. Failing to do so was adequate grounds for divorce.

* An espresso has one third of the caffeine of a regular cup of coffee.

Coffee was eaten before people began drinking it. African tribes mixed coffee berries (or beans, as we call them) with fat to form the first energy snacks.

* The Women's Petition Against Coffee (WPAC) was drafted in 1674 to represent 'Several Thousands of Buxome Good-Women, Languishing in Extremity of Want' who were upset that their men were always out at coffee houses indulging in the 'Excessive Use of that drying, Enfeebling Liquor'.

Beethoven was so fussy about his coffee that he counted 60 beans out before preparing each cup.

* Together America, France and Germany consume 65 per cent of the world's coffee.

Dark-roasted coffee contains less caffeine than medium-roasted. The longer the coffee is roasted, the more the caffeine burns off.

* The rise of Islam made a huge difference to the popularity of coffee. Since the Islamic religion prohibited alcohol, many turned to coffee to get their kicks.

☆ **All coffee comes from the 'bean belt', the area between the Tropics of Cancer and Capricorn. Hawaii is the only US state that grows it.**

✳ In 1675, in the belief that coffee houses were places where people would conspire against him, Charles II banned them. At the time, there were over 3,000 coffee houses in London, and the public outcry was so strong that the ban lasted only a fortnight.

☆ **The term 'Americano' comes from American GIs in Italy during the Second World War. They would order espresso with water to dilute the strong flavour.**

☆ ★ ON TOILETS ★ ☆

✳ The World Toilet Organization started the World Toilet Summit in 2001. It was held in Singapore.

☆ **The average person visits the toilet 2,500 times a year – about six to eight times a day.**

✳ Men and women were offered separate toilets for the first time at a ball in Paris in 1739.

☆ **The first toilet cubicle in a public toilet is the least likely to be used, and therefore is the cleanest.**

✳ Most toilets flush in the key of E flat.

☆ **World Toilet Day takes place on 19 November each year.**

* The flushing toilet as we know it was invented by Sir John Harrington, godson of Elizabeth I, in 1597. Elizabeth would not grant Sir John a patent for his toilet (because of the indecent nature of toileting), but she did have one installed at her Richmond residence.

Dylan Thomas once observed that, read backward, T. S. Eliot nearly spells 'toilets'.

* Marti Pellow, the lead Singer of Wet Wet Wet, was born in a public toilet.

In London, there is a public toilet for every 10,000 people.

* The first toilet to be flushed in a film was in Alfred Hitchcock's *Psycho*.

The life expectancy of a toilet is 50 years.

* The first toilet paper was developed in England in 1880 and sold, not on a roll, but as individual sheets in a box. Known as 'curl papers', they were sold from under the counter in chemists because members of the public were embarrassed to see them on display. Toilet rolls did not come on to the market until 1928.

The average toilet is flushed eight times a day.

* Hermann Goering refused to use regulation toilet paper – instead he bought soft white handkerchiefs in bulk and used them.

Pomegranates studded with cloves were used as the first attempt at making toilet air-freshener.

* Public toilets were known as 'halting stations' in the nineteenth century.

* **King George II died falling off a toilet on 25 October 1760.**

☆ ★ MONOPOLY ★ ☆

* The original game of Monopoly was dreamed up around 1905 by Lizzie Magie. She was opposed to capitalism and wanted the game to highlight the misery caused by the habits of buying and selling. She called it The Landlord's Game. Charles Darrow adapted the game thirty years later and called it Capitalism.

* **In Cuba, the game had a strong following until Fidel Castro took power and ordered all known sets to be destroyed.**

* Over 5,120,000,000 little green houses have been 'constructed' since the MONOPOLY® game was first introduced in 1935.

* **In 1964, a 95-pound board was sold for underwater use, and in 1983 350 members of the Buffalo Dive Club played Monopoly underwater non-stop for 1,080 hours.**

* A game was once held in an elevator – it lasted ten days. Another was played for 36 hours with all participants hanging upside down.

✦ **Escape maps, compasses and files were inserted into MONOPOLY® game boards smuggled into POW camps inside Germany during the Second World War. Real money for escapees was slipped into the packs of MONOPOLY® money.**

✶ The campus at Juniate College in Pennsylvania was once turned into a giant Monopoly game. Huge foam cubes were moved around the 'board', and players travelled by bike, communicating by walkie-talkie.

✦ **Trafalgar Square, Fenchurch Street Station and 'Go' are the three most landed on properties.**

✶ The character locked behind the bars is called Jake the Jailbird. Officer Edgar Mallory sent him to jail.

☆ ROYAL NICKNAMES ☆

Henry IV of Castile, the Impotent (ruled 1454–74) – After a marriage in which he refused to have sex with his wife for 13 years, the last of the late medieval kings of Castile married Joan of Portugal in 1455. Six years later Joan gave birth to a daughter, also named Joan. Another six years later, rebels claimed young Joan was not Henry's daughter. Rumours spread that Henry was impotent, although local prostitutes testified against this. There is a good chance they were bribed. A court doctor observed that Henry's penis was very thin at the base and 'huge at the head', which may explain his difficulties. Whatever the truth, Henry's second wife eventually did the dirty on him, and had

two children with the nephew of a local bishop. A divorce
ensued, and Henry eventually died. He is buried next to his
mother in the Royal Monastery of Santa Maria de Guadalupe (in
Guadalupe).

Alfonso IX of León, the Slobberer (ruled 1188–1230) –
Despite his attempts to modernise and democratise his kingdom
by founding the University of Salamanca and summoning the
first parliament with full representation in Western Europe (the
Cortes of León), poor Alfonso could not get away from the fact
that, whenever roused to anger, he drooled all over the place.

Vseslav of Polotsk, the Werewolf (ruled 1039–1101) –
According to legend, the Russian ruler was conceived by sorcery
and born with a caul (part of the foetal membrane) on his head.
Sorcerers told his mother the dried caul should remain on
Vseslav's head for good luck, which it did. Vseslav wore his 'wig'
day in, day out, and in his late twenties developed the ability
to turn himself into a werewolf. In 2005, a commemorative 20
rouble coin was issued in Belarus – in the foreground is Vseslav,
and in the background a werewolf.

Constantine V, the Dung-Named (ruled 741–75) – This
Byzantine emperor was the victim of a nasty rumour.
Constantine's adversaries spread the story that, as a child,
Constantine had defecated in the baptismal font. The name
derives from the Greek *kopronymos* (*kopros* – animal dung – and
onoma – name).

Harald I, the Lousy (ruled 872–930) – In order to persuade
Gyda, daughter of King Eirik of Hordaland (Hordaland being a
petty kingdom in Norway), to marry him, Harald did not cut his
hair for ten years. The logic of this is lost to modern historians
(who believe the story was cooked up by historians of the time).

Still, legend has it that various monikers – including Shockhead, Tanglehair and Lousy – were given to Harold, who eventually became the first king of a unified Norway and took Gyda for his bride.

Ivar the Boneless (ninth century) – Considering he was a Berserker (a Norse warrior said to have fought in an uncontrollable, trance-like fury), Ivar had a seemingly unfortunate epithet. Speculation is rife about precisely what Ivar's nickname referred to; some say his impotence, others his easily breakable bones, but there is a chance it was Ivar's astounding flexibility and lack of injuries that gave rise to the idea of him being without bones. More interesting still is the idea that 'boneless' meant 'legless' (as the English word 'bone' is cognate with the German word *bein*), and referred to his inability to walk. Boneless or not, we know Ivar was a ninth-century Viking who led his forces to capture York from the Northumbrians in 866.

☆ ⭐ SECONDS ⭐ ☆

* Every second, the sun flings one million tons of matter out into space, and produces enough energy (at the current rate of consumption) to supply the electrical needs of the US for 50 million years.

Between four and five people are born every second, and two people die.

* An area of the South American rainforest the size of a football field is cut down every second.

✶ **On average, Americans purchase 100 cans of Campbell's soup every second of every day in January.**

✶ Every second, you lose around three million red blood cells. In the same second, your bone marrow will produce the same number of new ones.

✶ **No high jumper has ever remained off the ground for more than a second.**

✶ A cheetah can complete four strides in a second, with each stride taking it between seven and eight metres.

✶ **Alligators and old people cannot hear sounds produced by more than 4,000 vibrations a second.**

✶ On average, birds need to fly at a minimum speed of 16.5 feet per second to stay in the air.

✶ **Cats purr at 26 cycles per second, the same as an idling diesel engine.**

✶ One hundred thousand cubic feet of water pours over the Niagara Falls every second.

✶ **A lobster can move through the water at a rate of up to 25 feet per second.**

✶ A space vehicle must move at a rate of at least seven miles per second to escape Earth's gravitational pull.

✶ **Some neutron stars (the remaining cores of collapsed stars) spin 600 times a second, which is as fast as a dentist's drill. They are around the size of Manhattan and weigh over one billion tons.**

✳ About 3,300 cups of coffee are consumed every second of the day worldwide.

☆ ★ HARRY POTTER ★ ☆

Harry Potter's birthday is 31 July 1980. Rowling's birthday is also 31 July, but in 1965.

Rowling found witchy-sounding names such as toadflax, gout-wort, grommel and others in *Culpeper's Complete Herbal*, a famous book of herbal lore dating from the 1600s.

When *Harry Potter and the Prisoner of Azkaban* was published in Great Britain, the publisher asked shops to put the book on sale on a non-school day – they wanted to prevent truancy.

In 2003, members of the Jesus Non-Denominational Church in Greenville, Michigan, burned Rowling's books on a bonfire because they believed they were evil.

J. K. Rowling's favourite childhood book was *The Little White Horse* by Elizabeth Goudge.

An outbreak of lice occurred among children in the cast during the filming of *Harry Potter and the Chamber of Secrets*.

Natalie McDonald, who appeared in *Harry Potter and the Goblet of Fire*, was by a nine-year-old fan who wrote to Rowling shortly before dying of leukaemia.

The driver and conductor of the Knight Bus, Ernie and Stan, are named after Rowling's grandfathers.

'Morsmordre' (the word that makes Voldermort's Dark Mark appear) sounds like the phrase for 'take a bite out of death' in French – a fitting call for Death Eaters.

Dumbledore's full name is Albus Percival Wulfric Brian Dumbledore. Dumbledore is an Old English word meaning 'bumble-bee'; *albus* is Latin for 'white'. Percival was a knight of King Arthur's Round Table and may also mean 'pierce the veil', suggesting an ability to return from the dead (by coming back from heaven through the veil of the Earth's atmosphere). Wulfric was the name of a twelfth-century saint who became a deeply holy man after seeing a homeless man in the street. Brian is a Celtic name, meaning 'strong'.

Rowling said that if she could take Polyjuice Potion she would become (former) Prime Minister Tony Blair for an hour. She also said that she would be dreadful at playing Quidditch as she does not consider herself sporty, is not great with heights and is clumsy.

A Platform 9¾ sign has been erected on a wall of King's Cross Station's building containing the real Platforms 9 and 10. Part of a luggage trolley has also been installed below the sign; while the near end is visible, the rest of the trolley appears to have disappeared into the wall.

The name Voldemort comes from the French words meaning 'flight of death' – Voldemort's main goal in the book is to conquer death. In the second Harry Potter novel, it transpires that 'I am Lord Voldemort' is an anagram of his full name, Tom Marvolo Riddle.

☆

MIKE THE HEADLESS CHICKEN

In 1945, Colorado chicken farmer Lloyd Olsen was preparing for dinner, which meant he had to slaughter one of his birds. He selected Mike. Using his axe, Lloyd chopped Mike's head off cleanly. As expected, the headless body kept moving, but Lloyd was most surprised when it ran out of the barn and out of sight. To his amazement, Lloyd found the body still alive and kicking the following morning. He'd never witnessed anything so peculiar, so began using an eyedropper to drip-feed water and grain into what was left of Mike's throat. The next morning, Mike was still running around.

Amazed and perplexed, Lloyd took Mike to the University of Utah so that scientists could take a look at him. On inspection, it became clear that Lloyd's axe had missed Mike's jugular vein by a whisker and that a blood clot had prevented him from bleeding to death. Moreover, the bird's brain stem was still attached, so many of his reflexes survived in tip-top shape. Mike continued to attempt to peck and preen himself like a normal bird – he even slept with his upper neck tucked under his wing.

In eighteen months, Mike grew from three pounds to an impressive eight, and Mike the Headless Wonder Chicken went on national tour with his owner, even appearing in *Time* and *Life* magazine feature articles. Eventually, and sadly, Mike choked on some grain in a hotel room, and it was all over.

To this day, Mike's fan club celebrates his will to live and every year there is a celebration of his life in Fruita, Colorado. Revellers are encouraged to run like a headless chicken and be merry.

☆ ★ MORE USELESS ★ ☆ ACTRESS FACTS

* Eva Longoria learned to shoot at the age of five. She hunted deer, turkey, quail and wild pigs with her family at their Texas ranch.

* **Jennifer Aniston ate the same lunch for nine years – lettuce, garbanzo beans, turkey and lemon dressing.**

* Sigourney Weaver's real name is Susan Weaver. She took Sigourney from a character in *The Great Gatsby*.

* **Kim Basinger collects inflatable ducks. She used to suffer from agoraphobia, which sometimes kept her indoors for up to six months at a time.**

* Jodie Foster was George Lucas's second choice to play Princess Leia in *Star Wars,* and she got the lead role in *The Silence of the Lambs* after Michelle Pfeiffer turned it down.

* **Halle Berry says she keeps a pair of jeans she wore as a teenager to make sure she stays in shape, and that when she was young she dreamed of a pill that would make her white.**

* Penelope Cruz collects coat hangers.

* **At the age of 50, Joan Collins posed semi-nude for *Playboy*.**

* In 1998, Dame Judi Dench won Best Supporting Actress for *Shakespeare in Love*, despite being on screen for only eight minutes, the shortest time ever for an Oscar winner.

* **During the filming of *Cleopatra*, Elizabeth Taylor's fourth husband, Eddie Fisher, was paid $1,500 a day to make sure that she arrived punctually on set.**

* Nicole Kidman suffered a broken rib while rehearsing a dance routine for *Moulin Rouge*.

* **Doris Day was approached to play the role of Mrs Robinson in *The Graduate*. She turned the part down because she thought the movie was 'trashy'.**

* Liv Tyler first thought she might be rock star Steve Tyler's daughter at the age of 11 when she went to an Aerosmith concert and realised how much she resembled him.

* **Tara Palmer-Tomkinson is a trained concert pianist who has played at the Royal Albert Hall, London.**

* Jordan (Katie Price) has an older brother called Daniel and a younger sister called Sophie. She speaks Greek. She once stood as a candidate in the Stretford and Urmston election, promising a 'Bigger and Betta Future', free breast implants, a ban on parking tickets and an increase in nudist beaches. Her campaign was designed only to bring a little fun to a dull election, but she still received 713 votes – 1.8 per cent of the votes cast. She once auditioned for a part on *Baywatch*.

* **Paris Hilton has size 11 feet – 'All those super cute shoes like Guccis and Manolos look like clown shoes on me.'**

BARD TRIVIA

* No portraits were painted of Shakespeare while he was alive.

* **Honorificabilitudinitatibus: one of the many words coined by Shakespeare, it means 'the state of being able to achieve honours'.**

* Most of Shakespeare's plays were not published until seven years after his death. The collection was called the First Folio.

* **Mark Twain did not believe that Shakespeare wrote his own plays.**

* There were two Globe Theatres. The first was built in 1599, and burned down in 1613 when a cannon was fired during a performance of *Henry VIII*. A second Globe Theatre was built on the original foundations in 1614. The roof of the second theatre was tiled, not thatched, and was demolished by the Puritans in 1644.

* **Shakespeare was rumoured to be the father of an illegitimate son called William Davenant.**

* Shakespeare's signatures were far from consistent. In the few examples that have survived, his name is never spelled 'William Shakespeare'. Rather, it reads variously as 'Willm Shaksp', 'William Shakespe', 'Wm Shakspe', 'Will Shakspere', 'Willm Shakspere', and 'William Shakspeare'.

* **Shakespeare's son was called Hamnet. Hamnet and his sisters, Judith and Susanna, were all illiterate.**

☆ Shakespeare was married to Anne Hathaway Shakespeare. Her gravestone records that she was 67 when she died in 1623, so it is believed that she was eight years older than her husband. However, the figures one and 7 are easily confused. If the 7 were a 1, Anne would be only two years older than her husband.

☆ **According to *The Oxford Dictionary of Quotations*, Shakespeare wrote about one-tenth of the most quotable quotations in the English language. The Bard also coined hundreds of phrases, including 'one fell swoop', 'vanish into thin air', 'play fast and loose', 'be in a pickle', 'foul play', 'tower of strength', 'flesh and blood', 'be cruel to be kind' and 'with bated breath'.**

✳ Shakespeare's tombstone in Stratford's Holy Trinity Church bears an inscription written by him:

> Good friend for Jesus sake forbear
> To dig the dust enclosed here!
> Blest be the man that spares these stones,
> And curst be he that moves my bones.

☆ **In his will, Shakespeare left his wife his 'second best bed'.**

PECULIAR LITERARY FEATS

The world's longest diary runs to 37.5 million words, and chronicles every five minutes from 1972 to 1997 of the life of former minister and schoolteacher Robert Shields. The American attempted to chronicle everything that happened to him, and wrote for four hours a day, even detailing blood pressure, received junk mail and toilet habits. The reverend allowed himself only two hours sleep at a time so that he could record his dreams, and left a diary that fills 91 boxes. It has been mooted that Shields suffered from hypergraphia, an overwhelming urge to write. Seems likely, considering his diary is nearly 30 times longer than *The Diary of Samuel Pepys*.

In 1998, Australian Les Stewart finally completed the manuscript for what has to be the most spectacularly pointless literary endeavour in history. After working at his typewriter for 16 years, Les typed the final line of his book: 'nine hundred and ninety-nine thousand, nine hundred and ninety-nine. One million.' During the writing process, he typed for 20 minutes, every waking hour, on the hour. He went through seven typewriters, 1,000 ink ribbons, and 19,890 pages, and once he'd finished he threw the manuscript away, keeping only the first and last pages.

Robert Louis Stevenson wrote *The Strange Case of Dr Jekyll and Mr Hyde* in six days while on a cocaine binge. 'That an invalid in my husband's condition of health should have been able to perform the manual labour alone of putting 60,000 words on paper in six days, seems almost incredible,' said his astonished wife, Fanny.

☆ DAFT BEHAVIOUR ☆

* Ken Edwards of Glossop, Derbyshire, England, ate 36 cockroaches in one minute on the set of Channel 4's *The Big Breakfast* in 2001. 'It's like having an anaesthetic at the back of the throat,' commented the former rat-catcher and part-time entertainer. He was also known for putting rats down his trousers.

* **Englishman and professional 'head balancer' John Evans balanced a 160.6 kilogram Mini Cooper on his head for 33 seconds in 1999.**

* The record for the most snails staying on someone's face for ten seconds was set by Alastair Galpin in 2007. Eight snails clung to his visage before deciding to move on.

* **The world record for farting was set on Japanese television. Gas was passed 3,000 times on the trot.**

* The world record for rocking non-stop in a rocking chair is 480 hours. It is held by Dennis Easterling. It can be assumed that he is now off his rocker.

* **The loudest burp recorded belonged to Englishman Paul Hunn, and measured 107.1 decibels.**

* The longest recorded ear hair is 18.1 centimetres, from the outer ear of Indian Anthony Victor.

* **Jim Lyngvild from Copenhagen, Denmark, holds the world record for most Ferrero Rocher chocolates eaten in a minute: seven.**

✳ Rolling an orange for a mile using his nose is one of Ashrita Furman's talents. He completed the record in 29 minutes at Terminal 4 of New York's JFK Airport.

✳ **Christian Adam cycled backwards for 60.45 kilometres in five hours and nine minutes while playing J. S. Bach on his violin. Christian sat on the handlebars and read sheet music from a stand fixed to the saddle.**

CHIMP DOCTORS

Chimpanzees seem to have a working knowledge of medicinal plants. Scientists have observed them using 13 different plants to treat a range of symptoms. In Tanzania, one chimp was observed using a plant called *Aspilia mossambicensis* to ease digestive problems caused by parasites. Chimps also appear to know which part of a plant will help them and, depending on the problem, will differentiate between the leaves, the pith and the roots.

☆ ✳ PLACES ✳ ☆

✳ Alaska is so vast that if you could view one million acres of the state every day, it would take an entire year to see it all.

✳ **A car could be driven round the world four times using the amount of fuel in one jumbo jet.**

✳ Europe is the only continent without a desert.

☆ **The oldest inhabited city is Damascus, Syria.**

* The first city in the world to have a population of more than one million was Rome. The most populated city in the world – when major urban areas are included – is Tokyo, with more than 37 million residents. Tokyo was once known as Edo.

☆ **On every continent there is a city called Rome.**

* Harvard University uses Yale brand locks on its buildings.

☆ **The Atlantic Ocean is saltier than the Pacific Ocean.**

* Quebec is the world's leading exporter of asbestos.

PEANUTS, PLANES
☆ ★ **& BRAINS** ★ ☆

* Peanut oil can be processed to produce glycerol, which in turn can be used to make nitroglycerin, one of the constituents of dynamite.

☆ **The wingspan of a Boeing 747 is longer than the Wright brothers' first flight.**

* The brain doesn't feel pain: even though it processes pain signals, the brain does not actually feel the sensations.

☆ **Your brain is more active when you are asleep than when you are awake.**

✳ There's no sand in sandpaper.

✳ **Eighty-five per cent of men who die of heart attacks during sexual intercourse are found to have been cheating on their wives.**

✳ American Green Cards have not been green since 1964.

☆ ★ SPIDERS ★ ☆

✳ Spiders do not get stuck in their own webs because they weave in non-stick silk strands, and walk on these. They also produce a special oil on their legs, which helps.

✳ **The silk of a spider starts out as a liquid – contact with air hardens it.**

✳ Only half of all spider species use webs for catching prey. The others use … other methods.

✳ **The much feared tarantula isn't poisonous. A tarantula's bite can be painful, but it isn't any more dangerous than a bee sting.**

✳ Australian crab spiders sacrifice their bodies as a food source for their offspring.

✳ **A strand from the web of a golden spider is as strong as a steel wire of the same size.**

THE MOST GROANWORTHY PUNS IN THE WORLD

(A man sent ten different puns to friends, in the hope that at least one of the puns would make them laugh. No pun in ten did.)

A pessimist's blood type is always B negative.

A Freudian slip is when you say one thing but mean your mother.

Marriage is the mourning after the knot before.

A hangover is the wrath of grapes.

Corduroy pillows are making headlines.

Sea captains don't like crew cuts.

Without geometry, life is pointless.

When you dream in colour, it's a pigment of your imagination.

Condoms should be used on every conceivable occasion.

A man needs a mistress just to break the monogamy.

A backward poet writes inverse.

In democracy your vote counts. In feudalism your count votes.

She had a boyfriend with a wooden leg, but broke it off.

A chicken crossing the road is poultry in motion.

If you don't pay your exorcist, you get repossessed.

With her marriage, she got a new name and a dress.

Show me a piano falling down a mine shaft, and I'll show you A flat minor.

Those who jump off a Paris bridge are in Seine.

Bakers trade bread recipes on a knead-to-know basis.

Santa's helpers are subordinate clauses.

Acupuncture is a jab well done.

Marathon runners with bad footwear suffer the agony of defeat.

The poor man fell into a glass-grinding machine and made a spectacle of himself.

THE FIRST BOYCOTT

Captain Charles Cunningham Boycott was a man unused to being ignored. That is, until he had no choice in the matter. An unscrupulous English land agent operating in Ireland's County Mayo on behalf of Lord Erne in the late 1800s, he was renowned for charging exorbitant rents, and was deeply disliked. In 1880 Charles Parnell and the Irish Land League campaigned for 'Three Fs' (Fair rent, Fixity of tenure and Free sale), but Captain Boycott would have none of it and did all he could to try to undermine Parnell's aims. Big mistake. Parnell suggested a comprehensive strategy of isolation against Boycott, and the local community didn't need much persuading. Before long, Boycott's labourers had deserted him, shops would not sell to him, the postman stopped ringing and nobody would talk to him. The campaign made national news in England and Ireland (unsurprisingly, the British press portrayed Boycott as a victim), and the verb to boycott entered the lingo.

☆ WEIRD EBAY ITEMS ☆

(LOT 2)

EX-WIFE WEDDING DRESS – A man was about to burn his ex-wife's wedding dress when his sister suggested eBay. The auction page included a description of the dress and a funny rant about the ex alongside a photo of the husband modelling it. The man claimed he wanted enough money to buy a case of beer and a ticket to a hockey game. The dress fetched $3,850.

JUSTIN TIMBERLAKE'S TOAST – In 2000, a leftover piece of Justin's toast was sold online for $3,154. After 40 bids, the 'winner' received the toast, the fork and plate Timberlake had used, along with his extra syrup.

IMAGINARY FRIEND – An English man sold his imaginary friend, a non-existent fellow called Jon Malipieman, stating, 'My imaginary friend is getting too old for me now. I am 27 and I feel I am growing out of him.' The man went on to detail his invisible chum's likes and dislikes, his hobbies, and even included a photo of him – a picture of a wall. The photo went for over £1,500.

SHRUNKEN HEADS – Twenty-six genuine shrunken heads were sold for just under £20. The heads were from the Jibaro Indians in the Ecuadorian jungle. The heads received only seven bids.

LEE HARVEY OSWALD'S WINDOW – The actual window and frame from which Oswald shot John F. Kennedy was auctioned in 2007. After 188 bids, the winning bid was $3,001,501.

RIGHTS TO NAME A BABY – In 2005, 33-year-old Melissa Heuschkel could not decide on a name for her new baby, so put the rights to name her daughter up for auction. The online casino GoldenPalace.com paid a staggering $15,100 and named the child Golden Palace Benedetto.

THE WORLD'S MOST MYSTERIOUS MANUSCRIPT

In 1912, Polish book dealer Wilfrid M. Voynich acquired one of the most peculiar books ever seen, a 240-page handwritten volume whose author and language remain completely unknown. A bizarre alphabet of sorts is contained within it, yet while the words follow some logic (certain marks tend, like vowels, to appear in every word), countless codebreakers, linguists and cryptographers have all failed to make any sense of it. More interestingly still, the lavish illustrations of herbs, astronomical phenomena, biological observations, maps and medicines often bear little relation to the world we know. In 2009, carbon dating showed the manuscript to have been written between 1404 and 1438. Opinions vary wildly as to whether the text is an encoded medieval language that could one day be decrypted, or an elaborate hoax. The Voynich manuscript is currently housed at Yale University.

COW IN FLIGHT

On 9 May 1962, a Guernsey cow in Iowa named Fawn was whisked up by a tornado and carried through the air for a few minutes before landing in the pen of a Holstein bull on a farm half a mile away. The flight is believed to be the longest unassisted solo cow flight in recorded history (there is scant evidence of other airborne cows). The brief encounter with the bull resulted in a calf. Or so the story goes.

☆ **'WELL I NEVER'** ☆

* Plastic surgery is nothing new. As early as 600 BC a Hindu surgeon reconstructed a nose by using a piece of cheek and by AD 1000 there was nose surgery using skin from the forehead.

* **One in five British homes has a foot spa, although mostly they sit idle, among more than £3 billion worth of useless gadgets to be found in UK homes.**

* Although Jimmy Carter's US presidency ended in 1981, he still receives about 4,000 letters a month.

* **More Brits die each year falling from their hotel balcony than do in diving accidents.**

* In 1911, Pablo Picasso was one of the suspects arrested for the theft of the *Mona Lisa*.

☆ **There is a world record for being able to squirt liquids out of a human eye. The existing record is 8.7 feet (2.65 metres), but a Turkish man claims to have broken the record with a 9.2-foot (2.8-metre) squirt.**

✳ Margaret Thatcher helped invent the chemical process that produces Mr Whippy ice cream.

☆ **Guests at the Queen's coronation in 1953 pilfered toilet paper from Westminster Abbey. 'It was found early on Coronation Day that much of the lavatory paper had been removed, and in future it will be necessary to take steps to prevent this,' official records revealed.**

✳ Up to 65 per cent of children with a father in jail eventually go to prison themselves.

☆ **Britons throw away enough rubbish every hour to fill the Royal Albert Hall.**

☆ TOUGH OLD JOBS ☆

Song plugger – In Victorian times, song pluggers were employed by music shops to play pieces of music to customers interested in buying sheet music. The occupation existed from the 1880s until the 1920s, when radio and the phonograph soon killed off the vocation.

Link boy – In the 1900s, link boys guided sleepy, often drunk people through the unlit city of London, and used a burning torch to light the way along tiny alleyways. It was hard and dangerous work – boys were prey to robbers, paedophiles and murderers, and the pay wasn't up to much either. Still, some boys worked in gangs, and would lead their charges straight into the arms of thieves.

Gong farmer – Often referred to as gong scourers, these lucky fellows got to remove the contents of cesspits and public toilets. They worked at night, in limited light and frequently died from the fumes.

Oakum picker – Boys in workhouses were given old hunks of rope to rip and pick apart until they were left with small strands (oakum). A tiring, messy job, the pay was awful – a meagre amount of food and a bed for the night was about as good as it got.

Pure collector – A misleading job description. In the nineteenth century, 'pure' was slang for dog mess, and collectors of it were normally old women and young girls. The poo was useful in the tanning industry as, when mixed with water, it was effective for softening hides and removing lime from them.

Crossing sweeper – Life as a crossing sweeper was a pretty dismal affair. These poor fellows, mainly children, earned a pittance by sweeping the filth of Victorian London's streets from the path of whichever lady or gentleman wished to cross. Most sweepers were lucky if they could make enough to eat, let alone afford somewhere to sleep. Their places of rest were most often very close to their working environment.

☆

RANDOM ENTERTAINMENT

* Fictional characters who boast stars on Hollywood's 'Walk of Fame' include Big Bird, Bugs Bunny, Donald Duck, Godzilla, Kermit the Frog, Mickey Mouse, Munchkins, Rugrats, Shrek, The Simpsons, Snow White, Tinkerbell, Winnie-the-Pooh and Woody Woodpecker.

* **Anti-American demonstrators protesting in Bangladesh after the September 11 terrorist attacks carried posters of Osama bin Laden sitting alongside Bert, a beloved *Sesame Street* Muppet character.**

* Mardi Gras translates as 'Fat Tuesday'.

* **In 1888, Hollywood was founded by Harvey and Daeida Wilcox, who named the district after their summer home in Chicago.**

* Barney, the famous purple dinosaur, is from Dallas.

* **At its height, the TV show *Doctor Who* had an audience of 110 million people.**

* The longest Hollywood kiss was from the 1941 film *You're in the Army Now*. It lasted for three minutes and three seconds.

* **The accent used by Mike Myers in *Shrek* is based on one his mother adopted when she was telling him bedtime stories.**

✳ In 1960 there were 16,067 slot machines in Nevada, home of Las Vegas. By 1999, this number had risen to 205,726 – one gaming machine for every ten people living there.

☆ **The word 'Muppet' was coined by creator Jim Henson, and is a combination 'marionette' and 'puppet', Kermit the Frog was named after Kermit Scott, a childhood friend of Henson, who became a professor of philosophy at Purdue University.**

✳ Close to three billion movie tickets are sold in India every year.

KARL JUNG COINCEDENCE

An anecdote from the founder of analytical psychiatry's *The Structure and Dynamics of the Psyche:* 'A young woman I was treating had, at a critical moment, a dream in which she was given a golden scarab. While she was telling me this dream I sat with my back to the closed window. Suddenly I heard a noise behind me, like a gentle tapping. I turned round and saw a flying insect knocking against the window pane from outside. I opened the window and caught the creature in the air as it flew in. It was the nearest analogy to the golden scarab that one finds in our latitudes, a scarabaeid beetle, the common rose-chafer *(Cetonia aurata)* which contrary to its usual habits had evidently felt an urge to get into a dark room at this particular moment. I must admit that nothing like it ever happened to me before or since, and that the dream of the patient has remained unique in my experience.'

POE'S PUSSYCAT

Edgar Allan Poe's short story 'The Black Cat' was inspired by his tortoiseshell cat, Catarina. Catarina would curl up in bed with Poe's wife to keep her warm while she was dying of tuberculosis.

'THING' WORDS YOU MAY NOT KNOW

AGLET	The plain or ornamental covering on the end of a shoelace
ARMSAYE	The armhole in clothing
CHANKING	Spat-out food
COLUMELLA NASI	The bottom part of the nose between the nostrils
DRAGÉES	Small beadlike sugar-coated confection, usually silver-coloured, used for decorating fairy cakes and sundaes
FEAT	A dangling curl of hair
FERRULE	The metal band on a pencil that holds the eraser in place
HARP	The small metal hoop that supports a lampshade
HYPNAGOGIC JERK	The weird jerk or falling sensation when you are drifting off to sleep
KEEPER	The loop on a belt that keeps the end in place after it has passed through the buckle
KICK or PUNT	The indentation at the bottom of some wine bottles. It gives added strength to the bottle but reduces its capacity
LIRIPIPE	The long tail on the hood of a graduate's gown

MINIMUS	The little finger or toe
NEF	An ornamental stand in the shape of a ship
OBDORMITION	The numbness caused by pressure on a nerve; when a limb is 'asleep'
PEEN	The end of a hammer head opposite the striking face
PHOSPHENES	The lights you see when you close your eyes hard (due to the excitation of the retina caused by pressure on the eyeball)
PURLICUE	The space between the thumb and extended forefinger
RASCETA	Creases on the inside of the wrist
ROWEL	The revolving star on the back of a cowboy's spurs
SADDLE	The rounded part on the top of a matchbook
SCROOP	The rustle of silk
SPRAINTS	Otter dung
WAMBLE	Stomach rumbling
ZARF	A holder for a handleless coffee cup

BREATH HOLDING

David Blaine holds the world record for holding his breath underwater. In 2008, live on *The Oprah Winfrey Show,* he remained inside a sphere filled with 1,800 gallons of water for 17 minutes and four seconds. Before the event, Blaine inhaled pure oxygen for 23 minutes. The average human can last for about a minute underwater, but many mammals fare a lot better. The northern bottlenose whale comes out on top (120 mins), followed closely by the sperm whale (112 mins). Nearly an hour behind is the Greenland whale (60 mins). Beavers can manage an impressive 20 minutes, while hippos and porpoises average around 15 minutes. More than ten minutes would pose a challenge to a duck-billed platypus, and a sea otter normally heads to the surface after five.

☆ SCRABBLE NUMBER ☆ CRUNCHING

The highest scoring 2–15 letter words are as follows (not including points from bonus squares):

2	QI (11)
	ZA (11)
3	ZAX (19)
4	QUIZ (22)
5	JAZZY (23)
6	MUZJIK (28)
7	MUZJIKS (29)
8	SOVKHOZY (30)
9	EXCHEQUER (30)
	EXOENZYME (30)
	MAXIMIZED (30)
10	ZYGOMORPHY (33)
11	HYDROXYZINE (37)
12	HYDROXYZINES (38)
. . . .	KATZENJAMMER (37)
13	SUBJECTIVIZED (37)
14	SUBJECTIVIZING (38)
15	OXYPHENBUTAZONE (41)

Word chains can be built up a single letter at a time, starting with a two-letter word, then adding another letter to the beginning or end to make a valid three-letter word, and so on. Two nine-letter words can be constructed in this manner:

SCRAPINGS – IN-PIN-PING-APING-RAPING-CRAPING-SCRAPING-SCRAPINGS

SHEATHERS – AT-EAT-HEAT-HEATH-SHEATH-SHEATHE-SHEATHER-SHEATHERS

CIGARETTES

* Around a trillion cigarettes are sold from country to country each year.

* **In the early 1950s, Kent cigarette filters contained asbestos.**

* Urea, a chemical compound found in urine, is used to add flavour to cigarettes.

* **A cigarette contains up to 10 per cent sugar.**

* Smokers draw harder on light and menthol cigarettes than they do on regular cigarettes. This causes the same overall levels of tar and nicotine to be consumed.

* **Roughly 25 per cent of cigarettes sold around the world are smuggled.**

* Fifty milligrams of nicotine is enough to kill an adult human within a few minutes.

☆ **In 1970, President Nixon signed the law that placed warning labels on cigarettes and banned television advertisements for cigarettes.**

BEATLE CATS

John Lennon's mother, Julia, owned a cat called Elvis. As a boy, John had three cats in Liverpool: Tich, Tim and Sam. He had a tabby named Mimi with his wife Cynthia, and with May Pang he had a white cat – Major – and a black cat – Minor. John and Yoko Ono shared their New York home with another black and white pair – Salt and Pepper. Sketches of his cats at play are featured in Lennon's books, *A Spaniard in the Works* and *Real Love: The Drawings for Sean*.

☆ CELEBRITY ANAGRAMS ☆

Occasional nude income – Madonna Louise Ciccone

Sprites nearby – Britney Spears

Icon mellows – Simon Cowell

Only scream jerk – Jeremy Clarkson

Merry wardrobe – Drew Barrymore

I'm a jerk but listen – Justin Timberlake

He's grown large 'n' crazed – Arnold Schwarzenegger

Seen alive? Sorry, pal – Elvis Aaron Presley

Fine in torn jeans – Jennifer Aniston

Blame, complain – Naomi Campbell

I warm billions – Robin Williams

End is a car spin – Princess Diana

Er, doesn't view – Stevie Wonder

Real dim, man-eating harlot – Madonna, the material girl

Sickener on TV – Kevin Costner

Rich hag is at tea – Agatha Christie

He grew bogus – George W. Bush

Meet a dear, rich man – The American Dream

Workable caramel lips – Camilla Parker Bowles

Manure plot – Paul Merton

Blob recreation – Robbie Coltrane

God I do complain – Placido Domingo

Mark a bitch voice – Victoria Beckham

Anal itch or I vomit – Victoria Hamilton

The kinky regal I – Keira Knightley

A demonic link – Nicole Kidman

CLASSIC RIDDLE #3
EINSTEIN'S RIDDLE

Einstein stated that only 2 per cent of the world could answer this puzzle. There are five houses in five different colours. In each house lives a person with a different nationality. The five owners each drink a different type of beverage, smoke a different brand of cigar, and keep a different pet.

The Brit lives in the red house.

The Swede keeps dogs as pets.

The Dane drinks tea.

The green house is on the left of the white house.

The green homeowner drinks coffee.

The person who smokes Pall Mall rears birds.

The owner of the yellow house smokes Dunhill.

The man living in the centre house drinks milk.

The Norwegian lives in the first house.

The man who smokes Blend lives next to the one who keeps cats.

The man who keeps the horse lives next to the man who smokes Dunhill.

The owner who smokes Bluemaster drinks beer.

The German smokes Prince.

The Norwegian lives next to the blue house.

The man who smokes Blend has a neighbour who drinks water.

Who owns the fish?

ANSWER TO CLASSIC RIDDLE #3

EINSTEIN'S RIDDLE

The person in house four owns the fish. The situation looks like this:

House	1	2	3	4	5
Colour	Yellow	Blue	Red	Green	White
Nationality	Norwegian	Dane	Brit	German	Swede
Drink	Water	Tea	Milk	Coffee	Beer
Smoke	Dunhill	Blend	Pall Mall	Prince	Bluemaster
Pet	Cats	Horse	Birds	Fish	Dogs

BAD POLITICAL
☆ ★ PREDICTIONS ★ ☆

'I see no good reasons why the views given in this volume should shock the religious sensibilities of anyone' – Charles Darwin, in the foreword to *The Origin of Species*, 1859.

'It will be years – not in my time – before a woman will become Prime Minister' – Margaret Thatcher, future Prime Minister, 26 October 1969.

'We will bury you' – Nikita Khrushchev, Soviet Premier, predicting Soviet communism would win over US capitalism, 1958.

'Stocks have reached what looks like a permanently high plateau' – Irving Fisher, Professor of Economics, Yale University, 1929.

ANIMAL BRAVERY

During the Second World War, thousands of animals served alongside soldiers, often performing remarkable acts of derring-do in the face of adversity. While their human counterparts received medals for bravery, the animals received little more than a pat on the back (or wing). Seeing the unfairness of this, the founder of the People's Dispensary for Sick Animals in England, Maria Dickin, created the Dickin Medal, the animal equivalent of the Victoria Cross. One of its most famous recipients is Simon, the only cat to have been awarded the decoration, albeit posthumously, in 1949. According to the Dickin Award website, Simon 'served on *Amethyst* during the Yangtze Incident [when the Chinese opened fire on HMS *Amethyst* during the Chinese Civil War, killing and maiming over 54 members of the crew], disposing of many rats though wounded by shell blast. Throughout the incident his behaviour was of the highest order, although the blast was capable of making a hole over a foot in diameter in a steel plate.' Another celebrated creature to have received the medal is a pigeon called White Vision. In October 1943, the bird flew more than 60 miles in terrible weather against a 25-mile-per-hour wind, carrying a message from a flying boat that had been shot down to a rescue team. The search had already been called off, but all the crew were rescued thanks to the pigeon's efforts. Another valiant pigeon, Beach Comber, was awarded the medal for 'bringing the first news to this country of the landing at Dieppe, under hazardous conditions in September, 1942, while serving with the Canadian Army'.

☆ CLASSICAL MUSIC ☆

* There are six versions of Franz Schubert's 'Die Forelle' ('The Trout') – whenever friends asked the composer for copies of the song, he wrote out new versions as best he could remember them.

* **In 1952, John Cage composed and presented '4 feet 33 inches', which consists of four minutes and 33 seconds of total silence.**

* Beethoven is the first well-known composer not to have held an official court position, which also makes him the world's first famous freelance musician. He often sold the same score to several publishers at once, and was notorious for demanding unreasonably large sums of money for even the simplest work. He also had syphilis, and was deaf by the time he composed his *Ninth Symphony*. When composing, he often poured iced water on his head.

* **For a while Frédéric Chopin, the composer and pianist, wore a beard on only one side of his face. 'It does not matter,' he explained. 'My audience sees only my right side.'**

* Arnold Schoenberg suffered from triskaidekaphobia – the fear of the number 13. He died 13 minutes to midnight on Friday the 13th.

* **Tchaikovsky adored Mozart. He once referred to him as 'the musical Christ'. Of other composers, Wagner bored him and he detested Brahms.**

* Bach had twenty children.

FANTASTIC HOAX #2
– THE WAR OF THE WORLDS

Perhaps the most famous hoax in entertainment history, the broadcast in 1938 of a radio play of H. G. Wells' *The War of the Worlds,* caused unprecedented listener hysteria. Narrated and directed by Orson Welles, the show was presented in the style of a stop-press news report, interrupting a CBS weather report to inform six million Americans that Martians were invading Earth. Thousands of distress calls were made to the police, and the broadcast was accompanied by an (accidental) power cut across the whole of one town in Washington State, resulting in residents taking up arms and running for the nearest hills. CBS were heavily criticised by the media for the stunt, and promised no such prank would ever be repeated. The incident did succeed in jump-starting Orson Welles' career, and it has been said that when the attack on Pearl Harbor was reported by the media three years later, many people received the news with scepticism.

☆ BOND, JAMES BOND ☆

James Bond began life in Ian Fleming's 1953 novel *Casino Royale*. The Bond name was borrowed from the author of *Birds of the West Indies*. In 1967, David Niven played Bond in a spoof version of *Casino Royale*, but the film is not part of the Bond franchise.

☆ **Since *Dr No* was released in 1962, the equivalent of half the world's population have watched at least one Bond film.**

✳ All the actors who have played 007 are over 1.8 metres (six feet) tall.

☆ **In Fleming's books, Bond drinks gin martinis rather than the vodka martinis he quaffs in the films. In the first 22 movies, Bond receives 23 vodka martinis. He orders six of these himself, yet receives only four of them. In his six appearances as Bond, Sean Connery said 'shaken, not stirred' only once, in *Goldfinger*.**

✳ The Bond character was based on Dr John Dee, the first known British secret agent. Dee (1527–1608) was an adviser to Queen Elizabeth I as well as being a brilliant mathematician, magician, philosopher, alchemist and astrologer. During England's war with Spain Dee was wary of spies and designed the 007 code for his correspondence with the Queen. The zeros meant 'for your eyes only' and '7' was a cabalistic, or cryptic, number.

☆ **Ian Fleming was attached to the British Naval Intelligence Division during the Second World War. When the war ended, Fleming moved to Jamaica, bought a plot of land and built a bungalow on it. He called his new home Goldeneye. On 14 July 1952 he wrote the opening line of his first Bond novel: 'The scent and smoke and sweat of a casino are nauseating at three in the morning.'**

✳ In the novels, James Bond and Q never actually meet. Fleming wrote about Major Boothroyd and the Q branch but never mentioned a character called Q.

In the first 22 movies, Bond has sex 81 times: in, near, under, or next to water (25), hotel room (20), at the girl's place (15), London flat (2), hospital (3), on a train (3), someone else's place (2), in a barn (2), in a forest (2), in a gypsy tent (2), in a plane (2), in a submarine (1), in a car (1), on a motorised iceberg (1). Roger Moore suffers from hoplophobia – fear of firearms. Thanks to his wincing, many of his Bond scenes had to be retaken several times. The Bond Girls sigh, 'Oh, James!' 16 times.

HEMP

For 3,000 years, until 1883, hemp was the world's largest agricultural crop, from which the majority of fabric, soap, paper, medicines and oils were produced. Both George Washington and Thomas Jefferson grew hemp. Benjamin Franklin owned a mill that made hemp paper. The US Declaration of Independence was written on hemp paper.

☆ LITERARY MATTERS ☆

Aristotle wrote *Meteorologica* in 350 BC – it remained the standard textbook on weather for 2,000 years.

Barbara Cartland wrote a novel every two weeks, producing a staggering 723 novels in her lifetime.

Ernest Vincent Wright's 1939 novel *Gadsby* contains 50,110 words, none of which contains the letter 'e'.

☆ **When John Berryman was 12, his father, John Smith, committed suicide by shooting himself. In 1972, at age 57, John Berryman followed in his father's footsteps by jumping from a bridge.**

✳ J. K. Rowling has no middle name. The 'K' was suggested by her literary agent, who thought it best if the author were known by initials rather than her real name, Joanne. The reason? He was worried that boys would not read a book written by a woman, but didn't think J. Rowling was enough.

☆ **Based on the dates of the historical battles mentioned in the novel *Gone With the Wind*, Melanie's pregnancy goes on for 21 months.**

✳ *Moby-Dick* did not sell all of its initial 3,000 copies during author Herman Melville's lifetime. His earnings from the book totalled a meagre $556.37.

☆ **Agatha Christie's *Murder on the Orient Express* was the first novel to be bought from a vending machine in the Paris Metro. Christie claimed she plotted most of her novels while eating apples in the bath.**

✳ Ernest Hemingway's four prerequisites to becoming a real man: plant a tree, fight a bull, write a book and have a son.

☆ **Goethe couldn't stand the sound of barking dogs and could write only if he had an apple rotting in the drawer of his desk.**

✳ Bibliophobia is the fear of books. Worldwide, around two billion people are illiterate.

☆ **The author of *Robinson Crusoe* changed his name in 1703 from Foe to Defoe. Daniel Foe believed that Defoe was 'more socially and upward sounding'.**

✳ Lewis Carroll invented the word 'chortle', a combination of 'chuckle' and 'snort'.

☆ **While writing *A Christmas Carol*, Charles Dickens toyed with Puny Pete, Little Larry and Small Sam before settling on Tiny Tim for the name of his crippled child. He wrote the novel in only six weeks.**

✳ John Keats was only about five feet tall.

☆ **Michel Thaler, a French writer, published a 233-page novel without using a single verb. The novel is *Le Train de Nulle Part* (The Nowhere Train). Thaler stated that verbs were like weeds among flowers; the weeds should be removed.**

✳ Virginia Woolf wrote her novels while standing up.

☆ **In Victorian times, Goldilocks was first known as Silver Hair. Later, she became Golden Hair, then Goldilocks. The three bears were only ever just the three bears.**

✳ Henry David Thoreau graduated from Harvard, but did not receive his diploma certificate, as he did not think it worth the $5 fee. The writer's last words before dying were 'moose' and 'Indian'. What he meant by this is anybody's guess.

☆ **Philosopher Immanuel Kant was opposed to reading novels, and expressed a dislike for folk music.**

NINE WAYS TO PRONOUNCE 'OUGH'

A rough-coated, dough-faced thoughtful ploughman strode through the streets of Scarborough and, after falling into his slough, he coughed and hiccoughed.

LITTLE-KNOWN
☆ ★ BEATLE FACTS ★ ☆

* The *Daily Mirror* coined the term Beatlemania in 1963.

* **At 2.58 in 'Hey Jude' Paul McCartney can be heard saying 'Oh, f***ing hell'. He had made a mistake in the song.**

* Some foods mentioned in Beatles records: truffles, cornflakes, honey, turkey, octopus, strawberries, eggs, peppers, pies and marshmallows.

* **The film *A Hard Day's Night* was named after an off-the-cuff remark by Ringo Starr while talking to DJ Dave Hull in 1964. 'We went to do a job, and we'd worked all day and we happened to work all night. I came up still thinking it was day I suppose, and I said, "It's been a hard day ..." and I looked around and saw it was dark so I said, "... night!"' In the film, Ringo reads Robert Traver's *Anatomy of a Murder* in a café with Paul's grandfather.**

* Eric Clapton played lead guitar on the George Harrison song 'While My Guitar Gently Weeps'. The song was about to be ditched when Harrison had the brainwave of getting Clapton on board.

In 2008 a topiary tribute to The Beatles was placed on a traffic island in Liverpool. It didn't last long – an angry Liverpudlian chopped Ringo's head off after the drummer admitted he missed nothing about Liverpool.

* Before she became known as Cher, the singer recorded the novelty song 'Ringo, I Love You' under the pseudonym Bonnie Jo Mason.

☆ REJECTED BESTSELLERS ☆

Chicken Soup for the Soul **by Jack Canfield and Mark Victor Hansen** – within a month of sending the manuscript out, the authors had received 33 rejections from publishers. They were told the book was too positive and that 'anthologies don't sell'. All in all, they received 140 rejection letters until, in 1993, they found a willing publisher, Health Communications. To date, the Chicken Soup series (65 titles) has sold over 80 million copies and been translated into 37 languages.

Dubliners, **James Joyce** – the young Irishman was rejected 22 times before finding a publisher for his collection of short stories in 1914. The first print run was small – 1,250 copies – and Joyce himself bought 120 of the 379 copies sold that year. The rest, as they say, is history.

***Zen and the Art of Motorcycle Maintenance*, Robert M. Pirsig** – Pirsig's spiritual quest for meaning in life was rejected 121 times before publication in 1974. Millions of copies later, the editor who took the book on remarked, 'It forced me to decide what I was in publishing for.'

***M*A*S*H*, Richard Hooker** – without this book there would have been neither TV series nor film, yet Hooker's Korean War tome was thrown back at him by 21 publishers.

***Carrie*, Stephen King** – had King's wife Tabitha not rescued the manuscript from the rubbish bin, *Carrie* would never have seen the light of day. After 30 rejections, King's first novel was published by Doubleday. The hardback sold only 13,000 copies, but the paperback, issued a year later, sold over one million copies in its first year.

***Gone With the Wind*, Margaret Mitchell** – rejected 38 times before publication, Mitchell's only book went on to win the 1937 Pulitzer Prize.

FIRST THINGS FIRST
☆ ★ **(THE 3RD)** ★ ☆

* Shirley Temple had made her first million by the age of ten. (And she always had exactly 56 curls in her hair.)

* **Sophia Loren's first beauty contest prize included several rolls of wallpaper and a tablecloth with napkins.**

✳ Uma Thurman's dad was the first Westerner to be ordained a Tibetan Buddhist monk.

✳ **Grace Kelly was the first actress to appear on a postage stamp.**

✳ Elton John's first job earned him 50p a night. He was a piano player in a Middlesex pub.

✳ **Naomi Campbell was the first black model to grace the cover of the French edition of *Vogue*.**

✳ Bill Clinton was the first left-handed American president to serve two terms.

✳ **'Billie Jean' by Michael Jackson was the first video to air on MTV by a black artist.**

TEETOTAL

Muhammad Ali	Jim Carrey	A. A. Gill	Stephen King
Prince Andrew	Kim Cattrall	Richard E. Grant	Bruce Lee
Adam Ant	Keith Chegwin	Richard Harris	Leona Lewis
Marie Antoinette	Winston	Adolf Hitler	Abraham Lincoln
Isaac Asimov	Churchill	Anthony Hopkins	Blake Lively
Tyra Banks	Eric Clapton	Barry Humphries	Jennifer Lopez
David Beckham	John Coltrane	Ana Ivanović	Rob Lowe
Tony Benn	Billy Connolly	Samuel L.	Tobey Maguire
Brian Blessed	Alice Cooper	Jackson	Bernard Manning
David Bowie	Fearne Cotton	Elton John	Chris Martin
Frankie Boyle	Tom Cruise	Griff Rhys Jones	Malcolm
Russell Brand	Kristin Davis	Franz Kafka	McDowell
George W. Bush	Michael Eavis	Natasha	Davina McCall
Alastair Campbell	Eminem	Kaplinsky	Ewan McGregor
Naomi Campbell	George Galloway	Peter Kay	Robert Mugabe

Andy Murray
Jimmy Nail
Friedrich Nietzsche
Ross Noble
Gary Oldman
Ian Paisley
Gwyneth Paltrow
Natalie Portman
Prince

Vladimir Putin
Christina Ricci
Anne Robinson
Henry Rollins
Cristiano Ronaldo
George Bernard Shaw
Frank Skinner
Dee Snider
Ringo Starr

Rachel Stevens
Catherine Tate
Pete Townshend
Donald Trump
Shania Twain
Stevie Ray Vaughan
Tom Waits
Rick Wakeman
Mae West

Jonny Wilkinson
Bruce Willis
Malcolm X
Mike Yarwood
Michael York
Angus Young
Frank Zappa.

☆ ★ **TEA** ★ ☆

* Tea was discovered in 2737 BC by Chinese Emperor Shen-Nun when some tea leaves accidentally blew into a pot of boiling water.

☆ **Those who know their facts about tea can tell you that all tea originates from the same evergreen plant: *Camellia sinensis*. There are over 3,000 varieties of the bush grown in mountainous areas around the world.**

* The Irish consume more tea per capita than any other nationality in the world.

☆ **Tea is a natural source of fluoride that can help protect against tooth decay and gum disease.**

* Eighty per cent of office workers now claim they find out about more about what's going on at work over a cup of tea than in any other way, and 96 per cent of all cups of tea drunk daily in the UK are brewed from tea bags.

☆ **Ninety-eight per cent of people take their tea with milk, but only 30 per cent add sugar.**

✳ The tea bag was invented by accident. In the early nineteenth century, New York entrepreneur and tea merchant Thomas Sullivan began mailing clients samples of tea in silk sachets. His customers assumed that the neat little bags were intended for the brewing of the tea. Sullivan received many letters commending him on his 'invention', but noted that the bags could be a little thinner to allow for a fuller flavour to develop. Sullivan began improving the design, but it was Joseph Krieger who found fame when he delivered the first finished tea bag to the world.

A VERY HORSEY PARAGRAPH

An adult horse's brain weighs 22 ounces, about half that of a human. Horses cannot vomit, but they do have long-term memory. If they are brought back to a place where they were once frightened, they will remember it and become agitated. Some horses wear nappies – in Charleston, South Carolina, it is illegal to bring a horse on to the streets unless it is wearing one. The nappies need to be rather large, as horses drink at least 25 gallons of water a day. Horses have 16 muscles in each ear, allowing them to rotate them 180°. If a horse is cold behind the ears, it means it feels cold all over. The Four Horsemen of the Apocalypse are said to signify the end of the world: conquest on a white horse, famine on a black horse, war on a red horse and plague on a pale horse. A horse's knee joint is the equivalent of a human wrist. The average lifespan of a horse is 20–25 years, but the oldest horse on record – Old Billy – lived to the age of 62 and died in 1822. The 100-metre long Uffington horse is carved in chalk in the Oxfordshire hills, and is linked to the Legend of King Arthur. It is said that Arthur is not dead, but merely sleeping until England is in peril, at which point he will wake up. When this happens, the Uffington horse is expected to rise up and dance on nearby Dragon Hill. When cantering, a horse takes a breath with every stride. The tradition of tying a ribbon to a horse's tail began many years ago. The idea was to warn riders on hunts of a horse's traits. Ribbons came in four colours: red meant the horse was a kicker; green meant the horse was inexperienced and might well misbehave; blue indicated a stallion (stallions can be very unpredictable), and white ribbons signified that the horse was for sale. The practice is still used today, but is less common. When racehorses die, most of their body parts are discarded. Only the head, heart and feet are buried – they symbolise intelligence, courage and strength. The only racehorse to have been buried whole was the great thoroughbred Man o' War. He won 20 of 21 races in a two-year period just after the First World War. When he died, he was embalmed and lay in state for several days in a specially made casket lined with his racing colours. Around 20,00 people attended his funeral.

☆ AS A MATTER OF FACT ... ☆

* Space is only 62 miles away. That's 100 kilometres.

* **Essex is the UK's book club capital, with more reading groups than any other county and spin-off events such as a walk-and-talk-about-books club.**

* On average, poets live for 62 years, playwrights 63 years, novelists 66 years and non-fiction writers for 68 years, according to California State University's James Kaufman.

One gigabyte of information – about a quarter of the memory of an iPod mini – is the equivalent of a pick-up truckload of paper.

* In the past 15 years, four people in the UK have died in cemetery accidents, crushed by falling tombstones.

The first person to die in a motor traffic accident was Bridget Driscoll, knocked down by a car travelling at 12 miles per hour in London on 17 August 1896. The coroner recorded a verdict of accidental death, and warned: 'This must never happen again.'

* A quarter of Australians were born outside Australia.

By some estimates, there are about 100 million unexploded landmines in the world.

* Lord Baden-Powell wanted to include a section on the dangers of 'self-abuse' in his *Scouting for Boys*. His original manuscript read: 'A very large number of the lunatics in our asylums have made themselves ill by indulging in this vice although at one time they were sensible cheery boys like you.'

Dom Perignon, the Benedictine monk, was originally employed by his abbey to get the bubbles out of the champagne.

* Bill Clinton sent just two e-mails while he was president.

BEST MAN VIOLENCE

A good best man has to be the 'best man' for the job – he must keep the ring safe, stay sober enough to make a speech and keep his hands off the bridesmaids until the disco starts. Easy enough for most mortals, but the trials of the original best men were far greater. In fourth-century northern Europe, legend has it that a groom would take his strongest, most trusted friend with him to aid him in the abduction of the chosen bride. Further duties included being on hand to beat back angry relatives attempting to halt the ceremony. Aggrieved in-laws-to-be were also the reason the groom and best man stood to the right of the bride – the position was optimal for the drawing of swords with the right hand.

☆ ★ **CASH** ★ ☆

* Winston Churchill was the first person other than a monarch to appear on a British coin, and economist Adam Smith was the first Scot to appear on a British banknote.

☆ **Paper money is made not from wood pulp but from cotton. This means that it will not disintegrate so quickly if it is put in the laundry.**

* The credit card was invented by the Diners Club. In 1949, American Frank McNamara was at a restaurant when he realised he did not have enough money to pay for his meal. He needed to call his wife to bail him out. This gave him the idea of the Diners Club – a credit system for restaurant goers.

☆ **The world's first ATM began life on 27 June 1967 at Barclays bank in Enfield, north London.**

✳ The Canadian dollar coin is nicknamed a 'loonie' because it depicts the loon, a bird, on one side. The two-dollar coin is nicknamed the 'toonie', a portmanteau word formed by combining 'two' and 'loonie'.

☆ **The Bank of England produces banknotes to the value of £26,731,450 every day. The Royal Mint issues 4.1 million coins a day.**

✳ It would take about fourteen and half a million notes of currency to build a mile-high stack.

☆ **In 2008, the town of Lewes in East Sussex issued its own currency. The Lewes Pound is designed to encourage local trade.**

✳ Approximately 40 per cent of US paper currency in circulation was counterfeit by the end of the civil war.

☆ **The life expectancy of a $100 bill is nine years.**

✳ Ten per cent of Americans have more than ten credit cards in their wallet. Collectively, the cards weigh the equivalent of 304 tons of plastic, or 61 elephants.

☆ **In 2009, a UK survey concluded that the average weekly pocket money for a child was £6.32.**

✳ The first cheque was issued in London on 22 April 1659. Its value was £10 and it was written by Nicholas Vanacker. In 1976 the cheque was auctioned for £1,200 at Sotheby's in London.

✧ **During the Second World War, forgeries of Bank of England pound notes were produced by prisoners in a German concentration camp. The project was code-named 'Operation Bernhard'. Five hundred thousand notes were produced every month in 1943. Germany hoped to ruin the British economy by flooding it with hundreds of millions of counterfeit pounds. It failed.**

☆ ★ APRIL FOOLED ★ ☆

✳ The most famous April Fool's joke of all time is surely the 1957 Swiss spaghetti harvest prank. BBC's *Panorama* reported that a mild winter and the disappearance of the 'spaghetti weevil' meant that Swiss farmers had yielded a bumper spaghetti crop. Footage was shown of farmers pulling spaghetti from trees. Surprisingly, a large number of viewers were fooled, and many called the BBC wanting advice on how to grow their own spaghetti. The BBC's advice was simple: 'Place a sprig of spaghetti in a tin of tomato sauce and hope for the best.'

✧ **In 1989, in an on-air prank, BBC staff were seen fighting behind presenter Des Lynam on *Grandstand*.**

✳ In 2003, The Comedy Network in Canada announced that it would produce and air a remake of the 1970s Canadian sitcom *The Trouble with Tracy*, widely considered to be one of the worst sitcoms ever made.

✳ **In 2004, British breakfast show *GMTV* aired a story claiming that Yorkshire Water had developed a 'diet tap water' that had already helped one customer lose a stone and a half in four months. The company claimed that a third tap would be added to kitchen sinks, allowing customers easy access to the water.**

✳ In 1962, Sweden's only TV channel convinced thousands of viewers that they could convert their black and white TVs to colour by pulling a nylon stocking over the screen.

✳ **In 1977, the *Guardian* printed a supplement devoted to San Serriffe, a small republic said to consist of several semi-colon-shaped islands in the Indian Ocean. Its two main islands were named Upper Caisse and Lower Caisse. Its capital was Bodoni, and its leader was General Pica.**

✳ In 1992, America's National Public Radio announced that Richard Nixon was to run for president again. His new campaign slogan, 'I didn't do anything wrong, and I won't do it again', was read by comedian Rich Little, impersonating Nixon.

✳ **In 1998, Burger King placed an ad in *USA Today* announcing the introduction of a new item to their menu: a 'Left-Handed Whopper'. All the condiments were rotated 180° for the benefit of their left-handed customers, and thousands of them requested the burger that day.**

✳ In 1976, astronomer Patrick Moore announced that the planet Pluto would soon pass behind Jupiter, and cause the force of Earth's gravity to weaken temporarily. Listeners were told that jumping in the air at 9.47 a.m. would cause a strange floating feeling. After 9.47, the BBC received hundreds of phone calls from listeners claiming to have felt the sensation. One woman even said that her friends had floated round the room.

☆ ★ A LITTLE FOOD AND DRINK ★ ☆

✳ Pepsi is used to remove mould from wooden decks of boats.

✩ **Aubergines belong to the thistle family.**

✳ Approximately 10 per cent of Russia's income is derived from vodka sales.

✩ **The cake on the front of the album *Let it Bleed* by The Rolling Stones was baked by Delia Smith.**

✳ Frisbees originate from pie-tin-throwing competitions in New England universities.

☆ ★  EYES ★ ☆

✳ Humans blink more than 10 million times per year.

✩ **Scallops have 35 blue eyes. The largest eyes in the world belong to the giant squid.**

✳ A duck has three eyelids and so does a camel.

✳ **Our eyes expand nearly 50 per cent when we see something that makes us happy.**

✳ The Tuatara lizard has three eyes.

✳ **The duck-bill platypus is blind for the first eleven weeks of its life.**

✳ Dolphins sleep with one eye open to protect themselves from danger.

✳ **The eye of an ostrich is larger than its brain.**

✳ The cornea has no blood supply, unlike every other part of the human body. It receives oxygen from the air.

✳ **Albert Einstein's eyes were stored in a safe place after he died. It wasn't until 1994 that they were brought out and sold at auction.**

✳ People generally read 25 per cent more slowly from a computer screen than from paper.

✳ **It is impossible to sneeze with your eyes open.**

✳ The space between your eyebrows is called the glabella.

☆ ANIMAL LONGEVITY ☆

Quahog clam	up to 405 years
Giant tortoise	up to 200 years
Parrot	up to 150 years
Homo sapiens	up to 122 years
Sturgeon	up to 100 years
Blue whale	up to 80 years
Flamingo	up to 80 years
Manatee	up to 60 years
Camel	up to 35 years
Wild cobra	up to 20 years
Mockingbird	approx. 10 years
Worker bee	1 to 4 months
Dragonfly	4 months
Gastrotich	3 days
Mayfly	between 30 minutes and one day

☆ MALE GENITALIA ☆

* Iguanas, koala bears and Komodo dragons all have two penises and some female hyenas have a pseudo penis.

* **The barnacle has the largest penis-to-body-size ratio of any animal.**

* 'Little Elvis' is said to be what Elvis called his penis.

* **It takes approximately 30 millilitres of blood to cause an erect penis in a man.**

* The fear of seeing or having an erect penis is called ithyphallophobia.

* **During his lifetime a man will ejaculate half a trillion sperm. This amounts to about 72 litres of semen.**

* The male bedbug has a curved penis for drilling a hole into the female bedbug because they do not have vaginas.

* **The average sperm count in the Western world is 30 per cent lower today than 35 years ago.**

☆ ★ DREAMS ★ ☆

* Medical experts report that babies dream in the womb. Once outside the womb the average human has about 1,500 dreams a year.

* **Smokers dream less than non-smokers.**

* Oneirology is the scientific study of dreaming.

* **In addition to cheese, vitamin B, St John's Wort, nicotine patches and melatonin also cause more vivid dreams.**

* Sigmund Freud's *The Interpretation of Dreams* (1900) sold only 415 copies in the first two years following publication.

☆ **People born with no sight have reported an exaggerated sense of taste, touch and smell but no visual imagery.**

✳ Abraham Lincoln dreamed he had been killed ten days before he was assassinated.

☆ **A dream can last for as little as a few seconds up to 45 minutes, but an average dream is about 15 minutes long.**

☆ ✦  ✦ ☆

✳ Oysters have a three-chambered heart and a pair of kidneys.

☆ **They filter out their food from the water and get through 60 gallons per day.**

✳ Oysters were a staple of the working-class diet in the nineteenth century, and became a delicacy only once stocks began to run out.

☆ **Just like warm-blooded animals, oysters are either male or female. But oysters have gonads that generate eggs, as well as sperm. So oysters have the ability to change sex, which they do, at least once in their lifetime.**

✳ There's one surefire way to tell if an oyster is alive. If its shell is open, tap it with your fingers. If it snaps shut, it's alive.

☆ **A species of crab, *Pinnotheres ostreum*, has evolved to live harmoniously inside an oyster's shell.**

✳ Oysters breathe much like fish, using both gills and mantle.

☆ **The largest oyster ever recorded was 13 inches long.**

✳ Long ago, people were advised never to eat oysters during months of the year that didn't contain the letter 'r' because the lack of proper refrigeration methods meant oysters didn't keep well in the warmer months, May to August.

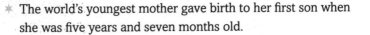

☆ ✦ **FAMILY** ✦ ☆

✳ The world's youngest mother gave birth to her first son when she was five years and seven months old.

☆ **Parents spend on average nine minutes playing with their children on Christmas morning.**

✳ The average four-year-old asks approximately 450 questions per day.

☆ **The highest number of children born to one woman: 69.**

✳ The highest number of reverse-charge calls from children are made on Father's Day.

☆ **The oldest woman confirmed to have given birth was 70.**

✳ The tiger shark can give birth to up to 80 young at once.

☆ **Almonds are a member of the peach family.**

✳ The Queen and Prince Philip are second cousins once removed.

FAMOUS STUTTERERS

Aristotle

Charles Darwin

Marilyn Monroe

Samuel L. Jackson

Winston Churchill

Bill Withers

Tiger Woods

Lewis Carroll

Somerset Maugham

John Montague

Ludwig Wittgenstein

King George VI

☆ FORMER CAREERS ☆

* Socrates trained as a stonecutter.

Keanu Reeves was the manager of a specialist pasta outlet.

* Peter Mayhew (Chewbacca) worked as a hospital porter.

Jim Carrey worked as a security guard.

* Johnny Depp used to sell pens over the phone and also fronted a Kiss cover band.

☆ **Tom Cruise had hoped to be a priest before his acting took off; and Johnny Vegas got as far as the interviews and was accepted into the priesthood but declined the offer.**

✳ Steve Buscemi was a firefighter in New York City.

☆ **Bill Murray used to sell roasted chestnuts.**

✳ Madonna worked in Dunkin' Donuts.

☆ **Jerry Seinfeld flogged light bulbs.**

✳ Warren Beatty chased rats away from the entrance of a cinema.

☆ **Brad Pitt moved refrigerators.**

☆ ✦ BLOOD ✦ ☆

✳ The blood of the grasshopper is white, lobster blood is blue and insect blood is yellow.

☆ **Coconut milk can be substituted for blood plasma in an emergency.**

✳ A leech can drink up to eight time its weight in blood at one sitting.

☆ **The Bloody Mary cocktail is named after Queen Mary I of England and Ireland. Catholic Mary shed a lot of Protestant blood.**

* When cornered and frightened, the horned toad can squirt projectile blood from its eyes up to a distance of nearly two metres.

* **Sharks can sense a drop of blood from 2.5 miles away. They can detect one part of blood in 100 million parts of water.**

* There is a drink containing lizard blood in Vietnam called Saigon Snake Blood Drink.

* **The blood used in *Psycho* for the shower scene was chocolate sauce.**

* Four hundred gallons of blood are filtered by the kidneys each day.

* **A woman has approximately 4.5 litres of blood in her body, while men have 5.6 litres.**

* Half your body's red blood cells are replaced every seven days.

BIG BEN

Big Ben is the name of the great bell inside the clock tower, rather than the tower itself. The crowning glory of the Houses of Parliament, the impressive clock tower looms 315 feet above the River Thames. It was designed by Augustus Pugin (the architect's final design before he lost his marbles and died) and erected in 1859. Pisa isn't the only place with a leaning tower. Big Ben's tower leans ever so slightly to the north-west thanks to the tunnelling for London Underground's Jubilee Line. As for Big Ben itself, the great bell was cast in 1856 by Warners of Norton near Stockton-on-Tees and transported by sea to London. On arrival at the Port of London, it was placed on a carriage and pulled across Westminster Bridge by 16 white horses. First hung in New Palace Yard, it was tested every day until 17 October 1857, when a one-metre crack appeared. Nobody would accept responsibility, and Warners quoted too high a price to recast the bell, so George Mears at the Whitechapel Foundry was called in. Mears cast the second bell in April 1858. It was too large to fit up the clock tower's shaft vertically so Big Ben was turned on its side and winched up. Big Ben rang out the following year but not for long. In September 1859, it cracked again and remained silent for four years while the hour was struck on the fourth quarter bell. A solution to Big Ben's silence was eventually found in 1863, when Sir George Airy, the Astronomer Royal, suggested the bell be repositioned by a quarter turn (so that the hammer struck a different spot), a lighter hammer be used and a small square be cut into the bell to prevent the crack from becoming worse. It worked, and has kept perfect time ever since. Big Ben may have been named after Sir Benjamin Hall, who oversaw the installation of the Great Bell.

PHARMACEUTICAL
☆ ★ NUGGETS ★ ☆

* Psammaplins, found in natural sea sponges, have been found to have anti-cancer properties.

A property in the saliva of leeches was once used as an anticoagulant in human blood.

* Coca-Cola was created by a pharmacist named John Pemberton and sold in his chemist shop. It was originally green.

Valium is used more than any other drug in the world.

* Asparagus was first cultivated in ancient Greece and used as a herbal medicine to cure toothache and ease the pain of bee stings.

FOUNDING FATHERS COINCIDENCE

John Adams, second president of the USA, and Thomas Jefferson, the third, were together among the principal authors to draft the Declaration of Independence. Jefferson did the writing, Adams the editing (among others including Benjamin Franklin, Robert R. Livingston and Roger Sherman). Congress signed the document on 4 July 1776. Fifty years later, Jefferson and Adams both died on the same day, 4 July 1826.

☆ BRITISH SPORT ☆

* Only teams to have played every season in the Premier League's top flight: Manchester United, Arsenal, Liverpool, Chelsea, Aston Villa, Liverpool, Tottenham Hotspur and Everton.

In 1969, while working as Controller of BBC2 David Attenborough held a meeting to put forward the idea for a new TV show to take advantage of colour television – the result was *Pot Black*, the snooker tournament programme. It was an instant hit.

* Iron Maiden singer Bruce Dickinson was also an international fencer. He was placed seventh in Great Britain, and has also founded a fencing equipment company named Duellist.

Hockey and polo are the only sports where left-handed play is banned.

* The first sport to allow women and men to play alongside each other was croquet.

There is an oft-touted story that, had the 1966 World Cup final ended in a draw, the toss of a coin would have determined the result. This is pure myth. There would have been a replay.

* Tennis attracts the third largest portion of British gambling money. The number one slot goes to football, and number two to racing.

☆ **The first Grand National took place in 1839. The lowest number of finishers was in 1928 when Tipperary Tim, a 100-1 outsider, was the first of two past the post. The highest number was 23 in 1984.**

✳ The oldest current football anthem is Norwich City's 'On The Ball, City', penned in the 1890s.

☆ **Blackburn Rovers are so-named because, once upon a time, they had no official ground and 'roved' from pitch to pitch.**

✳ Wimbledon Lawn Tennis Association provides free tea for life to competitors who reach the quarter-finals and beyond.

THE MEANING OF HEINZ 57

Heinz tell it this way: 'While riding a train in New York City in 1896, Henry Heinz saw a sign advertising 21 styles of shoes, which he thought was clever. Although Heinz was manufacturing more than 60 products at the time, Henry thought 57 was a lucky number. So, he began using the slogan "57 Varieties" in all his advertising.'

Heinz 57 is sometimes used to describe a dog which is a mix of multiple breeds, and bingo callers often call out 'Heinz 57' for number 57. Among trainspotters, Heinz 57 is also a nickname for British Rail Class 57 trains.

☆ QUIRKY WRITERS ☆

* Fairytale writer Hans Christian Andersen died falling out of bed. The chances of such an ending are one in two million.

* **Robert Louis Stevenson wrote most of *Kidnapped* while lying in bed.**

* Graham Greene once entered a competition to parody himself in the *Spectator*. He came third.

* **In 1937, F. Scott Fitzgerald drew up a will demanding 'a funeral and burial in keeping with my station in life'. Three years later, having fallen on hard times, Fitzgerald amended the document to read 'cheapest funeral ... without undue ostentation or unnecessary expense'.**

* John Grisham left a career as a lawyer to write his bestselling legal thrillers, but he returned in 1996 to represent the family of a railroad brakeman who was killed at work. He won $650,000 for the family.

* **Danielle Steel has been married five times – one of her husbands was a bank robber convicted of rape, another a burglar with a heroin addiction.**

* All the rights and royalties from J. M. Barrie's *Peter Pan* were bequeathed to the Great Ormond Street Hospital for Sick Children in London.

* **John Milton used 8,000 different words in his poem *Paradise Lost*.**

✳ Margaret Mitchell wrote *Gone With the Wind* between 1926 and 1929. In her early drafts, the main character was named 'Pansy O'Hara' and the O'Hara plantation we know as Tara was called 'Fountenoy Hall'.

✩ **Emily Dickinson, America's most famous female poet, published only seven poems in her lifetime. All of them were published against her will. Her poems were discovered after her death in 1886 and published four years later.**

CROSSING THE (PRODUCTION) LINE

In 1970, a draughtsman working for Quaker biscuits was made redundant. To express his bitterness, he made some subtle changes to the quaint picture he had prepared for printing on the biscuit tins. The amended scene included a pair of lovers in a flowerbed, a tiny jam jar with the word 'shit' printed on it and a pair of fornicating dogs. The X-rated tins went unnoticed for years until a shop worker noticed them. Production stopped while changes were made, but thousands of tins were already in circulation. Today, surviving examples have fetched up to £6,000 at auction.

☆ RECYCLE BECAUSE ... ☆

* Recycling a ton of paper saves 17 mature trees, 26,500 litres of water, 2.5 cubic metres of landfill space, two barrels of oil and 4,000 kilowatt hours of electricity – enough energy to power the average American home for five months.

* **Approximately 88 per cent of energy is saved when plastic is made from recycled plastic rather than the raw materials such as gas and oil.**

* Recycling one aluminium can saves enough energy to run a 100-watt light bulb for 20 hours, a computer for three hours and a TV for two hours.

* **When you throw away an aluminium can you waste as much energy as if you'd half filled it with petrol and poured it away.**

* Over 73 per cent of all newspapers are recovered for recycling. About 33 per cent of this is used to make newsprint; the rest is used to make paperboard, tissue or insulation.

* **Speaking of saving the planet, turning off the tap while brushing your teeth twice a day can save up to 30 litres of water. That's nearly 11,000 litres a year.**

☆

☆ ★ MUSICIANS ON ★ ☆ VALENTINE'S DAY

---

* On 14 February 1961, The Beatles played at the Casanova Club in Liverpool and were captured on film for the first time.

* **On Valentine's Day in 1972, John Lennon and Yoko Ono began a week-long stay as co-hosts on *The Mike Douglas Show*.**

* On the same day in 1972, *Grease* opened off Broadway, where it ran for the next decade for a total of 3,388 performances.

* **In 1973, David Bowie collapsed from exhaustion at the end of his Valentine's Day show at New York's Radio City Music Hall.**

* In 1998, Madonna performed her first club performance in more than ten years at the Roxy in New York.

* **In 1999, Elton John appeared as himself on a special Valentine's Day edition of *The Simpsons*.**

CATHERINE THE GREAT MYTH

Many have heard the story that Russia's empress had interesting sexual appetites and died when a horse was suspended above her bed and fell on her. This is nonsense, most probably French nonsense (as enemies of Russia back then, they are thought to have invented the story). The truth is, Catherine had a stroke while on the loo.

FAMOUS FOR THEIR NOSES

Rudolf I of Hapsburg. the German king and Holy Roman emperor (1218–91) – 'had so large a nose that no artist would ever paint its full dimension'. Royal portrait painters were advised to be flattering.

Michelangelo (1475–1564) – was well known for possessing a very squashed nose. A historian at the time noted 'his forehead almost overhangs it'. In his autobiography, sixteenth-century sculptor and goldsmith Benvenuto Cellini recounted the tale of how Michelangelo acquired his honker. According to Cellini, the young Michelangelo mercilessly teased the painter Pietro Torrigiano while he was studying inside a church. The story goes that, angered, Torrigiano turned and hit him, later recounting, 'I dealt him such a blow on the nose that he felt the bone and the cartilage yield under my fist as if they had been made of crisp wafer. And so he'll go with my mark on him to his dying day.'

Matthew Parker (1504–75) – may have been an English clergyman with an unremarkable nose, but he was also the original 'nosey parker'. Parker was Archbishop of Canterbury under Queen Elizabeth I and, though shy and modest, he was fussy about Church matters and couldn't help prying into everybody's business. At the time, to use one's nose meant to look into a matter, and this archbishop was so renowned for his nosy behaviour that his enemies began to call him 'Nosey' Parker.

Tycho Brahe (1546–1601) – was a celebrated Danish astronomer who lost the tip of his nose in a sword duel with nobleman Manderup Parsbjerg. The pair had argued on two occasions in the weeks leading up to the fight, which took place in dark conditions. For the rest of his life, Tycho wore a replacement nose tip made of silver and gold.

Cyrano de Bergerac (1619–55) – the French dramatist and duellist is often thought to be a fictional character thanks to Edmond Rostand's 1897 play. But Cyrano was a real man, and the play was loosely based on his life. The story goes that he fought over 1,000 duels because of jibes about the size of his enormous nose.

Thomas Wedders – was an English circus performer in the 1700s, and is thought to have had the longest known nose in history. It measured 19 centimetres, and earned him a living working in freak shows all over England. Thomas was considered mentally deficient, so his nose served him well career-wise. Today a waxwork of the Yorkshireman can be seen at Ripley's Believe It Or Not Museum in London.

PRINCE CHARLES FACTOIDS

When Charles was born, on 14 November 1948, the fountains in Trafalgar Square ran blue 'for a boy'.

His was the first royal birth since the seventeenth century that wasn't witnessed by a government minister.

The Duke of Edinburgh was playing squash at the time of the birth.

Charles was christened using water from the River Jordan, a royal tradition thought to stretch back to the Crusades.

Charles is often mocked for having his valet put toothpaste on his toothbrush, but that's a tall story. But it is true that his private secretary squeezed the tube for him when he had his arm in plaster after a polo accident.

During a trip to Fiji as a young man, topless women performed a fertility dance for him. 'It's better than the Changing of the Guard,' he commented.

He is a big fan of Leonard Cohen.

☆ ★ GAMBLING ★ ☆

* In 1950 at the Las Vegas Desert Inn, an anonymous sailor made 27 straight passes (wins) with the dice at craps. The odds against such a feat are 12,467,890 to 1. Had he bet the house limit on each roll he would have earned $268 million. As it is, he was so timid with his wagers that he walked away from the table with only $750. Today the dice are enshrined in the hotel on a velvet pillow under glass.

* **Gamblers in ancient Greece made dice from the ankle bones and shoulder blades of sheep.**

* Residents of Nevada bet an average of $846 a year in casinos.

* **Horse-racing regulations state that no race horse's name may contain more than eighteen letters. Names that are too long would be too cumbersome on racing sheets.**

✳ From a fifty-two-card deck it is possible to deal 2,598,960 different five-card poker hands. Of these 1,088,240 will contain a pair.

✳ **Eskimos don't gamble.**

✳ At race tracks, the favourite wins fewer than 30 per cent of all horse races.

✳ **When unable to gamble, compulsive gamblers often experience physical withdrawal symptoms resembling those undergone by heroin addicts. Their reactions range from restlessness to shakiness, severe headaches and diarrhoea.**

✳ According to *Gambler's Digest*, more cheating takes place in friendly, private gambling games than in all other gambling games combined.

✳ **Four large bells once hung in a clock tower of St Paul's Cathedral, London, but the tower was pulled down by Sir Miles Partridge in the reign of Henry VIII. Sir Miles got to keep the bells after winning them from Henry in a game of dice.**

✳ Madame de Montespan, mistress of Louis XIV, once lost four million francs in half an hour at the gambling tables.

✳ **In eighteenth-century English gambling dens there was an employee whose job it was to swallow the dice in the event of a police raid.**

✳ In poker, a pair of aces and a pair of eights is referred to as a 'dead man's hand'. The term was born in 1876 when Wild West gunfighter and lawman Wild Bill Hickok was shot down by Jack McCall during a card game in a saloon in Deadwood, South Dakota. As Wild Bill slumped over the table he exposed his hand for all to see.

☆ **There are no clocks in Las Vegas casinos.**

☆ LESSER KNOWN OLOGIES ☆

'Ology'	Area of study
Campanology	bell ringing
Cerealogy	crop circles
Cryptozoology	animals that may or may not be mythical
Dendrochronology	age of trees using tree-ring dating
Helminthology	parasitic worms
Nephology	clouds
Rhinology	the nose and its diseases
Selenology	the moon
Speleology	study or exploration of caves

MORE USELESS ☆ ★ ACTOR FACTS ★ ☆

✳ Sylvester Stallone swept the lion cages in Central Park Zoo, New York, when he was a struggling actor.

Chevy Chase nearly died when he was electrocuted during the filming of *Modern Problems*. During the sequence in which he is wearing landing lights as he dreams that he is an aeroplane, the current in the lights short-circuited through his arm, back and neck muscles. The near-death experience plunged him into a period of deep depression.

Nicolas Cage started life as Nicholas Coppola, but changed his name to disassociate himself from his famous film director uncle, Francis Ford Coppola. The name 'Cage' came from the comic book character 'Luke Cage'.

Kevin Spacey's older brother is a professional Rod Stewart impersonator.

As a child, Michael Caine had puffy eyes due to blefaritis, bow legs and a nervous jerk called Saint Vitus' dance. His ears protruded badly and his mother used to stick them back with plasters. Eventually, his ears were so close to his head that he would be slightly hard of hearing for the rest of his life.

Part of Arnold Schwarzenegger's fee for appearing in *Terminator 2* was a Gulf Stream GIII jet aircraft.

Pierce Brosnan entered showbusiness as a teenage runaway, working with the circus as a fire-eater. Years later, he purchased the typewriter of the James Bond creator, Ian Fleming, for £52,800.

At age 37 Jack Nicholson discovered that the woman he'd always thought was his sister was actually his mother.

* Ben Affleck caught the acting bug early on, appearing in ads for Burger King. When he was little, he asked his mother for a dog and she tested him by making him walk an imaginary pup for a week. In the end, he only lasted five days and didn't get the dog.

Steven Spielberg is Drew Barrymore's godfather. After she posed for *Playboy* in 1995, Spielberg sent a note that said 'cover yourself up' along with a quilt and a copy of the magazine with all her pictures altered so that she appeared fully clothed.

* Screen icon Tommy Lee Jones was a roommate of former vice-president-turned-environmental-champion Al Gore.

Martial arts specialist Bruce Lee was so fast that the film in his movies had to be slowed down to see his moves.

* O. J. Simpson was considered to play the role of the *Terminator* in the blockbuster movie, but producers rejected him as they thought he would not be taken seriously.

THE ORIGINAL SMART ALEC

Aleck Hoag was a pimp and petty thief who operated in New York in the 1840s. Hoag's wife, Miranda, was a wily prostitute who, while negotiating with potential customers in the street, would pick their pockets and pass their wallets on to her husband, who paid the police to turn a blind eye. Aleck came up with an inventive scam called the 'panel game', whereby Miranda would take clients to her room, undress them and draw a curtain around the bed. Once the fun was in full swing, a cough from Miranda cued Aleck to sneak into the room via a panel in the wall, steal any valuables from the punter's pocket, and exit quietly. Seconds later, Hoag would assume the role of an angry husband back from a trip and bang angrily on the door uttering all manner of threats. Encouraged by Miranda to dress quickly and escape through a window, their victim would be halfway home before realising what had happened. Hoag eventually came a cropper when he began dodging his payments to the police. He was sentenced to prison, but soon escaped, only to be recaptured and nicknamed Smart Alec by the police, who had to admit that, though irritating, he was a clever sort. By the 1860s, the phrase was common American slang.

TOP DOMAIN PRICES ☆

Domain	Price
insure.com	$16 million in 2009
sex.com	$12–$14 million in 2006
fund.com	$9.99 million in 2008
porn.com	$9.5 million in 2007
business.com	$7.5 million in 1999
diamond.com	$7.5 million in 2006
beer.com	$7 million in 2004
israel.com	$5.88 million in 2004
casino.com	$5.5 million in 2003
toys.com	$5.1 million in 2009

☆ ★ DR SEUSS ... ★ ☆

✳ ... was not a doctor at all. His real name was Theodor Seuss Geisel. Seuss was his mother's maiden name, and he began using it as a pseudonym at university. The Dr bit was added as a joke, for Seuss's father had hoped his son would gain a doctorate and become a professor.

✳ **Seuss's first book was rejected by over 27 publishers. In despair, he nearly burned it. He went on to publish over 40 books, with worldwide sales of half a billion.**

✳ *Green Eggs and Ham* was the result of a bet that he could not write a book using only fifty words. This and *The Cat in the Hat* are his biggest sellers. One in four American children receives a Dr Seuss book as their first book.

✳ **Seuss pronounced his name to rhyme with 'rejoice', and in 1950 coined the word 'nerd' in *I Ran the Zoo*. He disliked spending time with children, and never became a father.**

A LITTLE ABOUT EARTHQUAKES

More earthquakes occur in Alaska than in California. The largest ever recorded occurred in Chile on 22 May 1960 and had a magnitude of 9.5 on the Richter scale. Worldwide, there are approximately two earthquakes every minute. In Norse mythology, quakes were seen as the violent rages of Loki, god of mischief and strife. As punishment for murdering Baldr – god of beauty and light –

mischievous Loki was tied up in a cave with a venomous serpent above his head. Poison dripped from its mouth, and was caught in a bowl by Loki's wife, Sigyn. From time to time, the dear old girl had to empty the bowl, and the poison would drip on to Loki's face. Loki would jerk his head, thrash his rope around and cause the earth to tremble.

CHRISTMAS NUMBER ONES

Year	Song	Artist	Number of weeks at top spot
1960	'I Love You'	Cliff Richard and The Shadows	2
1961	'Moon River'	Danny Williams	2
1962	'Return to Sender'	Elvis Presley	3
1963	'I Want to Hold Your Hand'	The Beatles	5
1964	'I Feel Fine'	The Beatles	5
1965	'Day Tripper/We Can Work It Out'	The Beatles	5
1966	'Green, Green Grass of Home'	Tom Jones	7'
1967	'Hello, Goodbye'	The Beatles	7
1968	'Lily the Pink'	The Scaffold	3
1969	'Two Little Boys'	Rolf Harris	6
1970	'I Hear You Knocking'	Dave Edmunds	6
1971	'Ernie (The Fastest Milkman in the West)'	Benny Hill	4
1972	'Long-Haired Lover From Liverpool'	Little Jimmy Osmond	5

1973	'Merry Xmas Everybody'	Slade	5
1974	'Lonely This Christmas'	Mud	4
1975	'Bohemian Rhapsody'	Queen	9
1976	'When a Child Is Born'	Johnny Mathis	3
1977	'Mull of Kintyre'	Wings	9
1978	'Mary's Boy Child'	Boney M	4
1979	'Another Brick in the Wall (Part II)'	Pink Floyd	5
1980	'There's No-One Quite Like Grandma'	St Winifred's School Choir	2
1981	'Don't You Want Me'	The Human League	5
1982	'Save Your Love'	Renee and Renato	4
1983	'Only You'	The Flying Pickets	5
1984	'Do They Know It's Christmas?'	Band Aid	5
1985	'Merry Christmas Everyone'	Shakin' Stevens	2
1986	'Reet Petite'	Jackie Wilson	4
1987	'Always On My Mind'	Pet Shop Boys	4
1988	'Mistletoe and Wine'	Cliff Richard	4
1989	'Do They Know It's Christmas II'	Band Aid II	3
1990	'Saviour's Day'	Cliff Richard	1
1991	'Bohemian Rhapsody'	Queen	5
1992	'I Will Always Love You'	Whitney Houston	10
1993	'Mr Blobby'	Mr Blobby	2
1994	'Stay Another Day'	East 17	5
1995	'Earth Song'	Michael Jackson	6
1996	'2 Become 1'	Spice Girls	3
1997	'Too Much'	Spice Girls	2
1998	'Goodbye'	Spice Girls	1
1999	'I Have A Dream/Seasons in the Sun	Westlife	4
2000	'Can We Fix It?'	Bob The Builder	3
2001	'Somethin' Stupid'	Robbie Williams and Nicole Kidman	3

2002	'Sound of the Underground'	Girls Aloud	4
2003	'Mad World'	Michael Andrews and Gary Jules	3
2004	'Do They Know It's Christmas?'	Band Aid 20	4
2005	'That's My Goal'	Shane Ward	4
2006	'A Moment Like This'	Leona Lewis	4
2007	'When You Believe'	Leon Jackson	3
2008	'Hallelujah'	Alexandra Burke	3
2009	'Killing in the Name'	Rage Against The Machine	1
2010	'When We Collide'	Matt Cardle	3

 # ROYAL DEATHS ☆

Monarch	Cause of Death	Year
William I	Abdominal injury from horse saddle	1087
William II	Arrow in the back while hunting	1100
Henry I	Food poisoning after overeating	1135
Richard I	Arrow wound during siege of French château	1199
Edward II	Murder: a red hot iron in anus (rumoured)	1327
Richard II	Starved himself while imprisoned in Pontefract Castle	1400
Henry VI	Stabbed in the Tower of London on orders of Edward IV.	1471
Edward V	Murdered at the Tower of London, aged 12	1483
Richard III	Killed at Battle of Bosworth	1485
Elizabeth I	Tonsil abscess led to septicaemia	1603
Charles I	Beheaded for treason at Whitehall, London	1649
Charles II	Stroke (possibly from mercury poisoning)	1685

William III   Pneumonia after breaking collarbone falling
from horse 1702

George II   Aneurysm of the aorta while sitting on the toilet 1760

George IV   Gout and cirrhosis of liver, from eating and drinking
too much 1830

William IV   Alcoholism. 1837

WAR DOG AND CAT

The only known four-legged Japanese prisoner of war was a dog named Judy. In 1942, the pointer escaped from HMS *Grasshopper* and subsequently passed her time in a Medan military prison alongside her two-legged friends. She made herself very useful to the prisoners by catching lizards and rodents from around the prison, thus providing a welcome addition to their pitiful food rations. She also protected prisoners from many a beating from Japanese guards, biting and snarling until the guards relented. Leading Aircraftsman Frank Williams became Judy's best friend – he managed to bribe drunk guards into making the dog an official POW. Judy survived many more adventures before eventually making it back to Liverpool with Frank in 1945. She became a national heroine and won the Dickin Medal for animal bravery. Judy died in 1950. During the Second World War, a ship's cat named Oscar used up several of his nine lives. He was first rescued when the British torpedoed the *Bismarck* and given a new home on board HMS *Cossack*. When *Cossack* sunk a few months later, Oscar had another lucky escape and took up residence on HMS *Ark Royal*, only to find himself sinking again when *Ark Royal* was attacked by the Germans. After that Oscar was returned to solid ground, and lived safely until he passed away naturally in 1955.

ABRAHAM LINCOLN AND
☆ JOHN F. KENNEDY ☆
–COINCIDENCE OR NOT?

Lincoln was elected to Congress in 1846. Kennedy was elected to Congress in 1946.

Lincoln was elected president in 1860. Kennedy was elected president in 1960.

Both presidents were shot in the head and in the presence of their wives.

Both presidents were shot on a Friday. Lincoln was shot at Ford's Theatre. Kennedy was shot in a Ford car – a Lincoln limousine.

John Wilkes Booth shot Lincoln in a theatre and hid in a warehouse, while Lee Harvey Oswald shot Kennedy from a warehouse and hid in a theatre.

Lincoln was succeeded by a Johnson (Andrew). Kennedy was succeeded by a Johnson (Lyndon B.)

☆

☆ LANDLOCKED COUNTRIES ☆

Afghanistan	Ethiopia	Paraguay
Andorra	Hungary	Rwanda
Armenia	Kazakhstan	San Marino
Austria	Kyrgyzstan	Serbia
Azerbaijan	Laos	Slovakia
Belarus	Lesotho	Swaziland
Bhutan	Liechtenstein	Switzerland
Bolivia	Luxembourg	Tajikistan
Botswana	Macedonia	Turkmenistan
Burkina Faso	Malawi	Uganda
Burundi	Mali	Uzbekistan
Central African	Moldova	Vatican City
Republic	Mongolia	West Bank
Chad	Nepal	Zambia
Czech Republic	Niger	Zimbabwe

THE TELEVISION

In 1926, John Logie Baird made a public demonstration of his television set in London's Soho. A decade later there were on 100 televisions in the world – today there are approximately 1.5 billion. Perhaps unsurprisingly, Americans spend more time staring at the telly than any other nation – by the age of 65, the average US citizen will have spent nine years channel hopping, and seen more that 20,000 TV adverts. There are more TV sets in the US than there are people in the UK. The 'LNK Infotree' is the largest TV sculpture in the world. Constructed from 2,903 individual television sets, it covers 3,135 square metres at the Open Air Museum in Vilnius, Lithuania. A statue of Lenin lies in the middle of the labyrinth. The sculpture symbolises the absurdity of Soviet propaganda broadcast on television for over half a century.

☆ ★ ONE SENTENCE, ★ ☆
TWO MEANINGS

---

* Police help dog bite victim.

☆ **The man saw the boy with the binoculars.**

* The criminal experienced a seizure.

☆ **We saw her duck.**

* They are hunting dogs.

☆ **I once shot an elephant in my pyjamas. How he got into my pyjamas, I'll never know. ***

*Courtesy of Groucho Marx

GOATS AND HORSES

Goats have a calming effect on skittish horses, as many a horse trainer will testify. 'Stall walkers' – horses that pace around anxiously – benefit from bearded companions, which lends extra credibility to the story that the phrase 'Get your goat' finds its origin in horseracing. In the early twentieth century, it was common for owners to keep goats next to horses to make them more race-ready on race days, but this practice eventually led to thieves placing bets on a certain horse to lose before stealing its goat. This annoyed not only the goatless horse, but also the owner and anyone who'd bet on it to win. A phrase was born.

MORE LITTLE-KNOWN
☆ ★ BEATLES ★ ☆

☀ *Sgt. Pepper's Lonely Hearts Club Band* was the first British rock album to feature the lyrics on the back cover, and *A Hard Day's Night* was the one Fab Four album to contain only songs penned by Lennon and McCartney. For the *Sgt. Pepper* album cover created by the artist Peter Blake, cutouts of Adolf Hitler, Mahatma Gandhi and Jesus Christ were requested by Lennon, but ultimately they were left out, though a cutout of Hitler was made for use.

☆ **When the photograph for the cover of *Abbey Road* was taken, the VW Beetle was supposed to be moved but the owner was on holiday.**

☀ Paul is not McCartney's first name – it's James. Lennon changed his middle name from Winston to Ono after marrying Yoko Ono in 1969.

☆ **One of the original lines in 'With a Little Help From My Friends' was 'What would you do if I sang out of tune/ Would you stand up and throw tomatoes at me?' Ringo refused to sing it.**

☀ At the end of 'Strawberry Fields Forever', Lennon is heard mumbling what sounds like 'I buried Paul'. He's actually saying 'cranberry sauce'.

☆ **The first song ever written by Lennon was called 'Hello Little Girl'. McCartney's was 'I Lost My Little Girl'.**

✳ When Ringo left the group in 1968 by walking out of the
White Album sessions, the rest of the band took turns on the
drums for several tracks. When Ringo returned he found his
drum kit covered in flowers.

✳ **The BBC banned several Beatles songs – 'I Am the
Walrus' (it contained the word 'knickers') and 'Fixing a
Hole', 'Lucy in the Sky with Diamonds' and 'A Day in the
Life' (all seemed to contain drug references).**

OSCAR EXCEPTIONS

The shortest Oscar ceremony ever was the first, in 1929. It lasted
around 15 minutes – the winners had been announced three
months earlier. The longest ceremony took place in 2000, running
for four hours and 16 minutes. Bob Hope hosted the Oscars 18 times;
Billy Crystal is in second place with eight times. Kate Winslet is the
only actress to receive four Oscar nominations when under the
age of 30. The shortest ever Best Actor Oscar performance went to
Anthony Hopkins in 1992; Hopkins appeared for less than 16 minutes
as Hannibal Lecter in *The Silence of the Lambs*. George C. Scott and
Marlon Brando are the only actors who declined to accept their
Oscars, for *Patton* (1970) and *The Godfather* (1972) respectively. Meryl
Streep has received more Best Actress nominations than any other
actress – 13 in total, out of which came two awards. *The Turning Point*
(1977) and *The Color Purple* (1985) are the only films to have received
11 Oscar nominations, but no award. Vivien Leigh's Oscar for *Gone
With the Wind* (1939) sold at auction for $510,000 in 1994, making it the
only Oscar to sell for over half a million dollars.

A FLY IN THE EYE ... A TRUE STORY

While on a hunting trip one day, South African farmer Willie Spargenberg felt 'something flick' into his eye. Little did he know that a botfly had lodged itself in his eyeball and wasted no time in laying eggs behind his retina. That night, his face started to swell up. A week later, after suffering from severe headaches and blurred vision, Willie went to an eye specialist. The doctor zapped as many of the hatched maggots as he could, but some of them had begun to pupate and migrate to unreachable corners of Willie's eye socket. A scan showed the maggots had entered his sinuses, and there was nothing for it but to administer anti-parasitic veterinary medicine (botfly normally go for sheep's eyes). The maggots died, and Willie had been lucky. Without treatment he might have gone blind in one eye and the maggots could have burrowed into the brain, with potentially fatal results.

FAMOUS PEOPLE, NOT SO ☆ FAMOUS BANDS ☆

Celebrity	Band
Russell Crowe	30 Odd Foot of Grunts
Kevin Costner	The Modern West
Joe Pesci	Joey Dee and The Starlighters (disbanded)
Kevin Bacon	The Bacon Brothers

Stephen King and Matt Groening. . . Rock Bottom Remainders

Juliette Lewis . . . . Juliette and the Licks

Ricky Gervais . . . . Seona Dancing (disbanded)

Richard Gere . . . . The Strangers (disbanded)

Bruce Willis . . . . The Bruce Willis Blues Band

Tony Blair . . . . The Ugly Rumours (university days)

Dennis Quaid . . . . The Sharks

Billy Bob Thornton. . . . . Billy Bob Thornton and the Boxmasters

Steven Seagal . . . . Thunderbox

USELESS MUSICIAN
☆ ★ FACTS ★ ☆

* Jimi Hendrix, Janis Joplin and Jim Morrison were all 27 years old when they died.

* **Mick Jagger was a porter in a psychiatric hospital before he formed The Rolling Stones. He was also a student at the London School of Economics. Jagger turned down £3.5 million to write his memoirs, claiming he simply couldn't remember enough details from his own life.**

* Led Zeppelin were rumoured to have violated a groupie with a fish. The incident was mentioned in *Hammer of the Gods*, a sordid 1985 Led Zeppelin biography based on recollections of the band's then road manager Richard Cole.

* **Bryan Adams was arrested for smoking pot as a teenager. Years later he was nearly killed during a parachute jump.**

* Beatles George Harrison was arrested along with his soon-to-be wife on his wedding day in 1969. The charge? Marijuana possession.

* **Though Christina Aguilera is of Ecuadorian descent and recorded an album in Spanish, she doesn't speak the language. She once paid a visit to hospital after a plant fell on her head, and she sometimes sleeps with a night light burning.**

* Rod Stewart was a gravedigger before he became a famous rock star.

* **Janet Jackson's boob flash at the Super Bowl is the most searched event in the history of the internet.**

* The name Anastacia is Greek for 'She who will rise again'. Before she was famous, every music business person she met told her to get contact lenses if she wanted to succeed. Now, her glasses have become her trademark.

* **Naomi Campbell starred in Bob Marley and the Wailers' video for the song 'Is This Love' when she was just seven years old. She has no connection with Campbell's soup.**

* Lenny Kravitz once kept a marijuana joint he'd shared with Mick Jagger for a year.

* **Even though she appears in ads for Tommy Hilfiger's True Star fragrances, Beyoncé Knowles is reportedly allergic to perfume.**

✳ Moby's real name is Richard Melville Hall. According to the musician, his middle name and the nickname 'Moby' were given to him by his parents because of his ancestral relationship to *Moby-Dick* author Herman Melville.

✳ **Coldplay really like to live the life of a rock 'n' roll band when they tour: their rider includes a request for eight stamped, local postcards.**

✳ In 1985, a four-year-old Alicia Keys appeared on *The Cosby Show* as one of the guests at Rudy's slumber party.

✳ Eric Clapton grew up with his grandmother and her second husband and believed they were his parents and that his mother was his older sister. He never knew his real father. Clapton owns one-fifth of the planet Mars.

✳ **The R Whites lemonade song 'I'm a Secret Lemonade Drinker' was sung by Elvis Costello's dad, Ross MacManus. Elvis provided the backing vocals.**

✳ U2 singer Bono took his name from *bonavox*, the latin word meaning 'good voice'. It is said that a friend nicknamed him 'Bono Vox' after a hearing aid shop they regularly passed in Dublin because he sang so loudly he seemed to be singing for the deaf. Bono disliked the name at first. However, on discovering its meaning, he accepted it and shortened it to Bono.

✳ **As a child, Amy Winehouse wanted to be a roller-skating waitress.**

✳ Boy George was fired from a job in a supermarket for choosing to wear the store's carrier bags.

☆ **Goth rocker Marilyn Manson has often been said to have played nerdy Paul Pfeiffer in late-'80s sitcom *The Wonder Years*, but he did not. Actor Josh Saviano played Kevin's best friend, and the ex-actor is now a lawyer in New York.**

✳ On his first day at kindergarten, David Bowie was so nervous that he wet himself. He is also afraid of spiders and flying, but these days manages to control his bladder when facing his phobias. David has admitted that his claim to being bisexual was really a sham. He made up the story to create more mystery about himself in the 1970s.

☆ **When performing, Celine Dion requires a children's choir with 20 children of varying races.**

✳ When she was 16, Jessica Simpson tried to adopt a Mexican baby found in a dumpster.

☆ **Sheryl Crow's two front teeth are false – they were knocked out when she tripped on the stage earlier in her career.**

✳ Madonna is related to both Gwen Stefani and Celine Dion. Gwen's great-aunt's mother-in-law shares the same last name as Madonna Ciccone and an ancestor of Madonna's mother was married to a distant relative of Celine's dad. When Madonna wed Guy Ritchie, the minister gave the couple a toilet roll each. When interviewed, Susan Brown said she gave the gift because 'the toilet rolls are long and strong, which is what I hope their marriage will be.'

☆ **Elvis Presley's hip wiggling began as stage fright. He was so nervous that his legs would shake.**

* Simply Red are so named because they support Manchester United football club.

Apparently Christina Aguilera and her husband like to go nude on Sundays to keep the marriage alive.

* Avril Lavigne wrote the *Spongebob Squarepants* theme song. Her name means April the Vine when translated into English.

Madonna used to work in the cloakroom of New York's Russian Tea Room restaurant, but she was fired for wearing fishnet stockings.

* One of Halle Berry's unidentified boyfriends was so violent that he dealt her a blow to her ear which left her partially deaf.

Phil Collins lost his virginity in an allotment at 14 years old.

* Whitney Houston rides a Harley Davidson.

Dame Shirley Bassey once had a job packing chamber pots. She would write her name and address on them and says she received replies from all over the world.

* In recognition of her contribution to promoting Iceland around the world, Iceland's government gave Björk an island off the coast of her home country.

Elvis Presley's middle name was Aaron, in honour of his twin brother Jessie Garon, who died at birth. Elvis failed his music class at school and never once played an encore. His favourite food was fried peanut butter and banana sandwiches and he was at one time appointed Special Agent of the Bureau of Narcotics and Dangerous

Drugs; he weighed 230 pounds and had ten different drugs in his body at the time of his death.

* Mariah Carey was nicknamed 'Mirage' in high school because she never showed up for class.

☆ **Ozzy Osbourne has two smiley face tattoos on his kneecaps and he talks to them when he's feeling lonely or sad. In Jack Osbourne's autobiography, *21 Years Gone*, he writes that as a child he would watch his father down pills. Trying to be just like his dad, Jack would buy Tic Tac mints and swallow them.**

* US hip-hop star Missy Elliott is a big fan of biodegradable pants.

END-OF-THE-WORLD BRA

According to Nostradamus, the world should have ended in 1999. Back then around 30 per cent of Japanese people believed he had a point, a statistic that led Triumph International Japan to launch the Armageddon Bra. A fetching piece, it contained a sensor to detect incoming missiles, but the manufacturers failed to explain how this would help matters once the bra alerted the wearer to her imminent destruction. Another issue was that the device worked best if worn as outerwear.

☆ UNRELATED TITBITS ☆

* The founder of the Natural History Museum, Sir Richard Owen, was the man we have to thank for the word 'dinosaur', literally meaning 'terrible lizard'.

* **Just one in a hundred workers goes to the pub for their lunch. The same proportion spend lunchtime having sex.**

* It's 30 years since the world's first bar code was used. It was on a ten-pack of Wrigley's Juicy Fruit at a supermarket in Ohio. The gum is now an exhibit in the Smithsonian Institution in Washington, DC.

* **Reports of UFOs have dwindled since the late 1990s. In the UK, sightings have gone from about 30 a week to almost zero, a trend echoed in the US and Norway.**

* Ducks have regional accents. London ducks shout out a rough quack to be heard above the urban din; those in the West Country make a quieter, softer sound.

* **Freak conditions above Mt Everest can cause the sky to 'fall in'. An analysis of weather patterns in May 1996, by University of Toronto researchers, said that eight people died when the stratosphere sank to the level of the summit.**

* More than one billion birds crash into buildings in the US every year. Mirrored office blocks are a particular hazard.

ROMAN PLACE NAMES

Bath – Aquae Sulis
Cambridge – Cantabria
Canterbury – Durovernum
    Cantiacorum
Chester – Deva
Chesterholm – Vindolanda
Chichester – Noviomagus
Cirencester – Corinium
Colchester – Camulodunum
Corbridge – Corstopitum
Dover – Dubris
Dunstable – Durocobrivis
Durham – Dunelm
Exeter – Isca

Gloucester – Glevum Colonia
Halifax – Halifacium
Isle of Wight – Vectis
Leicester – Ratae Coritanorum
Lincoln – Lindum Colonia
London – Londinium
Manchester – Mamucium
Newcastle – Pons Aelius
Oxford – Oxonia
Silchester – Calleva
St Albans – Verulamium
Swindon – Durocornovium
Winchester – Venta Belgarum
York – Eboracum

HERE THERE AND EVERYWHERE

* You can send a postcard from hell. There is a small town located in the Cayman Islands called Hell. They have a post office.

☆ **Scotland has the highest proportion of redheads in the world. Thirteen per cent of Scots have red hair and approximately 40 per cent carry the redhead gene.**

✳ Davao City, located in the southern Philippines, is the largest city in the world in terms of area.

☆ **Alaska's coastline is longer than the entire coastline of the US (not including Hawaii).**

✳ In the dry valley region of Antarctica, it has not rained in two million years because of the cold climate.

☆ **The Netherlands has the highest concentration of museums in the world. Amsterdam alone has 42.**

✳ Canada has more lakes than the rest of the world combined.

☆ **For over ten years, the town of Tidikelt in the Sahara Desert did not receive a drop of rain.**

✳ Seven asteroids were named after the *Challenger* astronauts killed in the 1986 space shuttle launch.

☆ **The deepest part of the ocean is 36,198 feet (6.9 miles) at the Mariana Trench in the Pacific Ocean, south of Japan and near the Mariana Islands.**

✳ No point in England is more than 75 miles from the sea.

☆ **The largest recorded snowflake fell in Montana in 1887. It was 15 inches wide and 8 inches thick.**

✳ There is no land at all at the North Pole, only ice on top of sea. The Arctic Ocean has about 12 million square kilometres of floating ice and has the coldest winter temperature of −34° centigrade.

☆ **Antarctic means 'opposite the Arctic'.**

☆ **A huge underground river runs beneath the Nile, carrying six times more water than the river above**

✳ The word 'volcano' derives from Vulcan, the Roman god of fire.

☆ **Lloro, Colombia, is the wettest place on Earth, averaging 523.6 inches of rainfall a year, or more than 40 feet (13 metres). That's about ten times more than fairly wet major cities in Europe or the United States.**

✳ Mars days are 24 hours and 37 minutes long, compared to 23 hours and 56 minutes on Earth.

☆ **The moon is one million times drier than the Gobi Desert.**

☆ APRIL FOOLED AGAIN ☆

On April 1st ...

In 1986, *Le Parisien* announced that the Eiffel Tower was to be dismantled and reconstructed at Euro Disney. And what would replace the Tower? An Olympic stadium!

In 1959, residents of Wellingborough found a trail of white footprints painted along the main street of their town. At the end of the trail were the words, 'I must fly.'

In 1959, the BBC reported that Big Ben would be given a digital clockface, and the clock hands would be sold to the first four listeners to make a bid.

In 2008, the BBC announced that camera crews had captured footage of Adélie penguins taking to the air, and offered a video clip to prove it. *Monty Python's* Terry Jones explained how the penguins fly away to spend time in the tropical sun.

In 1975, an Australian news programme announced the imminent arrival of 'metric time'. Australia was to convert to the new system, where 100 seconds made a minute, and 100 minutes made an hour. Days would be 20 hours long.

In 1981, the *Daily Mail* reported on Japanese runner Kimo Nakajimi who began the London Marathon but, due to a misunderstanding, thought that he had to run for 26 days, not 26 miles.

In 1965, *Politiken*, a Copenhagen newspaper, reported that the Danish parliament had passed a new law requiring all dogs to be painted white. The purpose of this, it explained, was to increase road safety by allowing dogs to be seen more easily at night.

In 1991, *The Times* announced that the government had decided to ease congestion on London's M25 by making all the traffic travel in the same direction. Wednesdays, and Fridays would be clockwise only, and Tuesdays and Thursdays would be anti-clockwise.

In 1995 a statue of Lenin was seen to weep milky white tears in the Italian town of Cavriago. Hundreds gathered to watch the 'weeping Lenin' until the hoax was revealed.

In 2000, the *Independent* reported that Florida researchers had developed a Viagra-like pill to treat sexually frustrated pets, including hamsters. It was called Feralmone.

☆ ★ STUFF ★ ☆

* The US army packs Tabasco sauce in every ration kit given to soldiers.

☆ **An office desk has 400 times more bacteria than a toilet.**

* Sixty-five per cent of all Elvis impersonators are of Asian origin.

☆ **The WD in WD-40 stands for water displacer.**

* Teflon is the most slippery substance in the world.

☆ **Cow is a Japanese brand of shaving foam.**

* Ninety-three per cent of all greeting cards are purchased by women.

☆ **The best time for a person to buy shoes is in the afternoon. This is because the foot tends to swell a bit around this time.**

* Oral-B toothbrushes were the first to be sent to the moon when they were used aboard the Apollo 11 mission. Oral-B is a combination of oral hygiene and the letter B, which stands for the word better.

☆ **More than half the world's population has never made a telephone call.**

* Early Romans used porcupine quills as toothpicks.

☆ **Due to the shortages of lead and metals during the Second World War, toothpaste was packaged in plastic tubes and has been ever since.**

✳ Only 30 per cent of humans can flare their nostrils.

☆ **The Snickers Bar was named after a horse owned by the Mars family.**

URINE

An ostrich uses its own urine to cool itself down.

Urine was used as mouthwash in ancient China.

Cattle urinate backwards; the official term for this is retromingent.

Snakes do not urinate, instead they secrete uric acid.

Drinking the urine of a pregnant woman is said to boost the immune system.

☆ INTERNATIONAL RULERS ☆

✳ Nicaragua had 396 different leaders in 16 years (1839–55), making each reign only about 14 days.

☆ **There were once three presidents in one day in Mexico.**

✳ William Pitt, elected in 1783 at the age of 24, was the youngest English Prime Minister ever to hold the position.

☆ **Irish president Eamon De Valera was born in the United States.**

✳ Louis XIV owned approximately 1,000 wigs.

☆ **Teddy Roosevelt died from a tooth and gum infection.**

✳ US president John Quincy Adams kept a pet alligator in the White House.

☆ **Czar Alexander II of Russia sold Alaska to the USA for \$7 million to clear debts accrued from gambling.**

✳ Hitler was named 'Man of the Year' by *Time* magazine in 1938.

☆ **The first passenger elevator, known as 'The Flying Chair' was designed in 1743 for Louis XV of France. He didn't want to climb the stairs of his private apartments to visit his mistress Madame de Châteauroux. It was no more than a chair on the outside of the building with some weights to create a pulley system.**

☆ PLACE NAME MEANINGS ☆

Argentina	from *argentum*, Latin for silver
Bahamas	shallow sea or low tide
Burkina Faso	land of upright people
Cameroon	from the Portuguese *Rio de Camarões*, meaning river of shrimps
Croatia	rich in waters/lakes
Cyprus	copper

Dominica . . . . . Sunday, the day Columbus arrived on the island

Equador . . . . . . unsurprisingly means equator, where the country lies

Guam. . . . . . . .meaning 'we have' in the native Chamorro

Hong Kong. . . . . fragrant harbour

Japan . . . . empire of the sun

Kosovo . . . . . . field of blackbirds

Kyrgyzstan. . . . . land of forty tribes

Las Vegas . . . . . the meadows

Monaco . . . . . . single dwelling

Montserrat . . . . jagged moutain

Namibia . . . . . . area where there is nothing

Netherlands. . . . lowlands

Romania . . . . . . Roman realm

Samoa . . . . sacred centre

Sierra Leone . . . lion mountain

Singapore . . . . . lion city

Spain. . . . . land of rabbits

Taiwan. . . . . . . terraced bay

☆ ★ **THE RAT** ★ ☆

The first albino rats to be bred in captivity were born to a single albino rat captured by Jack Black, Queen Victoria's royal rat catcher. Peter Rabbit's creator Beatrix Potter was one of the first pet rat keepers – she owned one of Jack Black's albinos.

☆ **Rats are considered sacred in the Karni Mata temple in India. Thousands of them inhabit the temple and, should one of the rats be killed, the person responsible is obliged to replace it with a rat made of solid gold. According to local legend, Karni Mata, the fourteenth-century mystic and an incarnation of the Hindu goddess Durga, implored Yama, the god of death, to restore the life of the son of one of her storytellers. When Yama refused, Karni Mata reincarnated the dead son and all the storytellers as a rats. At Karni Mata's insistence, rats became sacred when her stepson Laxman drowned as he drank from a tank.**

✳ Rats make a laughter-like noise when tickled, though it is inaudible to the human ear.

☆ **The ancient Romans didn't distinguish rats from mice – they merely called them *rattus major* (big rat) and *rattus minor* (little rat). Either sized rat was considered good luck.**

✳ In China the rat is a symbol of prosperity.

☆ **Rats have terrible eyesight so are rarely seen where their whiskers cannot touch the perimeter of a landmark or wall. A rat in the middle of the room is a rare sight (thankfully).**

✳ The rat is the first animal in the Chinese Zodiac.

☆ **The kangaroo rat can go without water for longer than a camel.**

✳ Rats can hold their breath for three minutes and tread water for up to three days. They can multiply so quickly that within 18 months two rats could have over a million descendants.

In addition, they:

✳ ... can chew through concrete.

☆ **... can't vomit.**

✳ ... can distinguish the sound of different languages as proved in an experiment in which neuroscientists in Barcelona found that rats were able to differentiate between the rhythmic sounds of Japanese and Dutch.

☆ **... are not mentioned anywhere in the Bible.**

✳ ... have front teeth that grow approximately five inches every year but they grind them down with their continuous chewing on anything they can get hold of including cardboard, cement, brick and wood.

☆ **... eat their own faeces for its nutritional composition.**

✳ ... regulate their body temperature by contracting and expanding blood vessels in their tails which means they do not sweat.

☆ ★ DIGESTION ★ ☆

* A sloth digests its food over a two-week period.

Many cats cannot properly digest cow's milk and end up with diarrhoea.

* Pepsi was so named as it contained the digestive enzyme pepsin, and was originally marketed as a digestive aid.

Spiders digest food outside the body. After the prey is captured, spiders release digestive enzymes from their intestinal tract and cover the insect. The enzymes break down the body, which allows the spider to suck up its liquid prey.

* Once the housefly finishes eating, it vomits and eats it all over again. A frog vomits by ejecting its stomach so that it hangs out of its mouth and enables it to scrape out the contents with its front limbs before swallowing the stomach again.

A snake digests a frog over 50 hours. Its gastric juices are powerful enough to absorb bones and teeth.

* If a seabird ingests a fish that is too large to swallow whole, it can happily keep part of it in the oesophagus – the tail will dangle out of the bird's mouth until the digestion process has made room in the stomach for the rest of the fish to be swallowed.

EVEN MORE USELESS
☆ ACTOR FACTS ☆

* Sean Connery has to have tattoos declaring his love for his mum, his dad and his country covered by make-up when filming. When he was taking martial arts lessons from Steven Seagal for the James Bond film *Never Say Never Again*, Seagal broke his wrist – allegedly because Connery cracked a joke about his mother.

* **Christian Bale ate live maggots for his role as Dieter Dengler in the film *Rescue Dawn*. He played the only American ever to escape from a prisoner-of-war camp.**

* Peter Falk, best known for his role as TV detective *Columbo*, has a glass eye.

* **Colin Farrell says that Marilyn Monroe was the first woman he fell in love with. 'I used to leave Smarties, the Irish equivalent of M&Ms, under my pillow with a little note saying, "I know you're dead but these are very tasty and you should come and have a few. I won't tell anyone."'**

* Harrison Ford was bullied by classmates at school because he liked to hang out with girls. The scar on his face is from a car accident.

* **Hollywood heart-throb Hugh Jackman spurned the opportunity to be the next Jason Donovan when he turned down a part in *Neighbours* early in his career.**

✳ In all of his film contracts, Roger Moore stipulates that he be provided with an unlimited quantity of hand-rolled Cuban cigars.

✳ **Ben Stiller holds the Razzie Awards – the anti-Oscars, celebrating the worst of Hollywood for the year – record for most nominations in one year. In 2004 he was nominated for Worst Actor in five of the six films in which he appeared:** *Along Came Polly, Starsky & Hutch, Anchorman: The Legend of Ron Burgundy, Dodgeball* **and** *Envy*.

✳ Actor Bill Murray does not have an agent or a manager. He only considers offers for scripts and roles using a personal telephone number with a voice mailbox that he checks once in a while. In 1970 Murray dropped out of university after being arrested at Chicago's O'Hare Airport for trying to smuggle nearly nine pounds of marijuana.

✳ **Jake Gyllenhaal got his first driving lesson from family friend Paul Newman. He is a Buddhist and his favourite colour is green.**

✳ When Johnny Deep was engaged to actress Winona Ryder, he had a tattoo saying 'Winona forever' on his arm. After they separated, he had the 'n' and 'a' removed so that it read 'Wino forever!'

✳ **Tom Hanks is related to Abraham Lincoln. He collects 1940s typewriters.**

✳ *Austin Powers* and *Shrek* star Mike Myers has two streets named after him in Toronto, Canada. Mike Myers is descended from William Wordsworth.

☆ **As a teenager, actor-writer Matt Damon earned extra cash by being a sidewalk break-dancer.**

TOBY JUGS

Fashioned in the shape of a heavy-set, jolly old fellow holding a mug of beer in one hand and a pipe in the other, these ceramic mugs first became popular in the 1760s. They were produced by Staffordshire potters and may have been based on similar Delft jugs made in the Netherlands. The name most probably comes from the name of a notorious Yorkshire drinker called Henry Elwes, known to his friends as 'Toby Fillpot', for whom the old drinking song 'The Brown Jug' was written. Toby jugs are also known as fillpots, so that would make sense. These jugs would have been used for drinking, of course, and would sometimes have been caricatures of famous politicians, but nowadays they're mostly just tasteful ornaments ...

☆ **THIS SPORTING LIFE** ☆

✳ Basketball may find its origins in the game of *ollamalitzli*, a ball and hoop affair played by the Aztecs in Central America, but the game as we know it was devised in 1891 by Dr James A. Naismith at the International YMCA college in Springfield, Massachusets. The thinking was simple: the doctor wanted a game that was suitable for playing indoors. Peach baskets were used at first, and a ladder was provided to fetch the ball after a goal was scored.

✴ **Canada is the only country not to have won a gold medal while hosting the Olympic Games.**

✳ Karate actually originated in India, but was developed further in China.

✴ **In the United States, more Frisbees are sold each year than baseballs, basketballs and footballs combined.**

✳ Dart boards used to be made out of horsehair.

✴ **Ellen MacArthur, yachtswoman, had a total of 891 naps in 94 days, each of which was 36 minutes long while on her Vendée Round the Globe yacht race.**

✳ A squash ball moving at 150 kilometres per hour has the same impact as a .22 bullet.

✴ **Lacrosse was initially played by Native American Indians. They played it to prepare for war.**

✳ There are two golf balls on the moon. Astronaut Alan B. Shepard hit them on 6 February 1971 just before takeoff at the end of the Apollo 14 mission.

✴ **Australia and Greece are the only two countries to have taken part in every Olympic Games.**

✳ Before the introduction of the whistle in 1878, football referees waved handkerchiefs.

✴ **The fastest World Cup goal was scored by Turkey in 2002. Hakan Sükür put the ball over the line in an astonishing 10.8 seconds against South Korea.**

✳ In greyhound races, anise is used to scent the artificial hares.

☆ **Were it possible for a runner to complete a marathon at the same speed as the 100-metres race, he would cross the finishing line in 43 minutes.**

✳ The longest gloves-on boxing match was between American fighters Andy Bowen and Jack Bourke. It lasted seven hours and 19 minutes.

☆ **Sports dropped from the Olympics over the years include: croquet, water skiing, underwater swimming, pistol shooting duels, rugby, stone-throwing, lacrosse, archery with live birds, tug-of-war, club-swinging, rope-climbing.**

✳ The first person to swim the English Channel was Matthew Webb in August 1875. It took him 21 hours and 45 minutes. The record now stands at seven hours 25 minutes. The youngest swimmer on record is British 11-year-old Thomas Gregory, who made his 1988 crossing in 11 hours and 54 minutes.

☆ **Badminton descended from poona, a similar game played by British Army officers stationed in India in the 1860s.**

☆ PUTTING ONE'S FACE ON ☆

✳ Ancient Egyptians wore eye make-up made from the bodies of crushed beetles.

☆ **Before she was famous, Whoopi Goldberg worked as a bricklayer, a bank teller and a make-up artist in a funeral parlour.**

✳ Lipstick was made from finely ground, semi-precious stone in ancient Mesopotamia, and the ancient Egyptians mixed algae with iodine. Modern, shimmer-look lipstick may contain the silvery fish scales from herrings.

✩ **The word 'cosmetics' comes from the Latin word *cosmetae*, which referred to skilled female slaves who adorned their Roman mistresses with *cultus*, another Latin word referring to make-up, perfume and jewellery.**

✳ Modern-day mascara was invented by T. L. Williams in 1913. Williams worked as a chemist in New York and wanted to help his sister Mabel look more beautiful in order to attract a good man. He concocted a mixture of coal dust and Vaseline, and applied it to his willing sister's eyelashes. Williams felt his invention a success, as his sister was soon married. The chemist went on to found Maybelline – the name is said to be a combination of Vaseline and his sister's name.

✩ **Roman Britons mixed a potion of tin oxide, starch and animal fat and plastered it on their faces as an early form of foundation.**

DANCING TO DEATH

Dancing mania is a phenomenon that reared its bizarre head largely between the fourteenth and seventeenth centuries, when thousands of people might be observed dancing together uncontrollably to the point of collapse. Dancing mania finds its origin in the word *choreomania*, from the Greek *choros* (dance) and *mania* (madness), and has often been put down to religious fervour. One of the first major outbreaks occurred in 1374, with incidents being reported in England, Germany and the Netherlands. In July 1518, one of the most extreme examples of the 'dancing plague' kicked off when Strasbourg resident Frau Troffea began dancing in the street. Still at it four days later, she had amassed a following of 33 fellow ravers. Within a month this number had swelled to 400. Participants were observed to jump around, scream, make animal noises, brandish wooden sticks and even have sex with each other. Many of the dancers collapsed from exhaustion and heart attack, and a number of people died. Treatments included isolation, exorcism, prayers and the playing of calming music, but it was all observers could do just to allow people to dance themselves out. Theories abound about the possible causes of the condition, but the most prominent is that victims may have been suffering from ergot poisoning – damp conditions during floods in the Middle Ages meant the fungus (which causes hallucinations) grew plentifully. Encephalitis, epilepsy and typhus have also been suggested as triggers, but ultimately the whole affair remains rather a mystery.

EMOTICONS

(.V.)	Alien	:'(	Crying	$_$	Greedy
O:-)	Angel	|_P	Cup of coffee	:->	Grin
X-(	Angry	*-*	Dazed	=)	Happy
~:o	Baby	:o3	Dog	:-)	Happy
:-#	Braces	#-o	Doh!	<3	Heart
</3	Broken heart	:*)	Drunk	{ }	Hug
=^.^=	Cat	//_^	Emo	:-|	Indifferent
:O)	Clown	<><	Fish	X-p	Joking
:-S	Confused	:-(	Frowning	\VVV/	King
B-)	Cool	:-P	Frustrated	:-)*	Kiss
:_(	Crying	8-)	Glasses	(-}{-)	Kissing

=D	Laughing out loud	=(	Sad	:-{ }	Talking
		:-(	Sad	(:|	Tired
<3	Love	:-7	Sarcastic	:-J	Tongue-in-cheek
=/	Mad	:-@	Screaming		
:-)(-:	Married	=O	Shocked	:-&	Tongue-tied
<:3)~	Mouse	:-o	Shocked	=-O	Uh-oh
~,~	Napping	O-\-<]:	Skateboarder	:-\	Undecided
^_^	Overjoyed	:-)	Smile	**==	United States flag
<l:o	Partying	:-Q	Smoking		
:-/	Perplexed	:>	Smug	:-E	Vampire
=8)	Pig	-@--@-	Spectacles	=D	Very happy
\&&&/	Princess	:P	Sticking tongue out	;-)	Winking
\ %%%/	Queen			|-O	Yawn
@~)~~~~	Rose	:o	Surprised		

GOLD

All the gold that has ever been mined *(approximately 120,000 – 140,000 tons)* would make a cube measuring only 20 metres on each side. Divided equally among the world's population, it would give us roughly 24 grams each. Almost all rocks and soil contain traces of gold that are invisible to the naked eye and could not be mined for profit. Gold may be safely ingested and is famous for its non-allergenic properties. Both the EU and US authorise the use of gold for the decoration of food – this is referred to as food-grade gold. Gold leaf is referred to as food additive E175. Tutankhamun's inner coffin is made of 110 kilograms of pure gold. Gold has always been recycled – there's a decent chance that any gold you own will contain gold once worn by a Roman. The near-Earth asteroid Eros is estimated to contain approximately 20 billion tons of gold, and similar amounts of other metals.

☆ ★ CHINA ★ ☆

* Fortune cookies are not a Chinese tradition. They were invented in 1920 by a worker in the Key Heong Noodle Factory in San Francisco.

The Chinese are said to have invented the toilet roll in sixth century AD, though it was used only by emperors.

* Many Chinese children keep crickets as pets, and cricket fighting is a popular sport.

More people speak English in China than in the USA.

* Historically the lotus was a symbol of purity, the peony a symbol of spring, the chrysanthemum a symbol of longevity and the narcissus a symbol of good luck. The bat was also a symbol of good luck and the lantern a symbol of wealth, the carp a symbol of perseverance, the cicada a symbol of rebirth.

Before the civil war in 1949, there were five time zones in China. After the war, the unified China decided on one time zone for the whole country – GMT + 8.

* Mahjong, a game of both chance and skill, using 152 tiles bearing Chinese characters and symbols, is the nation's most popular pastime.

Pigtails in the hair were once used to indicate a girl's marital status. A young girl would wear two pigtails but, once married, would wear her hair in a single pony tail.

✳ There are approximately 50 million philatelists (stamp collectors) in the world, and a third of them reside in China. The hobby is a status symbol, and is seen to signify an honourable, middle-class existence.

✳ **White, not black, is worn as a symbol of mourning at funerals. Red is a symbol of happiness.**

✳ Live crabs are a popular commuter snack sold from vending machines in south-eastern China.

✳ **First discovered or invented in China: the horse collar, wheelbarrow, mouldboard plough, paper money, cast iron, the helicopter rotor and propeller, the decimal system, the seismograph, matches, circulation of the blood, paper, printing, the kite, the rocket, mechanical clocks, the crossbow, silk, stirrups, the suspension bridge, gunpowder.**

BREAKING UP IS (NOT) HARD TO DO

In 2002, a Taiwanese carpenter identified only as 'Mr Lee' purchased a pornographic DVD, *Affairs With Other Wives*, only to discover secretly recorded motel footage of his wife having sex with his friend, the local butcher. Lee immediately divorced his wife, and the butcher fled the village. Six years later, Mr Lee ran into his old buddy in Chungli City and promptly stabbed him in the leg. The butcher sued Lee for causing bodily harm, but Mr Lee could not countersue for adultery due to a five-year statute of limitations. A definite case of too much, too little, too late.

SMARTIES FACTS

All the Smarties tubes sold in one year laid end to end would make a 63,380-mile chain – that's two and a half times around the world. Originally known as 'Chocolate Beans', Smarties have been around since 1882. They became officially known as Smarties in 1938. The original colours were dark-brown, light-brown, green, orange, pink, violet and yellow. Until 1958, the dark-brown, light-brown and orange Smarties had plain chocolate centres, a coffee flavoured centre and an orange-flavoured centre respectively. The blue Smartie was introduced for a limited period in 1988 to celebrate 50 years of the product, but it was so popular that it eventually replaced the light-brown Smartie.

☆ ★  ★ ☆

* An African elephant survives with just four teeth while an alligator has eighty.

* **Frogs have teeth but toads do not. Anteaters have no teeth or jaws, just a very sticky one-foot-long tongue.**

* Lemon sharks grow around 24,000 teeth per year – the equivalent of a new set every fortnight.

* **Porpoise teeth were once used as currency in the Pacific islands.**

✳ Biting another human with your own teeth in Louisiana is classed as 'simple assault' but biting him with false teeth is 'aggravated assault'.

THEY SAY HELLO AND
☆ ✦ YOU SAY ... ✦ ☆

Language	Hello	Goodbye
Arabic	Al salaam a'alaykum	Maasalaama
Bengali	Ei je	Nomoskaar
Chinese	Ni hao	Zài jiàn
French	Bonjour	Au revoir
German	Hallo	Tusch
Hawaiian	Aloha	Hui Hou
Hebrew	Shalom	Anee ohev otakh
Hindustani	Namaste	Alavidha
Italian	Ciao	Arrivederci
Japanese	Konichiwa	Sayonara
Malay-Indonesian	Selamat pagi	Selamat tinggal
Portuguese	Bon dia	Adeus
Russian	Zdravstvuite	Do svidaniya
Spanish	Hola	Adios
Swahili	Jambo	Kwaheri
Thai	Sawatdee	Lar-korn

☆

☆ FAMOUS TIPPLES ☆

Queen Victoria – Claret and whisky mix

Napoleon Bonaparte – Absinthe

Charles Bukowski – Boilermaker – a shot of Four Roses bourbon with a Carlsberg Elephant beer chaser

Anthony Burgess – Hangman's Blood – gin, whisky, rum, port brandy, stout, champagne

Raymond Carver – Bloody Mary

Humphrey Bogart – Martini

Winston Churchill – Highball – whisky and water

Carson McCullers – Sunny Boy – hot tea and sherry

Richard Nixon – Dry martini

William Faulkner – Mint julep – bourbon, syrup and mint

Raymond Chandler – Gimlet – gin and lime juice

☆ REPRODUCTION ☆

* The three things pregnant women dream most of during their first trimester are frogs, worms and potted plants.

☆ **The female blue crab can produce as many as a million eggs per day.**

❋ Beavers mate with one partner for life. If one of them dies, the surviving beaver will seek a replacement.

❋ **A male fox also sticks to one mate and if the female dies it remains single. Conversely, the female fox will find another mate.**

❋ The ovum is the largest cell in the female human body.

❋ **It's a case of survival of the fittest in the womb of a tiger shark. The embryos fight with each other and the mother gives birth to the survivor.**

❋ Rather than copulate to reproduce, the male salamander merely secretes a jelly-like substance containing sperm so that the female can inseminate and fertilise the egg independently.

❋ **The American opossum gives birth less than two weeks after conception. Gestation for giraffes is around 15 months.**

❋ A kangaroo is only 0.8 inches/2 centimetres in length at birth.

☆ ★ EGG FACTS ★ ☆

❋ Oology is the study of eggs (and the 'ology' with the fewest letters).

❋ **Average number of eggs laid by the female American oyster per year: 500,000,000.**

* The queen of a termite colony may lay 6,000 to 7,000 eggs per day, and may live 15 to 50 years.

Red Amazon ants invade other ant colonies to steal eggs or larvae, which they either eat or raise as slave workers. Amazon ants are incapable of feeding themselves and need captured workers to survive.

* Mosquitoes prefer children to adults, and blondes to brunettes. But only female mosquitoes bite – they need protein from the blood in order to produce eggs.

Ostrich eggs are between six and eight inches long and six inches in diameter, the largest egg produced by any living bird, and they take 40 minutes to hard boil. The smallest avian egg is around 0.4 inches in diameter, produced by the hummingbird. The Aepyornis, an extinct Madagascan creature, laid the largest egg ever reported. It was thirteen inches long, up to three feet in circumference and had an internal volume of nearly 2.5 gallons.

* On average world egg consumption per capita is 230 per year.

Eggshells have thousands of tiny pores that allow moisture to leave the egg and oxygen to replace it. In the 21 days it takes for a chicken's egg to incubate, it will absorb about eight pints of oxygen, release nearly seven pints of carbon dioxide and about 18 pints of water vapour.

A COMEBACK WHEN
☆ YOU NEED ONE ☆

Of all the people I've met, you're certainly one of them.

I'm busy now. Can I ignore you some other time?

If I throw you a stick, will you leave?

It's a case of mind over matter. I don't mind because you don't matter.

Can I borrow your brain? I'm building an idiot.

I'm not as dumb as you look.

Your hairdresser must really hate you.

I think of you when I get lonely. Then I'm perfectly happy to be alone.

You know what I like about you? Nothing.

What do you look like with your mouth shut?

If you ever become a mother, can I have one of the puppies?

I hope you stay single and make some poor girl happy.

Keep talking. I need the sleep.

Isn't such a tiny mind lonely in such a big head?

Next time you throw out your old clothes, stay in them.

I really think you're going to go places. The sooner the better.

When I want your opinion, I'll rattle your cage.

☆ ★  ★ ☆

* The fattest oak tree in Britain would take about nine adults to hug it, finger tip to finger tip.

☆ **An oak spends 300 years growing, 300 years resting and 300 years dying gracefully.**

☆ The Sunday edition of the *New York Times* requires nearly 65,000 trees' worth of paper.

☆ **The record for the tallest tree is the giant redwood measuring 367 feet (112 metres) the smallest grows to 2 inches/5 centimetres and is known as the Greenland dwarf willow.**

* The oldest tree is nearly 4,770 years old; it is the Methuselah pine found in eastern California's White Mountains.

☆ **The baobab tree can stock 35,800 gallons/163,000 litres of water in its trunk, making it resistant to drought.**

* Trees shrink when they get very old, becoming shorter and squatter. It's a great survival strategy as it means they can cope better with high winds.

- **The manchineel is the most dangerous tree. Every part of this Caribbean beach-dweller causes burns and blisters, and consuming the apple-like fruit can lead to death.**

- It can take 250 years before a tree is a suitable home for certain lichens.

- **Queen Elizabeth I was sitting beneath an ancient oak in Hatfield Park when she first heard that she would be the next Queen of England.**

- The hollow Bowthorpe oak is so large that 20 people once dined inside it.

- **The Milking Tree in Northamptonshire was considered so important in the landscape back in 1790 that a naval report, commissioned by King George III, declared that it must not be sacrificed for shipbuilding. The tree can still be visited today.**

MOST TRADED ITEMS AROUND THE WORLD

Oil	Soybeans	Handbags
Coffee	Fresh pork bellies	Caviar
Maize	Ferrous scrap	Watches
Smoked salmon	Oranges	Maple syrup

☆ TRULY USELESS JOKES ☆

* Phone answering machine message: 'If you want to buy marijuana, press the hash key ...'

* **A guy walks into the psychiatrist's wearing only clingfilm for shorts.**
The shrink says, 'Well, I can clearly see your nuts.'

* I went to the butcher's the other day and I bet him 50 quid that he couldn't reach the meat on the top shelf. 'Sorry,' he replied, 'the steaks are too high.'

* **I went to a seafood disco last night and pulled a mussel.**

* An ice-cream man was found covered with hundreds and thousands. Police say that he topped himself.

* **Did you hear about the restaurant on the moon? Great food, no atmosphere.**

* I recently went on a cannibal holiday. I won't be going back. It cost an arm and a leg.

* **He said, 'You remind me of a pepper pot. I said 'I'll take that as a condiment.'**

* A man walks into a bar with a roll of tarmac under his arm and says, 'Pint, please, and one for the road.'

* **What do you call a fish with no eyes? A fsh.**

✳ Two hydrogen atoms walk into a bar. One says, 'I've lost my electron.'
'Are you sure?' says the other.
The first replies, 'Yes, I'm positive ...'

☆ **WHAT THE DICKENS?** ☆

✳ Dickens wrote about epileptic fits and seizures with such accuracy that today's doctors believe he may have suffered from them himself.

☆ **Besides** *A Christmas Carol*, **Dickens wrote five Christmas books:** *The Chimes, The Cricket on the Hearth, The Battle of Life, The Haunted Man* **and** *The Ghosts*.

✳ Dickens was introduced to mesmerism – an early form of hypnosis – by Professor Joseph Elliotson at University College London. The writer is said to have become a master at mesmerism and was fascinated by its power to control minds.

☆ **Dickens' younger brother Augustus nicknamed him 'Boz', a name Dickens later adopted as a pseudonym.**

✳ Dickens always slept with his head to the north and wrote facing the same direction.

☆ **Dickens died in the middle a novel:** *The Mystery of Edwin Drood* **remains unfinished, though two films based on the work have been made.**

CLASSIC RIDDLE #4

There is a small town with precisely two barbers, one on each side of town. The barbershop on the west side of town is pristine. Its floors are spotless, the windows are always perfectly clear, and the air always smells fresh. The barber has a friendly smile, polished shoes, a well-groomed head of hair and a fancy shirt. The barbershop on the east side of town is a mess. Its floors and windows are dirty, and it smells disgusting. The barber always has a grimace on his face. His skin is oily, his hair is short and ragged and he has food on his clothes all the time. A man travelling through town realises he needs a haircut. Knowing the stories of the two barbers, the man decides to go to the dirty barbershop on the east side of town. Why does he do this?

ANSWER TO CLASSIC RIDDLE # 4

Because there are only two barbers in the town, the barbers must cut each other's hair. The barber on the west side of town has a nice haircut, so the eastside barber must be a good barber. On the other hand, the barber on the east side of town has ragged hair, meaning the westside barber must not be very good. So the man goes to the east side barber to get a better haircut.

DEVILISHLY DIFFICULT
☆ TONGUE TWISTERS ☆
(REPEAT AD INFINITUM)

* The sixth sick sheik's sixth sheep's sick.

* **I slit a sheet, a sheet I slit, upon the slitted sheet I sit.**

* Unique New York.

* **Irish wristwatch.**

* The strap slipped off the soldier's shoulder.

* **A big black bug bit a big black bear and the big black bear bled badly.**

* Slipper snakes slither southwards.

* **The Leith police dismisseth us with six thick thistle sticks.**

* Three witches watch three watches. Which witch will watch which watch?

* **Mrs Smith's fish sauce shop.**

* Toy boat.

* **Peggy Babcock.**

* Free-flying fruit flies flying freely.

☆ **Black bugs' blood.**

✳ Good blood.

☆ **If Stu chews shoes, should Stu choose the shoes he chews?**

✳ What time does the wristwatch strap shop shut?

☆ **That Blake's black bike's back brake bracket block broke.**

✳ She was a thistle sifter and sifted thistles through a thistle sieve.

☆ **A truly rural frugal ruler's mural.**

KITES

Kites were first used by the Chinese military to transport long-distance messages. The colour relayed the information being sent. They were also used to measure wind speed in the eighteenth century. The smallest flyable kite in the world is five millimetres high, while the largest is the Megabitem, which measures 55 x 22 metres.

Kite flying was banned in China during the Cultural Revolution; anyone found flying a kite was jailed for up to three years and their kites destroyed. The Chinese name for a kite is *fen zheng,* meaning 'wind harp'. This derived from early kites which had wind instruments attached to them.

Kite flying was banned in Japan in 1760 because it was feared that people preferred flying kites to working.

Kites were used in the American Civil War to deliver letters and newspapers.

Large kites were banned in East Germany to ensure people did not fly themselves over the Berlin Wall.

Worldwide, more adults fly kites than children.

Approximately 12 people are killed each year in kiting accidents throughout the world.

When making *Mary Poppins*, Walt Disney asked his songwriters to write a song about a kite as a tribute to his daughters, who were members of the Kappa Alpha Theta sorority. The sorority's symbol is a kite.

YOU COULDN'T MAKE IT UP

In 1974, 17-year-old Neville Ebin, while riding his moped in Hamilton, Bermuda, was struck and killed by a taxi. Neville's passenger lived to tell the tale. One year on, Neville's brother Erskine went the same way. Moreover, Erskine was riding on the same moped along the same street, carrying the same passenger and was hit by the same taxi.

☆ SOME FAMOUS ☆ BILINGUALS

Al Gore – Spanish

Alanis Morissette – French

Antonio Banderas – Spanish

Audrey Hepburn – Spanish, French, Dutch/Flemish, Italian

Bill Clinton – German

Claudia Schiffer – French

Clint Eastwood – Italian

Condoleezza Rice – Russian

Hugh Grant – French

Jodie Foster – French

Johnny Depp – French

Morgan Freeman – French

Natalie Portman – Hebrew, some French, German, Japanese and Spanish

Queen Elizabeth II – French

Renée Zellweger – German

Will Smith – Spanish

William Shatner – French

☆ OLD JOB NAMES ☆

OLD JOB NAMES

Aurifaber . . . . Goldsmith

Baxter . . . . Baker

Brewster . . . . Beer manufacturer

Brightsmith . . . . Metalworker

Carter . . . . Wagon driver

Castor . . . . Hat maker

Caulker . . . . One who filled up cracks (in wood or iron)

Chandler . . . . Candle maker

Chiffonnier . . . . Wig maker

Colporteur . . . . Pedlar of books

Cooper . . . . Barrel maker

Cordwainer . . . . Shoemaker

Costermonger . . . . . . Pedlar of fruit and vegetables

Crocker . . . . Potter

Currier . . . . Curer of hides

Draper . . . . Dealer in dry goods

Dyker . . . . Stonemason

Ferrier . . . . Blacksmith

Fletcher . . . . Arrow maker

Fowler . . . . Bird hunter

Granger . . . . Farmer

Haymonger . . . . Dealer in hay

Hayward . . . . Fence inspector

Hillier . . . . Roof tiler

Hind . . . . Farm labourer

Hooper . . . . Barrel hoop maker

Hostler . . . . Horse groom

Jagger . . . . Fish pedlar

Keeler . . . . Bargeman

Kempster . . . . Wool comber

Lavender . . . . Washerwoman

Lederer	Leather maker
Marshall	Horse doctor
Mercer	Cloth merchant
Pitman	Coal miner
Scrivener	Professional writer
Spittleman	Hospital attendant
Tanner	One who cures animal hides into leather
Tinker	Travelling salesman
Wainwright	Wagon maker
Webster	Weaver
Whitesmith	Tinsmith
Whitewing	Street sweeper
Yeoman	Farmer who owns his own land

FLIES

Pope Adrian VI choked to death when a fly got stuck in his throat as he was drinking from a fountain. Flies can react to visual stimuli and change direction in 30 milliseconds. They are the only insects to have two wings – all others have four. If all the offspring survived, the offspring of a single pair of flies could produce 190,000,000,000,000,000,000 flies in four months. Flies taste with their feet, and housefly feet are ten million times more sensitive to the taste of sugar than the human tongue. A fly can travel 300 times the length of its body in one second – a jet travelling at the speed of sound only travels 100 times its length. The average housefly lives on average 21 days and beats its wings 200 times per second (having jumped up and backwards when taking off). Average speed of a fly in flight is 4.5 miles per hour. Coffin flies live for up to a year inside a sealed coffin, producing many generations, which live off the corpse.

☆ CELEBS AT SCHOOL ☆

* When Richard Branson left school, his headmaster said, 'I predict you will either go to prison or become a millionaire.'

Kate Winslet was bullied because of her weight, and nicknamed 'Blubber'.

* Actor Robin Williams was voted least likely to succeed by classmates at school.

Davina McCall went to the same school as Kate Beckinsale and Nigella Lawson.

* Former Prime Minister Tony Blair was called 'the most difficult boy I ever had to deal with' by his school housemaster.

Sylvester Stallone was voted 'most likely to end up in an electric chair' by his classmates.

* US actress Cameron Diaz was nicknamed 'Skeletor' when she was at school because she was so skinny.

Anthony Hopkins had a talent for drinking Indian ink.

* Jack Nicholson was a bit of a bad boy – one year he was in detention every day.

Sharon Osbourne dropped out of school at 15, saying that she was bored.

* Anne Robinson's maths teacher told her she 'would never make anything of herself'.

- **US actress Denise Richards was nicknamed 'Fish Lips' when she was at school.**

- Steven Spielberg was nicknamed 'The Retard', and once lost a race to a boy in the class who was actually mentally retarded.

- **US actress Gwyneth Paltrow was bullied at school because she was 'gawky'.**

- Damon Albarn was bullied at school because other kids thought he was a 'gayboy'.

- **Felicity Kendal's nickname was Fatty Foo.**

- Noel Gallagher was nicknamed Brezhnev.

- **Elle Macpherson was nicknamed Smelly Elly.**

- Sophie Anderton was nicknamed thunder thighs at school.

- **Boy George was expelled from school for bunking off and not doing any work.**

- Salma Hayek was expelled from school for setting all the clocks back three hours.

☆ ★ CLOTHING ★ ☆

- The YKK on the zipper of your Levis stands for Yoshida Kogyo Kabushibibaisha, the world's largest zipper manufacturer.

☆ **The reason why women's dress-shirt buttons are on the left and men's on the right is because when buttons were first used during the Victorian period maids used to dress the ladies, and since the maids put on their shirts the buttons were put on the servants' right side, hence the women's left.**

✳ Castaways Travel, a Houston-area travel agency, offers an all-nude flight to Cancún, Mexico. Once the plane reaches cruising altitude, you are allowed to take off all your clothes and roam about the cabin.

☆ **Warner Brothers Corset Company created the bra cup sizing system, which is now used universally by manufacturers.**

✳ Silk was developed in China where it was kept a secret for more than 2,000 years. Anyone found trying to smuggle silkworm eggs or cocoons out of the country was immediately put to death.

☆ **Two hundred and fifteen pairs of jeans can be made with one bale of cotton.**

HEARTY FACTS

The heart beats approximately 100,000 times per day and 2.5 billion times during the average human lifespan. The pressure created by the human heart is sufficient to squirt blood to a distance of nearly ten metres. Women's hearts beat faster than men's. The blue whale's heart beats just nine times per minute. The heart of a brachiosaurus is reported to have been as big as a pick-up truck. An octopus has three hearts and an earthworm has five. The heart of a shrimp is located in its head. The heart was thought to be the centre of human intelligence during the Middle Ages. A giraffe's heart can measure up to two feet in length and weigh as much as 25 pounds

---

☆ ★ CLOCKWISE ★ ☆

* Northern hemisphere: hurricanes go anti-clockwise.

* **Southern hemisphere: hurricanes always go clockwise.**

* If you see an object spinning in a clockwise direction you are using the right side of your brain more than the left side. The opposite is true if you see an object spinning anti-clockwise.

* **Windmills in Ireland turn in a clockwise direction, whereas windmills in the rest of the world turn anti-clockwise.**

* Hair grows from the scalp and swirls in a clockwise direction around the crown in the majority of people. Like left- or right-handedness, though, some people's hair grows in the opposite direction.

* **The planet Venus rotates clockwise whereas most other planets rotate anti-clockwise.**

SKIN

The outer layer of skin on the human body is in a continuous process of shedding and every 28 days it is replaced completely. The total weight of human skin weighs up to 4 kilograms/8.8 pounds, double the weight of the human brain. Total skin shed in a lifetime is around 18 kilograms /39.7 pounds. Dead skin cells make up approximately 70 per cent of household dust.

LAST DEATHS BY PUNISHMENT IN THE WEST

Last execution in tower of London. 1941

Last guillotine execution 1939

Last person burned at the stake in London 1786

Last public execution in United States 1936

Last woman hanged in England 1955

☆ ENTERTAINMENT 'LASTS' ☆

* The Beatles' last concert was at Candlestick Park, San Francisco, on 29 August 1966. The last song they played was 'Long Tall Sally'. The Beatles recorded their last song together, 'I Me Mine', in 1970.

☆ **Beethoven's last symphony was his Ninth.**

✳ The last song Elvis performed was 'Bridge Over Troubled Water', at his final concert in Indianapolis in June 1977.

☆ **The last line ever spoken by Marilyn Monroe on the silver screen was 'How do you find your way back in the dark?' The line is from 1961 film *The Misfits* with Clark Gable. Monroe died in 1962.**

✳ The last feature-length British movie released without a soundtrack was *Paradise Alley* (1931), starring John Argyle and Margaret Delane.

☆ **The last feature-length US movie released without a soundtrack was *The Poor Millionaire* (1930), starring Richard Talmadge and Constance Howard.**

☆ **LAST IN THE WORLD** ☆

Last matriarchal society – In matriarchal societies, the female rules the roost. The Mosuo tribe is thought to be the last 'kingdom of women' on the planet. Near Lake Lugu in south-west China, 40,000 people reside in a community whose language does not have a word for 'husband' or 'father'. Women are responsible for all decisions, own all the land and bring up any children without the help of men. 'Walking marriages' enable this. From the age of 13, women are permitted as many lovers – male companions known as *axias* – as they desire, and any offspring are raised without question of paternity. All men are referred to as 'uncle' and spend their time fishing and raising animals before discreetly visiting women's homes at night.

Last handwritten newspaper – *The Musalman* is thought to be the only handwritten newspaper in the world. Every day since 1927, calligraphers have gathered in a room in Chennai, India, to transcribe the news in Urdu by hand on to four pages before sending them off to be copied and printed. National and local news, as well as sport and the arts, are covered, and the paper's daily circulation is around 23,000. Wisely, the calligraphers always leave a corner of the front page blank in case breaking news needs to be added before going to press.

Last to abolish slavery – Believe it or not, the State of Mississippi didn't abolish slavery until 1995. Despite the 13th Amendment in 1865, the state held out for years because citizens originally wanted reimbursement for their freed slaves. By 1995, it was naturally more of a symbolic gesture than anything else, but a welcome one nonetheless.

☆ THE LAST WORDS ☆

THE FAME GAME – A SELECTION OF QUOTES

'So, where's the Cannes Film Festival being held this year?' – Christina Aguilera

'I don't want to achieve immortality through my work; I want to achieve immortality through not dying' – Woody Allen

'There are two types of actors: those who say they want to be famous and those who are liars' – Kevin Bacon

'I definitely want Brooklyn to be christened, but I don't know into what religion yet' – David Beckham

'You would think a rock star being married to a supermodel would be one of the greatest things in the world. It is' – David Bowie

'Talking about art is like dancing about architecture' – David Bowie

'Fame means when your computer modem is broken, the repair guy comes out to your house a little faster' – Sandra Bullock

'My favourite review described me as the cinematic equivalent of junk mail' – Steve Buscemi

'I love England, especially the food – there is nothing I like more than a lovely bowl of pasta' – Naomi Campbell

'Whenever I watch TV and see those poor starving kids all over the world, I can't help but cry. I mean I'd love to be skinny like that but not with all those flies and death and stuff' – Mariah Carey

'One day there may be a wife, but for now I'm just interviewing for the position' – 50 Cent

'The problem with beauty is that it's like being born rich and getting poorer' – Joan Collins

'I admit I'm being paid well, but it's no more than I deserve. After all, I've been screwed more times than a hooker' – Sean Connery

'I haven't done anything particularly harsh. Harshness to me is giving somebody false hopes and not following through. That's harsh. Telling some guy or some girl who's got zero talent that they have zero talent actually is a kindness' – Simon Cowell

'I don't worry about image. I don't know what that is. I'm just myself' – Tom Cruise

'I am the Fred Astaire of karate' – Jean-Claude Van Damme

'Who the **** said that? Oh man. I want to live the life I read about. I've never even met Anna' – Matt Damon, on rumours tennis beauty Anna Kournikova had pole-danced for him

'I don't like to watch my own movies. I fall asleep in my own movies' – Robert De Niro

'After a while you learn that privacy is something you can sell, but you can't buy it back' – Bob Dylan

'Television is an invention that permits you to be entertained in your living room by people you wouldn't have in your home' – David Frost

'I hate ridiculous names; my weird name has haunted me all my life' – Peaches Geldof

'My mother said it was simple to keep a man, you must be a maid in the living room, a cook in the kitchen and a whore in the bedroom. I said I'd hire the other two and take care of the bedroom bit' – Jerry Hall

'There are many dying children out there whose last wish is to meet me' – David Hasselhoff

'It's funny how most people love the dead. Once you're dead you're made for life' – Jimi Hendrix

'What's WalMart, do they sell like wall stuff?' – Paris Hilton on the American supermarket chain

'Me and Janet really are two different people' – Michael Jackson

'I think everyone who says they don't like watching themselves in movies should stop lying' – Samuel L. Jackson

'You know, obviously, I have this sort of strange animal magnetism. It's very hard for me to take my eyes off myself' – Mick Jagger

'I definitely believe in plastic surgery. I don't want to be an old hag. There's no fun in that' – Scarlett Johansson

'Madonna, best f***ing live act? F**k off! Since when has lip-synching been live? Anyone who lip-synchs in public on stage when you've paid £75 to see them should be shot. That's me off her Christmas card list, but do I give a toss? NO!' – Elton John

'Everyone in Hollywood is either not drinking alcohol because of their diet, or is a reformed alcoholic, or is in rehab. Hollywood is just so boring' – Catherine Zeta Jones

'If you wanted to torture me, you'd tie me down and force me to watch our first five videos' – Jon Bon Jovi

'In my films my breasts are definitely computer animated, because I don't have any. They spend most of the money in the film's budget just making my breasts. That's why producers never like me' – Milla Jovovich

'I'm allergic to drugs. They bring me out in handcuffs' – Robert Downey Jr

'Well, I can wear heels now' – Nicole Kidman on life after Tom Cruise

'Hook me up with a great photographer, a clever stylist and an expert retoucher, and together we create a beautiful illusion' – Heidi Klum

'I'm kind of ashamed to be a celebrity. I don't understand wanting to read about other people's dirty laundry. I think celebrity is the biggest red herring society has ever pulled on itself' – Jude Law

'I curse like a sailor, I show my boobs, I'm a rock star and I smoke like hell' – Courtney Love

'I saw losing my virginity as a career move' – Madonna

'Being naked on set is like swimming naked – it makes you feel powerful' – Ewan McGregor

'If you want to get the girl, tell them you're gay. That's my advice' – Sir Ian McKellen

'The whole business is built on ego, vanity, self-satisfaction, and it's total crap to pretend it's not' – George Michael

'It was no great tragedy being Judy Garland's daughter. I had tremendously interesting childhood years – except they had little to do with being a child' – Liza Minnelli

'I don't try to be a sex bomb. I am one' – Kylie Minogue

'Hollywood is a place where they'll pay you a thousand dollars for a kiss and fifty cents for your soul' – Marilyn Monroe

'I can honestly say all the bad things that ever happened to me were directly attributed to drugs and alcohol. I mean, I would never urinate at the Alamo at nine o'clock in the morning dressed in a woman's evening dress sober' – Ozzy Osbourne

'Plastic surgeons are always making mountains out of molehills' – Dolly Parton

'It makes you feel permanently like a girl walking past construction workers' – Brad Pitt (on fame)

'Prince Charles asked me if I was in the original *Star Wars*. I was like, "What are you smoking?"' – Natalie Portman

'I think that gay marriage is something that should be between a man and a woman' – Arnold Schwarzenegger

'Alcohol may be man's worst enemy, but the Bible says love your enemy' – Frank Sinatra

'People always ask me, did I ever learn anything when I was a stripper? Yeah, I did. One man plus two beers equals 20 dollars' – Anna Nicole Smith

'If you haven't turned rebel by 20, you've got no heart; if you haven't turned establishment by 30, you've got no brains!' – Kevin Spacey

'The movies are weird. You actually have to think about them when you watch them' – Britney Spears on the Sundance Film Festival

'My biggest nightmare is I'm driving home and get sick and go to hospital. I say, 'Please help me.' And the people say, 'Hey, you look like …' And I'm dying while they're wondering whether I'm Barbra Streisand' – Barbra Streisand

'People ask me if I went to film school. And I tell them, "No, I went to films"' – Quentin Tarantino

'I, along with the critics, have never taken myself very seriously' – Elizabeth Taylor

'I kiss people with my soul. I don't kiss them with my mouth' – Justin Timberlake

'In three movies I was overweight. And they all made 100 million, so I knew people weren't coming to see my body' – John Travolta

'When I was in prison, I was wrapped up in all those deep books. That Tolstoy crap – people shouldn't read that stuff' – Mike Tyson

'These are two consonants and a vowel I'm very proud of' – Carol Vorderman on being awarded an MBE

'I want to be like David Bowie or Iggy Pop and I'm more like Norman Wisdom' – Robbie Williams

'Ah, yes, divorce, from the Latin word meaning to rip out a man's genitals through his wallet' – Robin Williams

'All my life I have always known I was born to greatness' – Oprah Winfrey

P.S. ONE MORE THING
☆ ★ **FAMOUS LAST WORDS** ★ ☆

'Wait a minute …' – Pope Alexander VI, talking to God

'Am I dying, or is this my birthday?' – Nancy Astor

'Pardonnez-moi, monsieur' – Marie Antoinette, after stepping on her executioner's foot.

'Now I shall go to sleep. Goodnight' – Lord Byron

'Take a step forward, lads – it'll be easier that way' – Robert Erskine Childers, to his firing squad

'I can't sleep' – J. M. Barrie

'I should never have switched from scotch to martinis' – Humphrey Bogart

'I am about to – or I am going to – die: either expression is correct' – Dominique Bouhours, French grammarian

'Damn it . . . Don't you dare ask God to help me' – Joan Crawford to her housekeeper, who had begun to pray aloud

'I've never felt better' – Douglas Fairbanks

'I'm bored with it all' – Winston Churchill

'Please put out the light' – Theodore Roosevelt

'God will pardon me, that's his line of work' – Heinrich Heine

'Go on, get out – last words are for fools who haven't said enough' – Karl Marx, to his housekeeper, who urged him to tell her his last words for the sake of posterity

'I've had eighteen straight whiskies, I think that's the record' – Dylan Thomas

'Go away. I'm all right' – H. G. Wells

———●·✦·●———

P.P.S

'Books are a load of crap' – Philip Larkin